*f*P

DRIVING CHANGE

*How the Best Companies
Are Preparing for the
21st Century*

JERRY YORAM WIND
JEREMY MAIN

THE FREE PRESS
New York   London   Toronto   Sydney   Singapore

THE FREE PRESS
A Division of Simon & Schuster Inc.
1230 Avenue of the Americas
New York, NY 10020

THE FREE PRESS and colophon are trademarks
of Simon & Schuster Inc.

Manufactured in the United States of America
10 9 8 7 6 5 4 3 2 1

Library of Congress Cataloging-in-Publication Data

Wind, Jerry Yoram.
    Driving change : how the best companies are preparing for the 21st
century / Jerry Yoram Wind, Jeremy Main.
        p.   cm.
    Includes bibliographical references and index.
        1. Organizational change.   2. Business forecasting.
    3. Technological innovations.   I. Main, Jeremy.
    II. Title.
    HD58.8.W56   1998
    658.4'06—dc21   97–40195
                                                                      CIP

ISBN 0-684-82744-1

To

DINA WIND

and

PATRICIA MAIN

CONTENTS

PART III: THE RESPONSE—THE WEAPONS

PART IV: THE RESPONSE—THE ORGANIZATION

INTRODUCTION

E very generation likes to think that it lives in a time of unique challenge and change. Peter Drucker and Warren Bennis have made change a theme of their writing about management for decades. However, ever since American companies—particularly the auto and electronic firms—discovered around 1980 that they no longer owned the world, that others had become much better than they were (and might even destroy them or buy them), they have been driven to change on a scale that really *is* unprecedented. Indeed, one of the hazards of researching a book of this type today is that companies are changing so much so fast that remaining current during the process of producing a book becomes difficult. While we were researching this book, in 1995 and 1996, at least five of the companies that we studied, AT&T, Digital Equipment Corporation, Hewlett-Packard, 3M, and Xerox, put themselves through major remakes aimed directly at preparing themselves for the 21st century. Others have tied their basic strategies to what they believe will fit the 21st century, the "Vision 2000" at General Motors and Astra Merck, "Ford 2000" and "Xerox 2000" (updated to "Xerox 2005" in 1997). Having reorganized its computer sales force to face the customer in 1995, Hewlett Packard did it again in 1997. Some companies, such as SEI Investments, rather than announcing major restructurings, with all the anxiety they cause, have adopted a strategy of quiet, continuous change.

The corporation as we know it, the corporation that was the engine of prosperity throughout the 20th century, will emerge as something different in the 21st century. The transition to the next enterprise is most visible in the United States, but companies in Asia and Europe must make a similar transition because the forces of change are global. The markets, the technology, and the demands of employees, of customers, and of citizens are driving companies to change boldly and bravely. Today inaction is the riskiest strategy.

Business is bursting with promising, innovative ideas about management, work, products, and processes, and with new management tools to make better use of them. Set beside other types of organizations, especially those in education and government, the ground-breaking corporations appear enlightened, agile, and open-minded. The response of schools to demands they improve has been sluggish at best, and our politicians are mostly going off in the wrong direction, babbling themselves into irritating irrelevance. However, even the most enlightened companies don't get much credit for what they are doing. The "good" side of business is obscured by too many reports of outrageous benefits for CEOs, of wholesale and often callous "downsizing," of a lack of trust and humanity, of a focus on short-term financial gain, and of plain lying, stealing, and cheating.

Moreover, business does a very poor job of explaining itself, and too often puts its foot in its mouth. On TV, CEOs show up as tongue-tied grouches, and corporate-speak squeezes the life out of language. Thus: "Human Resources goes beyond the traditional personnel function by partnering with internal customers to discover meaningful solutions to people-related issues and needs."[1] This deadening sentence comes not from some hoary bureaucracy, but from one of the newest and most innovative large companies in the United States, Astra Merck, a pharmaceutical joint venture between America's Merck and Sweden's Astra.

Executives are prone to keep reaching out for new solutions, hoping to find the one, preferably quick, simple, and cheap, that will solve their problems, permanently. New management ideas often suffer from too much early hype. When the idea is new, the expected performance is touted by consultants, eager to build new business, and by the business press, eager to appear to be on top of the latest trend. When the actual performance turns out to be less than the expected performance, the idea is judged to be a failure, and the trend is declared dead. Since the idea has been oversold in the first place, the result will likely be disappointing.

Executives who follow the fads flip-flop from Quality of Worklife to

Total Quality Management to Just-in-Time planning to Reengineering to Growth, snatching up the next one before they have even understood, much less fully implemented, the last one. If doctors were to treat their patients the way executives run their companies, then one year they would all prescribe Valium (Rx Quality of Worklife) for all their patients, regardless of the ailment, and the next year they would prescribe amputation (Rx: Reengineering) for all ills.[2]

Business leaders seem to need to think they have found the true way. But we are not talking about religion. We are talking about how to change the way we run our companies. That is often a matter of plain common sense. It means reviving ideas that have been obvious for a long time but not widely practiced, like knowing the customer and caring for the employee. Today a whole set of new tools allows us to manage better than we ever have before, by using information technology and teams, by improving quality, improving innovation, creating the right corporate architecture, and many, many other ways. These are practical instruments, now well tested, not matters of faith. They need to be used in a balanced, thoughtful way that is fitted to the particular corporation.

The business world is littered with corporate graffiti. To the word corporation you add some vivid or grabby adjective such as biological, boundaryless, cluster, democratic, federated, fishnet, hollow, horizontal, intelligent, learning, open-lattice, open-book, orchestra, organic, shamrock, virtual, or visionary, and Presto! you have a new theory of the corporation. A pithy metaphor does not describe the next enterprise or solve complex problems. This book will not offer any quick or easy rules. If we wanted a metaphor we might call this book "a fad-free diet for saturated executives."

Having said that, the authors would obviously be fools to add to the corporate graffiti by offering their nostrums for creating a successful enterprise in the 21st century. However, like any business today, a book needs a vision or an overarching theory. Instead of catchy metaphors, we offer in these pages a framework for thinking and acting that we hope will help business leaders drive the changes they need to make. American business, or at least a few enlightened or beleaguered companies, began to make the transition around 1980. We have been accumulating experience in what works and what doesn't work, what is needed and what isn't needed for nearly two decades.

This book arises out of research at the SEI Center for Advanced Studies in Management at the Wharton School at the University of Pennsylvania in Philadelphia. The SEI Center, a nonprofit research organization initially funded by SEI Investments and Xerox Corporation, was established in 1989 as a think tank to focus on the future of management. The Center has sponsored research projects, organized conferences and discussions, and listened to some of the world's top business leaders (who come to its meetings and serve on its board), as well as to consultants and academicians. The result is a picture of the characteristics of a 21st century corporation that will distinguish it from the 20th century version that we are familiar with. Here is a comparison of the two:

Old characteristics	**Emerging characteristics**
Goal-directed	Vision-directed
Price-focused	Value-focused
Product quality mind-set	Total quality mind-set
Product-driven	Customer-driven
Shareholder-focused	Stakeholder-focused
Finance-oriented	Speed-oriented
Efficient, stable	Innovative, entrepreneurial
Hierarchical	Flat, empowered
Machine-based	Information-based
Functional	Cross-functional
Rigid, committed	Flexible, learning
Local, regional, national	Global
Vertically integrated	Networked, interdependent

We will deal with these emerging characteristics throughout the book. The ideas are already fairly familiar; they do not spring fully formed from our imaginations. Today's executives have probably all introduced one or more of these new characteristics in their own companies, with mixed results. All of the ideas have been tested to some degree over the last decade or more. They are not all equally important. Nevertheless, these are the features that will differentiate tomorrow's corporation from today's. In the fall of 1996, the SEI Center surveyed many of the executives engaged in these changes and asked them to say how important each characteristic was to them and how far their companies had come in adopting them. The answers, furnished by 53 executives about equally divided between North America, Asia, and Europe, are shown in the chapters relating to each question and in summary form in the appendix.

The new ideas will not necessarily drive out the old. Obviously attention to profits will remain critical to every corporation. Hierarchies are not going to disappear altogether in team-driven, flattened organizations. You can't become totally global and ignore local and regional factors. You can't become altogether cross-functional and let go of functional excellence. Rather than a complete shift, we are talking about a change in balance here, new emphases, and tradeoffs. Although most companies will probably end up being a mixture of the old and the new, they will all have to adjust to new realities—to the needs of their employees, customers, and communities, to new technology, to global markets, to demands for more speed and innovation and adaptability.

This book carries the work of the SEI Center a step further by looking at what actually happens when companies try to change their characteristics. Since we cannot propose one model for the next enterprise, we will look at the drivers of change that all companies are going to have to deal with, and then the various means of responding to these drivers. Here is how we have organized the book:

- **Part I** describes the drivers of change—the obsolescence of the old corporation, the eruption of information technology, globalization, the new intensity of competition, society's expectations, and customers' expectations.
- **Part II** describes how the new enterprise is reshaping the way business views people, including the customer, the leader, and the employee.
- **Part III** analyzes how companies are using the new tools they have in information technology, innovation, speed, and quality.
- **Part IV** takes up the changes in the corporation itself, how companies are becoming global, how they network, how they learn, how they can best respond to society's demands, how they can redesign their architecture.

We sought particularly to describe how business is preparing itself for the 21st century by talking to CEOs and other executives—the people in charge of driving change. We have gone to dozens of American, Japanese, and European companies, mostly the ones that have had the perseverence to try to execute the new ideas well for years. We have asked their chief executives what they have learned from the experience, and we have gone down into the companies to talk to others, as well as to consultants, former employees, and business professors familiar with the companies. Therefore, we hope to go beyond the fairly familiar characteristics of the next enterprise and describe what is less known—how they work in practice. We also stress what is often ignored both in management theory and executive planning—how to integrate all the elements of the next enterprise. The executive too often will seek a narrow solution, the infamous "silver bullet" rather than taking a coherent view of the whole and trying to match all the new pieces to each other. Throughout the book we will stress the links between one change and another. At the end of many chapters we highlight some links that need to be considered, along with pointers and cautions. We hope to create a practical guide to help today's managers and executives drive change in their companies as they reach into the 21st century. Rather than describing the changes and the new organization in the abstract, we have chosen to do so more by telling the stories of the companies that are leading the way.

The Duke of Wellington said "the battle of Waterloo was won on the playing fields of Eton." A sports metaphor might describe what is happening—or should be happening—to the corporation, and, for that matter, to the concept of organization. If Wellington were alive today, he might say the war in Vietnam was lost on the playing fields of West Point. The U.S. Army at that time was like a football team, a huge, clanking force of armored heavyweights, dependent on mass, directed by a domineering if not egomaniacal coach who second-guessed the people in the field. The classic 20th century corporation is like that Army. It's as inappropriate for modern business as the Army was for guerrilla warfare. Ban football thinking! Think soccer! The corporation needs to learn how to play a fluid, constantly changing game that demands agility, improvisation, and adaptability from players who can slip into each others' roles and who are not dominated by a tyrant.

1
WHY CHANGE?

MOONING THE CUSTOMER

Unflattering descriptions of the corporation abound. It is called authoritarian, control obsessed, feudal, hierarchical, mechanical, militaristic, rigid, shortsighted, secretive, slow, and unenterprising, to single out just a few of the epithets. It has even been described as the only remaining totalitarian institution in the world, now that Communism is dead. How could it ever have survived, much less succeeded? Perhaps it succeeded only too well. Inevitably it became complacent and closed its eyes to change around it. It really does need to be reinvented, and many of the epithets are true. Jack Welch, probably the most famous of America's modern reforming executives, puts the problem in his pungent way. Today's hierarchical structure, giving the CEO control over strategy, organization, and information, says General Electric's chairman, creates an organization with "its face toward the CEO and its ass toward the customer" (according to the *Harvard Business Review*). Over the years, he says, GE had created "a management approach that was right for its time, the toast of the business schools. Divisions, strategic business units, groups, sectors—all were assigned to make meticulous, calculated decisions, and move them smoothly forward and upward. The system produced highly polished work. It was right for the 1970s, a growing handicap in the 1980s, and it would have been a ticket to the boneyard in the 1990s."[1]

SEI Survey	
Reinventing the corporation is critical	74%
We are successfully reinventing it	19%

The modern corporation has a lot of history and legacies to overcome. Human organization has always been hierarchical, in churches, in armies, in feudal monarchies, and in modern bureaucracies. Business was no exception. The modern corporation grew, logically enough, out of the coming of the railroads and the telegraph beginning in the mid-19th century. Before then, companies had been relatively small and localized, with modest needs for controls, information, and capital. But the railroads created the first large, dispersed organizations and required firm controls and rapidly delivered information when the small local lines merged into big regional and national lines.

The business historian Alfred D. Chandler Jr. describes how the railroads, especially the Erie under its general superintendent, David C. McCallum, produced the first large, modern corporation. He created a structure for the administration of a complex organization, enunciated the principles of administration that would govern it, and created a flow of information to track and evaluate the operations of a far-flung enterprise. McCallum believed in the strict adherence to hierarchy so that subordinates dealt only with immediate superiors. He was the first to use information technology, in this case the telegraph, not only to transmit urgent news but to gather information to help management monitor the railroad.[2]

It is interesting that Chandler's history, *The Visible Hand: The Management Revolution in American Business,* attributes to that 19th century revolution two of the same drivers that we today think especially important in our management revolution: information and speed. Then it was the telegraph that created new information technology; today it is the computer and all its electronic links. Then it was the railroads that made business move faster; today it is automation, TV, the jet, the telephone, the fax, e-mail, and the rest of our electronic paraphernalia, and a whole array of management devices to make business act and react faster.

THE LAZY IDIOT THEORY

The completion of the classic corporation required three more elements: the detailed ordering of human activity, the invention of the assembly line, and the perfection of the corporation as an organization. The first came with "scientific management," the invention of Frederick Winslow Taylor, a mechanical engineer, who laid the basis at the turn of the century for dividing work into minute, repetitive components and then telling the worker just how to do it, with no deviation. Scientific management assumed the worker was ignorant, stupid, and would spend as much time "soldiering" as he could get away with.[3] The worker did exactly what the foreman told him to do, and management planned the work. Taylorism did greatly raise factory output but it also dehumanized work.

New manufacturing machinery, plus the huge demand for Model T Fords around the world, pushed Henry Ford into making the next major advance in industrial organization, the invention of the moving assembly line. After experimenting with moving lines to produce auto components, Ford started making the entire Model T on an assembly line at Highland Park, Michigan, in October 1913. The labor needed to assemble a car dropped immediately from 12 hours, eight minutes to two hours, 35 minutes. By the following spring the time spent assembling a car fell to one hour, 35 minutes.[4]

The finished model of the classic 20th century corporation emerged after World War I out of the near-ruin of General Motors caused partly by the postwar recession and partly by the loose if inspired management of its founder, Will Durant. Alfred P. Sloan Jr. became president in 1923 and set about organizing, in his carefully analytical and intellectual way, the large modern corporation. GM survived pretty much as he created it until the 1990s, and was enormously successful most of that time. Sloan believed a big company had to be decentralized, so that the divisions would have operational autonomy. But they would be guided, helped, coordinated, and above all held accountable by a corporate staff, especially by a finance committee. Management relied heavily on what soon became a huge staff. Sloan saw his own role as "selling ideas, rather than simply giving orders,"[5] demonstrating more wisdom than many CEOs have shown since. As early as the 1940s, Peter Drucker saw that GM needed to begin changing, but that piece of wisdom escaped GM until the 1990s.[6]*

In human terms, the 20th century corporation created "the organization man," the title of William H. Whyte's famous book about corporate life in the 1950s.[7] The young corporate manager then believed that his goals and the corporation's were the same. He (at the time there was no question of "she") cherished "the idea that his relationship with The Organization is for keeps." He was optimistic, not cynical, about the system. He did not think his bland fellowship needed to recruit any geniuses, but if any eccentrics were recruited by mistake the organization could iron out their rough spots. The organization man wanted to rise, but not so high that his neck would stick out. In the view of executives and personnel officers of the 1950s the leader in those stable times should be an administrator. If the organization needed a new idea from time to time, let it come from the staff. The corporation did not want people with drive and imagination.[8]

HIERARCHY LIVES

The corporate culture after World War II may have been hypocritical and deadening, but before dismissing it as a hopeless anachronism, we should point out that it worked well. Loyalty gave managers security and the many tiers of hierarchy promised them a lifetime of possible promotions. If the old AT&T had 100 levels of hierarchy, as sometimes seemed the case to those dealing with the company, and promotions came on the average once every two years, then AT&T could promise an ambitious

---

*Drucker's book started off as a study of General Motors, where he had the run of the company for 18 months towards the end of World War II. But, as he notes in a 1983 epilogue to the book, GM was so angry with the results that he became a non-person to GM. While the book was a best-seller all over the world, GM did not even catalogue it in its library. One reason for the fury was that Drucker perceived then, when GM was at the pinnacle of its success, that GM needed reorganization, 40 years before the board or management realized it. Another reason was Drucker's call for "social responsibility." For instance, he said GM should be concerned for the health of the cities where it had plants. Alfred P. Sloan, GM's great chairman at the time, responded that GM had no responsibility where it had no authority. Selling cars was hard enough. It would be irresponsible for GM to enter another field, particularly one where it lacks authority as well as competence.

trainee a satisfying career path for 200 years. The corporation was something solid to hold on to. It replaced some of the social context and ties that were disappearing elsewhere, in the school, the church, the community, and the family. The classic corporation was, in fact, a huge success. It excelled at mass production. It worked well too where control was especially important, in the airlines, for example. With its intricate division of labor, it created functional excellence. People could get very good at their jobs. In a stable, predictable environment, the classic corporation could do what it was supposed to do very well. It made possible the American manufacturing revolution, which raised standards of living to a level unimaginable a century ago. And it still does most of the work of sustaining our economy. Hierarchy has not disappeared. Jobs have not disappeared. Mass production has not become superfluous.

However, the classic corporation had inherent weaknesses that became more of a handicap as time passed. The hierarchies designed to control work became so cumbersome they were an obstacle to getting work done. The staffs meant to think for the organization and help the operational people became oppressive burdens that drove out innovation and entrepreneurship. The people doing the work had no real power; the people with the power did little real work. The classic corporation may have bred functional excellence, but it did not encourage coordination. Staffs and divisions feuded among each other; Chevrolet viewed Pontiac as being as much of a competitor as Ford. Mass production pushed products out on the market, but was not sensitive to what the market might want to pull out of the factory. In fact, the corporation grew more and more distant from the customer. Instead of spreading to the people who needed it to do their work, information got bottled up in the hierarchy. Ideas and conflicts got suppressed by a form of "teamwork" that meant playing along and not rocking the boat rather than working as a team to generate the best possible results.

THE IMMEDIATE THREAT

In short, corporations worked much as organizations of all kinds have worked through history. Catholics who strayed from Church doctrine by a hair confronted the Holy Inquisition. Medieval guilds would expel a member who dared to experiment with the way things were made traditionally (just as today unions seem to be the defenders of the status quo). In ancient Egypt physicians were trained to perform exactly 128 procedures, each in only one way. Egyptian artists learned there was only one way to paint a crocodile or a person.[9] Even in our lifetimes, armies prepared, as they always have, to fight the last war. Human nature seems to dislike change, whether it be in the way we kill, cure, worship, or work.

It takes a war to shake up an army and it took something like a war to shake up the American corporation. Its faults suddenly magnified and multiplied in 1979 and 1980 when a superior competitor strode onto the world market. America discovered that Japanese copying machines were better and cheaper than our own, that Japanese integrated circuits were far more reliable, and their exports of excellent cars brought Chrysler and Ford to the edge of ruin. The postwar complacency of the American corporation came to an end, although not all at once. The most immediately threatened companies, such as Xerox and Ford, began to change quickly. Companies cushioned for a while from competition by their size and success, such as General Motors and IBM, did not understand the new reality until more than a decade later.

Even the virtues of the classic corporation became a handicap. Skill at mass production is less of an advantage when new technology and organization allow you to meet the market by changing the product frequently and quickly, and by mass customizing. Big staffs and hierarchies become even more of a burden because they slow decisions and smother initiative. A rigidly functional structure stands in the way of the kind of teamwork that can produce rapid and innovative responses to competition. A company that insists rigidly on a chain of command cannot take advantage of new information technology.

The old corporation no longer made a good fit with the people that ran it, the people that worked for it, or the people that bought from it. The assumption that lay behind Taylorism—that the worker was stupid, ignorant, and lazy—is certainly not true now, if it ever was. Until 1910, when the great expansion of secondary school education began in the United States, barely 10% of young Americans were high school graduates.[10] In the mid-1990s, 70% of the students who entered ninth grade graduated, and 62% of them went on to college. As well as being better educated, people are more independent-minded today. Americans raised in the 1960s and later question authority and are not about to do just what they are told. They can make their own decisions. Customers are also more demanding. In the following chapters we will describe in more detail the drivers of change—new information technology, tougher competition, and the demands of society and the customer—all of which contribute to the obsolescence of the classic corporation.

JERKING HONDA'S WHEEL

The same need to change exists in Europe and Asia as well as in the United States, of course, but it is muffled if not suppressed by other, different, and even contrary pressures. Perhaps only in Britain is the corporation as free to experiment and innovate as it is in the United States. On the Continent and in Japan a whole set of social, economic, and political constraints forces executives to react differently from the way American executives react to the same problems. Cozy relationships between politicians and executives, between banks and corporations have inhibited independent behavior. The stockholders who might rebel against incompetent managers in the United States have been generally too insignificant or well-behaved to revolt in Europe or Japan. In France and Germany, especially, labor unions have a power they have lost elsewhere. In Germany some of the very features of the economy that made it such a success after World War II have inhibited change. The "social market economy" is a market economy with a social side meant to limit the pain the market can inflict on workers. Germany's "industrial democracy" puts the workers in positions of power on corporate supervisory boards. When confronted with the need to change, European executives have one overwhelming fact to consider—that the unemployment rate in Europe is double what it is in the United States. Ironically, the very changes that might create jobs in Europe are inhibited by the high rate of unemployment.

Jobs are also a major inhibitor of change in Japan. The 1990s recession in Japan forced corporations there to take another look at the guaranty of lifetime employment so that they might be freer to change and raise productivity. But they backed off the thought of dropping lifetime employment contracts, although they have done some tinkering. Ryuzaburo Kaku, CEO of Canon Inc., says that the restructuring of Canon does not include an end to the lifetime employment system. Only business, not government, can offer employment, he says, therefore "companies have a responsibility to maintain the existing social system." Kaku believes that only companies that come up with ways of maintaining employment will survive in the 21st century, and those that pursue only profits will not survive.[11]

Japan, which only a decade or two ago had so much to teach Americans about improving management, now finds itself hobbled from keeping up with American management. However, global competition is forcing Japan to change. The cartels that keep prices high are eroding, companies such as Matsushita and Canon and Honda are restructuring, with the constraint of not laying off large numbers of employees. The Japanese feel the need to change. When Nobuhiko Kawamoto became CEO of Honda in 1990 he "sensed something had to be done quickly to prepare Honda for the future. . . . As a result, I made a decision to jerk Honda's steering wheel."[12] Beyond what his own company should do, Kawamoto believes Japan should move to share common standards, values, and perceptions with the rest of the world. In the last 50 years, he says, Japan has "forced or coerced" its own way in the world. The country has changed twice radically in the last century, after the Meiji Restoration and after World War II, but the Japanese psyche is still back in the Tokugawa period of isolation and rule by shoguns. That has to change, says Kawamoto.[13]

FED UP AT DAIMLER

In Europe, in spite of regulations, restrictive trade practices, old boy networks, strong unions, and high unemployment, business has started to respond to the urgent need to change. The privatization of major companies, such as British Telecom, Deutsche Telekom, Pechiney, Saint-Gobain, and scores of others has forced them to become more efficient. Being competitive in international markets is at least as important to European firms as it is to the Japanese, and more so than to Americans. Much of German business has always been export-oriented. In the cases of big companies based in small countries, such as Electrolux in Sweden, Nestlé, Roche Holdings, and Sandoz in Switzerland, Philips in the Netherlands, and Solvay in Belgium, domestic sales are a very small fraction of total sales.

European executives and investors are rebelling against the comfortable, established ways of doing business in Europe. When Deutsche Bank got fed up with huge losses and poor acquisitions at Daimler-Benz AG it used its position as majority stockholder to force out CEO Edzard Reuter in 1994. What a shock to the German business establishment! His successor, Jürgen Schrempp, set about doing other shocking things, mainly abandoning the money-losing Dutch aircraft subsidiary, Fokker N.V., in 1996. A cozy collective bargaining system that sets industry-wide agreements has produced labor peace but has also given German workers the shortest work-week and the highest pay in the industrialized world. But when the metals industry federation, Gesamtmetall, agreed in 1995 to a pay increase well above the rate of inflation *and* a one-hour cut in the work-week to 35 hours, rebellious companies forced the head of Gesamtmetall to resign. Some companies quit the federation; others just negotiated their own deals with labor.

In France, graduates of the "grandes écoles" at the summit of business and government have looked after each other nicely. They formed a tight network which pretty well has run the country. When a small bank, Banque Pallas-Stern, got into trouble in 1995 it naturally turned for help to France's biggest company, Elf Aquitaine SA, a depositor and shareholder. Instead of helping, Philippe Jaffre, the Elf chairman, pulled his $200-million deposit out of the bank and said, "This bank is not my problem." The bank sank.[14] The network is losing its solidarity.

Europe offers one example of what may be a model of the corporate form of the future. ABB Asea Brown Boveri Ltd., a $36-billion-a-year electrical engineering company, is an obsessively decentralized organization with a minimal staff at corporate headquarters in Zurich. Percy Barnevik, the Swede who pulled together the Swiss-Swedish giant in 1987, cut the combined headquarters staff of 6,000 people to 171. They supervise 1,300 operating companies with 5,000 profit centers in 140 countries. The difference between ABB and earlier decentralized large organizations, such as GM, is that the entrepreneurs are out in the field, at the fingertips of the company, and not in the home office. Just one layer of managers separates the top of the company from managers in the field. A proprietary automated information system ties the company together.

A QUANTUM WORLD

ABB may be the model of the next enterprise, or one model, or it might even become irrelevant. In the United States there does not yet exist a model for the 21st century company and maybe there never will be. What emerges may come in many different shapes and styles. Perhaps it is even wrong to think of the next enterprise in terms of the organization. John Sculley has mutated from being the formal head of a formal organization (PepsiCo) to the formal head of a somewhat informal organization (Apple Computer) to the informal head of an informal organization: he runs a network of interests and companies which are themselves networks rather than organizations. He says, "I don't think that it makes too much difference how you organize companies anymore." What really matters, he argues, is being able to reach your customers and serve them in a manner that is going to be satisfactory to them and competitive in the marketplace. "As long as you have set up the processes that allow you to implement successfully, I do not think it makes much difference which particular organization design you end up choosing."[15]

Rather than looking at themselves as pyramids or structures defined by hierarchical tables, companies are more inclined today to look at themselves as a series of related processes. What matters is how you do things, not how you design the organization chart.

Our concepts of organization may be changing fundamentally, paralleling fundamental changes in our ideas about physics and the environment. We can look to our understanding of science for guidance in our understanding of organizations. Newtonian physics sees a mechanical world which can be explained by studying each of its parts separately in increasing detail. But 20th century quantum physics explains the world not in terms of stable pieces of matter, but in terms of electrons, neutrons, photons, protons, and other particles of energy that are constantly responding to and changing each other. Likewise, the organization may be seen not as a stable, mechanical arrangement of parts, but as a network of relationships. In a Newtonian world you manage by control, by linear thought, by reduction, by mechanical means, by specializing. In a quantum world you manage—if you can manage at all—by being adaptable, open, conscious of relationships and of the whole. In the first, things predominate; in the second, people.[16]

The complexity of corporations has to be recognized and, once recognized, demands a different view of how to run a business. Corporations can be included among the "complex adaptive systems," a concept developed by the Santa Fe Institute, a think tank that has attracted many scholars and businessmen dissatisfied with the way things are. Complex systems can be found in many places in the natural world—the ecology, an ant colony, the human brain—and in our society—political parties, cultural and social groups, the economy, companies. Each system is a network of agents (nerve cells, in the case of the human brain) constantly acting and reacting to each other. "There is no master neuron in the brain, for example, nor is there any master cell within a developing embryo," explains Mitchell Waldrop, a *Science* magazine writer who has pursued ideas about complexity at length. "If there is to be any coherent behavior in the system, it has to arise from competition and cooperation among the agents themselves."[17] Without the benefit of human boss or biological control center, these complex systems do indeed behave coherently. They are especially good at adapting to change. Because their world is so complex, they could not adapt successfully under unified control. If the corporation is viewed as one of these complex systems, then the old command-and-control model becomes inadequate.

A similar view of organization emerges from chaos theory, which sees chaos not as a total lack of order, but as turbulence, movement, change that is unpredictable but that actually has rules of its own. The founder of VISA International, Dee Hock, who warns of "massive institutional failure" in our future, talks of the "chaordic" organization. Like VISA or the Internet, the chaordic organization has no head, but is self-organizing, self-regulating, organic, adaptable, and complex. Perhaps what makes the chaordic idea appealing is the complexity of modern organizations; the parts can't know the whole, and the whole can't know all the parts.[18]

Our social organization suggests another way of looking at business organization that has been developed by Russell Ackoff, a management consultant who used to be a professor of unorthodox leanings at the Wharton School. Ackoff traces the evolution of the corporation from the bad old mechanical model to the better biological model (after World War I) to the even better social model (after World War II). He describes a "democratic hierarchy" in which there is no ultimate authority. Rather, each individual can participate directly or through a representative in decisions that affect him or her. Ackoff describes such power as "circular" because anyone with authority over others in a democracy is subject to the collective authority of those others.[19] Some companies have actually organized themselves by Ackoff's principles (see Chapter 9), although his ideas have so far had wider appeal than application. But they need to be considered in the creation of the next enterprise.

Before we let ourselves be carried off into a chaordic or chaotic future, let's not lose our heads. We haven't seen the organization of the future, we don't know what the model looks like. We aren't about to discard hierarchies, functions, controls, and linear thinking. We do know, however, that corporations have no choice but to respond to certain irresistible drivers: information technology, new levels of competition, new standards and expectations of consumers and society. These are discussed in the next four chapters. The response by corporations to these drivers is discussed in the subsequent chapters.

Pointers

It would be hard to find a corporation that can do business as it did at the beginning of the 1980s. Many have attempted to respond to the massive changes that have washed through business since then. Few have responded effectively. One reason for the ineffectual response is that business leaders simply have not appreciated how different their world has become. Here are some of the questions that should signal to a company how much it needs to change:

- Have the organization, leadership, and style of management remained pretty much the same for the last two decades?
- Has the idea of change, frequent if not constant, been accepted?
- Has the company's culture become innovative, open, and receptive?
- Has the company embraced information technology?
- Have competitors, foreign or domestic, changed the nature of the market?
- Has deregulation or privatization affected the business?
- Has new technology changed the products and services?
- Have the customer's total needs been fully understood?
- Has the company opened itself up to alliances and partnerships?

I
THE DRIVERS

2

THE COMPUTER'S REIGN

The information system is the firm.

—Thomas N. Urban, ex-chairman, Pioneer Hi-Bred
International Incorporated

P ioneer Hi-Bred sells more corn (maize) seed to farmers in America and around the world than anyone else. Henry A. Wallace, who liked to experiment with plant genetics while he was still in high school, founded the firm in 1926. "HA," as he is still known in Des Moines around the modest company headquarters, where his bust stands in the lobby, went off to Washington to become Franklin Roosevelt's secretary of agriculture. Wallace became vice president in 1940, then turned political mystic, ran for president on the Progressive Party ticket in 1948, and never returned to Des Moines. But the company flourished. Pioneer grew into the most successful seed company in the world. It provides 43% of the hybrid corn seed sold in North America and its worldwide sales reached $1.5 billion in 1996.

Pioneer remains much the same company it has been for nearly seven decades. People are expected to work there a long time and if their relatives come to work too, that's fine. Many of the salesmen are still part-

SEI Survey	
Reorganizing around information technology is critical	70%
We are doing it	13%

time farmers who will take the time to stop and chat with neighboring farmers. A critical piece of equipment remains the "weigh wagon," hauled behind the sales reps' pickups and used to analyze crops, comparing the yields of different hybrids. "We don't get all shook up about the revolution of the moment," says Tom Hanigan, vice president and director of information management.

Yet within this solid midwestern framework Pioneer is racing to become a 21st century company. Electronic data and communications provide the fuel that powers and shapes the transformation of Pioneer. Salesmen still use their weigh wagons, but the more important tools today are the laptop computers they carry. With one of them the salesman can give the farmer a mass of data about seeds, yields, cost-benefit ratios, diseases, pesticides, and herbicides. Today's farmer is often a businessman with a degree from an agricultural college, a PC in the house, and a consulting agronomist at his elbow. He wants ideas—and very detailed, specific information. With a portable printer, the Pioneer rep can run off copies of Iowa State University pamphlets identifying plant diseases. The salesman can also log on to Pioneer's data base on 505,000 farmers, which includes names, addresses, phone numbers, previous crops, planting yields, animals, orders, and the farmer's payment record.

Anyone who thinks information systems have simply made Pioneer more competitive misses the point. Thomas Urban, whose father was Wallace's first salesman and who became Pioneer's CEO, puts it more dramatically. A sober, thoughtful man, Urban retired as Pioneer chairman at the end of 1996 and now teaches at the Harvard Business School. Here is how he describes what information technology has done to Pioneer:

> The cost and speed of the new information technologies now allow us to think of our businesses quite differently. The idea of a firm has always been embedded in its information flow. Increased speed and reduced cost of management information now allows us to extract that idea and manipulate it to our advantage. Information effectively represents the discrete elements of our business. We can now relate each element in new ways, creating a seamless flow of activity resulting in a significant improvement in meeting customer needs. Assets, customers, products, and employees are, in reality

information sites which generate, receive, and send data and ideas. The most useful description of the firm today is, in fact, a description of the content and flow of the information between those sites. I submit this is a more revolutionary idea than it might first appear to be. . . . The organization of information at Pioneer is now redefining our structure as well as job descriptions, reward systems, and finally, the distribution of power, authority, and responsibility. Repositioning the firm around the information process, in fact, has become the critical organizational tool allowing us to speed product development and relate those products to our customers' needs. . . . Our information system is, in fact, the business, not an adjunct to it, or a support system for it. . . . The company is organized around, and driven by, the flow of information. . . . The information system is the firm.[1]

We have all been told often enough, even if we haven't exactly experienced it or plain don't understand it, how electronic information systems are changing our lives. With a computer and modem, we can send e-mail almost free and delivered almost instantly to a friend in Hong Kong, download the text of the president's latest Saturday radio chat, reserve seats on a flight to Lexington, join a forum to play chess, dig up information on a company that interests us, shop for a new bed, or learn about a disease that has stricken a friend. Very interesting, entertaining, fascinating as a novel way of doing things electronically, and often very useful. But hardly enough to change the life of the individual, although it may come to that.

However, as the Pioneer story shows, computerized information does change the life of a business. It changes the way companies are organized, the way they are managed, the relationships among their people and with their customers, suppliers, and partners. It changes the scope and understanding of a business, the organization and flow of work, the way work is performed. It changes marketing and distribution, it lowers the barriers confronting entrepreneurs, and reduces the differences between big and little companies.

The existence of new information technology does not assure us it will be used profitably or productively. Look at television, which might be considered the new information technology of the 1950s and 1960s. TV's record is so mixed that its influence on our lives might well be on balance negative. TV has certainly debased politics and our taste in entertainment. Another advance in information technology, automated menus driven by touch-tone phones, is at best a mixed blessing. The menu system may save the company money, but does the customer prefer to flounder through a series of menus listening to mechanical voices, quite likely ending up at the starting point or in the wrong place, or does he prefer to find a responsive, intelligent being at the other end of the line? Would Federal Express be a success today, or even exist, if customers' calls weren't answered promptly by helpful agents and instead were shunted into a multiple choice menu and interrupted by plugs and blurbs, irrelevant information, and the discouraging news that the average waiting time on hold is currently 13 minutes—which is what happens when you call a computer company for help in deciphering its unintelligible manual.

The problems raised by the adoption of information technology can be momentous. "Someone in St. Petersburg with a $3,000 computer can put our networks at risk," says Colin Crook, Citibank's senior technology officer. "The sheer problem of running networks, managing them, and protecting them to avoid systemic failure becomes a key concern. Planning is no longer possible in the world we live in, and it is really risk management that we need to focus on."[2]

The enormous importance of information technology to American business, if any proof were needed, is shown convincingly by trends in capital spending. (See Figure 2.1.)

THE COST OF SINGLE-PRICING

A decade ago People Express Airlines demonstrated convincingly the cost of failing to use advanced computer systems. For a while in the early 1980s, it looked as if People Express might be leading corporate America into the 21st century. It was innovative, used imaginative management approaches, and was briefly the fastest growing company in the United States. But its success rested on People's ability to price tickets below the prices charged by the major carriers.

American Airlines changed the whole game in January 1985. American had been developing its sophisticated computerized reservation system and now began using it to sell seats for as many as ten different prices on a single flight. The businessman making a last-minute trip

FIGURE 2.1

Business Investment in Computers

The Survey of Current Business tracks private spending on durable capital equipment in the United States and the growing portion of it devoted to information technology. The figures include the cost of software supplied with the hardware, but not the cost of additional software, which could be as much again as the hardware spending.

Year	Total Durable Equipment	Information Processing Equipment	Ratio
1960	$ 74.3 billion	$ 3 billion	4%
1965	$115.9	$ 5.5	5%
1970	$149.5	$ 10.7	7%
1975	$183.9	$ 16.9	9%
1980	$268.2	$ 45.4	17%
1985	$342.4	$ 88	26%
1990	$381.9	$116.2	30%
1995	$535.2	$201.8	38%
1996	$578.6	$241.9	42%

Source: Department of Commerce, *Survey of Current Business,* April 1996 and April 1997, National Data, Tables 5.4 and 5.5. Dollar figures are in "chained" (adjusted) 1992 dollars.

would pay the full price and the retiree or student sitting beside him might pay a fraction of that. Since American could track its loads accurately, it might not offer any discounted seats on a Friday night but sell off the whole flight cheap on a Wednesday. As far as most customers could see, it became as cheap to fly American as People. People's computers simply could not handle multiple-priced seating on a single flight. People could only offer one price. By the end of 1985 People had lost half its market share. Donald Burr, the founder and CEO, tried various desperate maneuvers to save the company, but they failed and he sold the airline in 1986. Lack of information technology was not the only reason, but it was a major one.[3] Airline reservation systems are so sophisticated today that they can make millions of price adjustments a day, changing the mix on each flight according to what has been sold and what needs to be sold. Passengers who can't get the price they want for a flight may call back an hour later and find that it is now available. Passengers also have sophisticated price information within easy reach. So the challenge to the airlines becomes one of yield management, to create the pricing model that can fill the most seats at the most profitable level.

Understanding the significance of information technology may be hard because we don't have the right frame of reference or frame of mind. Business people are literal minded, used to dealing with physical things, assets, inventories, machines, buildings, products. They even treat people as physical items, rather than as feeling, emotional beings. So we have looked at business information as a collection of physical items, something fixed and absolute that can be hoarded or tucked away. No wonder "lack of communication" often surfaces as one of the chief complaints people have about their employers. And how do we usually answer that complaint? Create an employee newsletter, set out a suggestion box, put slogans on the wall, hold a seminar, send out a memo! All of them amount to more *things.*

But if you think about matter (physical things) and memory (information) you can turn conventional thinking upside down and see that memory is more permanent than matter and that similarly, in business, knowledge is more substantial than physical assets. Margaret Wheatley, in her provocative book, *Leadership and the New Science,* shows how science can give us a new perspective on information. The human body appears solid and stable, but the materials in our physical cells are constantly being replaced. Even the atoms in our brain cells are replaced every 12 months or so, while the knowledge in the brain remains. Our cells change, but the information in our DNA does not change. "Information organizes matter into form, resulting in physical structures," Dr. Wheatley writes. But instead of recognizing the life-giving properties of information, we treat it as inert, something to be squashed down into averages and statistics that miss the details and the peculiarities.[4]

THE DECISIVE FACTOR

The new view of information combines powerfully with the recognition that knowledge is critical to business. Peter Drucker, Daniel Bell, and others have written of the transformation we are experiencing today. Neither land nor capital nor labor are decisive today, as they were in the past. Knowledge is the decisive factor of production. Drucker likens the knowledge revolution to what occurred after Gutenberg invented printing with movable type in 1455 and what occurred at the end of the 18th century, which witnessed the beginnings of capitalism, communism, and the industrial revolution. The knowledge revolution, he says, began with the G.I. Bill of Rights that sent so many returning World War II veterans to college and will end somewhere around 2010 or 2020.[5] (That would coincide approximately with the time when engineers may hit the theoretical limit of their ability to cram transistors into a single chip—which is believed to be one trillion transistors.)

Paul Allaire, the CEO of Xerox Corp., grew up with the computer. He took the first courses on computers offered at Worcester Polytechnic Institute four decades ago and then worked as an engineer with Univac. He saw the use of computers emerge from plain calculating in the 1950s, to data processing in the '60s, to information processing in the '80s, and then to "knowledge creation" in the '90s. This latest step, he says, allows us to devise significantly different organizations for the first time since the Church and the military established the hierarchical model as the standard way of organizing human endeavor.[6]

The knowledge made available by computers allows us to know that which used to be unknowable. For example, we can know exactly what is selling today in every store in a chain. It allows us to react immediately through computer-integrated flexible manufacturing, to produce exactly what the market wants at that moment, whether the quantity be one or one million.

Information technology permits us to choose whether to centralize an organization or decentralize it to a degree impossible before, while retaining whatever level of control and information we wish at the center. It democratizes the organization because now everyone in the organization can have the information needed to make decisions. But it also allows top management an unprecedented opportunity to monitor in detail and in real time the performance of people all over the company, or the levels of quality or productivity they are achieving. Information technology creates enormous efficiencies in the routine or backroom operations of corporations, to the point where they can function with a fraction of the people they once had. One major bank estimates that the full application of information technology and electronic cash could eliminate the need for nearly nine out of ten of its current employees, already reduced in numbers.

THE 24-HOUR DAY

The competitive advantages achieved by those who use information well are formidable. Some of the most effective new business techniques, such as just-in-time production, flexible manufacturing, and fast cycle time, depend on computerized information. It gives the small company the opportunity to compete with larger companies, because computers do much of what large staffs used to do. With communications virtually free worldwide, the local company can act like a global company. With their more intense use of information technology, American companies have an advantage over their European and Japanese competitors that may last well into the 21st century. Instead of being the Asian century, as it is often described, the 21st could be another American century, thanks to information technology!

Electronic information is especially useful in helping the corporations follow, analyze, classify, select, satisfy, court, stroke, cling to, or herd (or cull) the almighty customer to a degree once impossible. Corporations can know more about their customers and their habits and react more precisely to their wants. They can carve markets into segments they didn't even know existed before, and create new products for those segments. They can create market segments of one, or mass-customize products by individual customers. Retailers can send individual specifications direct to the factory, which means Levi Strauss can "mass-customize" a pair of jeans for you from a central factory. They can serve their markets differently too, for instance by going directly to the customer through the Internet. Customers can look into the UPS or FedEx computers to find out the status of their shipments.

Information technology reduces generally the need for intermediaries in sales, in management, and in the handling of information itself. Executives can integrate and understand their operations better and make connections they never could make before. With good information technology, corporations can refine their behavior to a format called "sense and respond," in contrast to the old ways of doing things, known now somewhat disparagingly as "make and sell."

All these advantages come at a price, of course. The speed of change imposed by computer technology adds disruption and uncertainty to our lives, which is never comfortable. Our jobs become less secure. Corporations face new risks, the risk that their information systems can be invaded or sabotaged, and the risk that a single employee, empowered and wired, can create havoc, even bring a corporation crashing down, as happened at Barings. When any corporation is so close to oblivion, then risk management has to be a company priority. Information technology makes it possible to develop and market new products rapidly, but by the same token the competition can imitate you quickly too. You can no longer use technology to hang on to an advantage long-term, as Henry Ford did for years with the Model T. Another risk is that you become so dazzled with computerized information that you lose the ability to think critically. As secretary of defense during the Vietnam War, Robert McNamara offered computerized summaries of the trends in the number of villages declaring loyalty to South Vietnam and of comparative casualties on both sides as convincing evidence that the United States was winning. We were perhaps more naive about information technology then than we are now, but the very fact that the data about Vietnam had been entered on computers conferred some legitimacy on spurious information.

Our own lives can be both blessed and cursed by information technology. The speed of change and the automation of work adds to our job insecurity, of course, but technology creates new jobs and opportunities too. Cheap and rapid global communications give us the 24-hour business day, which means work on research and other projects can continue around the clock somewhere in the world. We can call for help from anywhere in the world in a few moments. But all that information also means interruptions at any time, maybe less sleep and less time to think.

Information technology gives us more freedom to choose where and how we work, to set our own hours, but it also may separate us even more than we are already from other people. Instead of moving from the city to the suburb, we can move to the country and spend our days "interacting" with the computer. The computer can divide society in other ways as well. For the young and well-educated, dealing with the computer is as easy as breathing. Teenagers are the most at home with the computer. But older people—that is, those over 40—may find the computer age frightening. Many top executives just don't have firsthand experience with the computers that are making so much difference to their companies. The poorly educated cannot make the transition to the computer age. The age handicap will resolve itself as those raised on the computer get older, but the education handicap could get worse. Computers may create another category of haves and have-nots.

A meeting of some of America's most knowledgeable users of information technology, from business and from the universities, held at the University of Pennsylvania in mid-1996 to commemorate the 50th anniversary of the creation there of ENIAC, the first computer, was notable for the mild pessimism or gloom of some of the participants. They were concerned with some of the negative effects of information technology. They were also baffled by the increasing unpredictability of the future, not only long-term but short-term too. Yet the power of information technology to change business is unquestioned. It is one of the irresistible drivers that business has to accept.

Pointers

- Information technology (IT) can change almost everything about a company, its structure, its products, its markets, its processes.
- IT increases the value of invisible assets, such as knowledge, skills, and training.
- IT makes it possible to segment the market and customize products down to units of one.
- IT democratizes a company because employees have more information and can talk to anyone in the company.
- IT increases the flexibility of work by allowing more people to work at home, on the road, or at hours that suit them.
- IT helps make fast, fact-based decisions.
- IT allows companies to unify their global operations and to work a 24-hour day around the world.
- IT gives American corporations a competitive advantage since they have advanced the furthest in its application to management.

Links

- IT changes relationships with suppliers, customers, and partners, and allows all these parties to peer inside each others' systems to get the information they need directly.

- IT requires a better educated, better trained, and better motivated employee.

Cautions

- IT products better information faster, and may even create knowledge, but it doesn't furnish wisdom or intuition, which remain essential to good management.
- IT can create new social divisions, between the young and the middle-aged, between the educated and the uneducated, between rural, suburban, and city people.
- IT raises huge concerns about the vulnerability of organizations to sabotage, espionage, and vandalism.

3

THE MARKET'S IMPACT

> We are living through a transformation that will rearrange
> the politics and economics of the coming century. There will
> be no *national* products or technologies, no national corpora-
> tions, no national industries. There will no longer be national
> economies. . . . All that will remain rooted within national bor-
> ders are the people who comprise a nation. Each nation's pri-
> mary assets will be its citizens' skills and insights.
>
> —Robert Reich[1]

Trade among the world's nations, at least among the richer ones, exploded after World War II and, like the universe itself, keeps getting bigger and bigger faster and faster. At first, American corporations were the prime beneficiaries. They ruled world trade. But then the terms of competition began to change. Others acquired the technical and managerial skills and the capital that made American companies so successful, improving on them in some spheres, and often enjoying advantages conferred by cheaper labor and newer equipment.

Around 1980 the competition became qualitatively different. Before then, corporations with sizable foreign business had called themselves

SEI Survey	
Adopting a global posture and perspective is critical	77%
We are achieving it	34%

multinationals. With few exceptions they were basically "flag planters," domestic companies with foreign trading or manufacturing arms, or both, which might be very profitable but which were adjuncts to their domestic business. But in the 1980s the multinationals began to go "global." "Globalization" became a popular management mantra. *The Economist* soon called the idea "the stalest of buns." Yet it would be hard to find more than a handful of companies today that have become truly global, in the sense that they operate as one borderless company throughout the world. The need to be global becomes stronger every day, so there's still a long way for corporations to travel on the road to globalization. How they are trying to get there will be covered in Chapter 14. For the moment we will focus just on the competitive pressures that are pushing companies to do so.

The world's markets are merging and heating up. Lower trade barriers, the spread of information technology, the merging of consumer tastes and needs, and the easy movement of capital have all contributed to the creation of a global market. Companies whose home markets are close to saturation need and see new opportunities in markets opening elsewhere. They are willing and able to introduce new products around the world all at once, or with only slight pauses between launches in one country and another. If knowledge has become the prime factor of production (see Chapter 2), it is also the easiest way to move across boundaries. With faxes, computers, modems, cellular phones, the Internet, and private intranets, information flashes around the world. So does money. The global executive follows close behind by jet. In some businesses, especially those based on service and "knowledge" work, the ease of entry into global markets has intensified competition. A one-person software company operating out of a basement in Connecticut or an apartment in Calcutta can expand its business in Australia almost as readily as it can in, say, Pennsylvania. And in businesses requiring huge capital investments, such as aircraft, drugs, and computer chips, only a global market can pay back the investment.

The volume of international financial transactions has increased more than trade in goods and services, which in turn have grown more than the world's gross national product. The greatest acceleration came from direct foreign investment by multinational corporations and from international bond issues, international loans, and international currency transactions. Direct foreign investment reached a new high of $318 billion in 1996, up 57% from 1992.[2] Worldwide currency transactions grew 30% between 1992 and 1995 to a daily total of $1,190 billion—so that one week's exchange transactions amounted to about the annual total of exports of goods and services.[3]

"The global paradigm shift is unprecedented, unwitting, and irreversible," says Howard Perlmutter, a professor at the Wharton School who specializes in global business. "No one is in charge, most organizations and institutions are unprepared. You have a global overlap of sovereignty in most fields. You have global prices, a global exchange market, in which $1 trillion is traded daily. All countries want foreign investment."[4]

FINDING PROFITS ABROAD

The number and size of transnational corporations participating in that global market have grown enormously. In the 14 wealthy nations for which the United Nations Conference on Trade and Development has data going back 30 years, the number of transnational corporations nearly quadrupled between 1969 and 1995, from 7,000 to 26,000. If you include all 38,000 transnationals in the world, their 1993 sales amounted to $5.2 trillion, one billion dollars short of the gross domestic product of the United States that year.[5]

These multinationals grow their business faster and make more money than companies that stay home. A Conference Board survey of 1,250 American manufacturing firms reveals that the sales of companies with international operations grow twice as fast as the sales of purely domestic companies. The true multinationals—that is, companies with plants in all three major world markets—produce markedly better returns on assets and returns on equity than the domestic companies and than companies with a lesser international presence. All 64 companies in the survey with annual sales greater than $5 billion had some foreign activity but the handful with the minimal connections—licensing agreements and export offices—were the least profitable.[6]

Smallness appears to be no barrier to competing internationally because 91% of the companies with sales below $500 million a year had business outside the United States and they grew more briskly than purely domestic companies.[7] In another survey, *Inc.* magazine's 1995 list of 500 fast-growing small private companies (average sales $23 million), 46% reported international sales in 1994, up from 19% in 1990.[8] Small European companies naturally export more vigorously. In his study of *Hidden Champions,* Hermann Simon unearthed 122 German companies with sales of less than $1 billion, mostly much less, that had a dominant share of their world markets. On average, 51.2% of their sales were outside Germany. These were only the companies that agreed to answer Simon's questions. Many more chose to remain hidden.[9]

Competition has intensified for many other reasons. Massive deregulation and privatization has forced or freed up many monopolies and protected industries to fight for their lives. More demanding customers create new competitive opportunities. New techniques for improving the quality of goods and services and speeding their development and delivery heighten competition. However, the coming of world markets is the overwhelming reason for the intense competition that draws tight the nerves of business today. Even companies based in the United States, with its huge domestic market, are dependent for survival on international sales. A random selection of 1996 annual reports put out by large corporations gives even a casual reader a remarkable view of the importance of international markets in a year when the American economy was more robust than the European or Japanese economies and the dollar gained strength:

- **Baxter International** reported that 48% of its sales are outside the United States, but they produce 73% of its profits.
- **General Electric's** foreign revenues reached $33.3 billion or 40% of total revenues, up from 20% a decade earlier. By the millennium, GE expects foreign sales to overtake domestic sales; they are growing three times as fast as domestic sales.
- **General Motors** reported 37% of its automotive sales were outside the United States and expects that number to reach 50% in the near future. GM's net profit margins were 1.2% in North America and 4.3% on international operations.
- **IBM's** 1996 sales in the United States accounted for 52% of total sales but only 14% of profits.

Without their international sales, these companies and many other companies would stagnate. (For a comparison of sales and assets of the largest transnationals, see Figure 3.1.)

FIGURE 3.1

The Top Transnationals

The ten largest transnational corporations, ranked according to their foreign sales, are almost equally divided between the United States, Europe, and Japan. The list looks much different if the companies are ranked by the size of their foreign assets, which is how the United Nations Conference on Trade and Development ranks them. By assets, they come out in this order: Royal Dutch Shell, Ford, Exxon, General Motors, IBM, Volkswagen, General Electric, Toyota, Daimler-Benz, Elf Aquitaine. Here is the ranking by foreign sales (all figures are for 1994 and are in billions of dollars except the employment numbers):

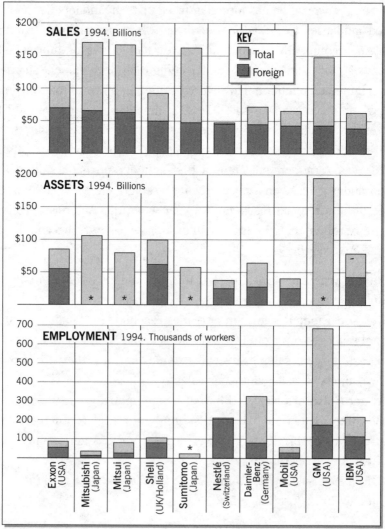

*Foreign data not disclosed

Source: United Nations Conference on Trade and Development, *World Investment Report 1996* (New York and Geneva: United Nations, 1996), pp. 31–32.

GROWING WITH ASIA

Business has to go where the growth is. For the past 20 years, economic growth in the industrialized countries with their mature markets has lagged behind growth in the rest of the world, especially Asia. The gap has widened recently. Figures compiled by *The Economist* in 1997 showed the United States and Japanese gross domestic products advancing 3.1%, Germany's by 1.9%. But look at the growth numbers for the developing countries in Asia: China 9.4%, Thailand 8.6%, Malaysia 8.1%, Indonesia 7.8%, South Korea 7.2%, India 7%, Taiwan 6.6%, Singapore 5.8%, the Philippines 5.2%. Latin America also has some promising growth, although it is erratic. Argentina's GNP was growing by 9.2%, Chile's by 7.7%, and Mexico's by 7.6%.[10]

These growth figures explain the interest, for example, of the auto companies in pressing into new markets in Asia. Excluding Japan and South Korea, sales of new vehicles expanded 17% in 1995 in East Asia and are expected to continue to expand rapidly for the next few years, in spite of the appalling pollution and traffic jams in many Asian cities. These figures explain why Honda, General Motors, and Toyota either have built or plan to build auto plants in Thailand. GM, a late starter, produces vehicles in new plants in Indonesia and India, has begun construction of a new plant in Thailand, and has approval to start a joint venture to make midsize sedans in Shanghai. Ford completed a new Escort plant in India in 1996, plans another there in 1998, and has launched a $500-million joint venture with Mazda to build pickup trucks in Thailand.

While Asia is the best, it is not the only region of new opportunity. Latin America has shifted fundamentally from the populist, protectionist policies that went back to the mercantile economics of colonial days to more realistic free-market policies. Falling tariffs, reduced inflation, and privatization of large enterprises have created new trade and investment opportunities—with some serious risks attached. The collapse of the Soviet Union opened up a vast portion of the earth to new business for those brave enough to work with instability and even physical danger. The competition to grab a share of growing economies pulls other companies along into the global market. Ford and GM want suppliers who can work with them around the world. All the big players want bankers, data processing companies, travel agencies, advertising agencies, consultants who can provide them with "global solutions," in the current business jargon. These suppliers have to follow their clients wherever they go.

The top advertising agencies and accounting and consulting firms are all global and enjoy a huge advantage over their local or regional competitors. The advantage will likely grow as their clients sell more of the same products around the world and consolidate their business into one or a handful of firms. "We don't have a major advertiser who hasn't consolidated," says Joseph Plummer, vice chairman of DMB&B, a New York agency.[11] IBM replaced some 40 firms with just one in 1994; Fiat, GM, Kellogg, Kodak, and Philips have only two; Bristol-Myers and Ford have three; Procter & Gamble three, and Nestlé five. (Coca-Cola, on the other hand, replaced one firm with some 30 agencies in 1991 because it felt captive to the one company, but it did consolidate each brand under one firm.)

THE NEW DYNAMICS OF DRUGS

The pharmaceutical companies, to take the example of one industry, have to be global in a much tougher market. "The drug industry had been a very profitable gentleman's club," says Robert C. Holmes, executive director for strategic planning and management at Astra Merck. "All could make money and there was no pressure on prices. The doctors determined the treatment. Then came the health care debate and a revolt against double-digit price inflation. The whole industry's dynamics changed. It became more competitive. Now people are very conscious of costs and the consumer is involved. So to cut costs, health organizations look, for example, at the 12 ACE [angiotension-converting enzyme] inhibitors [to control blood flow and pressure] and maybe put just two on the formulary and then negotiate the price of those two with the pharmaceutical company. In the 1980s all 12 could sell profitably. The market for secondary products is disappearing. You have to be the first or second to market."[12] A second generation of somewhat better drugs that have fewer side effects but are six times as expensive as the ACE inhibitors came to market in the 1990s with a much reduced potential. Until the 1980s a "me-too" drug could be brought out at a lower risk than the trailblazer with prospects of selling very well (and with a patent that would last beyond the patent of the first drug). Peak-year sales of a late entrant could run to $1 billion or more, but today the follow-on drug's best year probably would not exceed $500 million.[13]

The new dynamics of the pharmaceutical industry put particular pressure on small or medium-sized companies to go global one way or another, by expanding, merging, or seeking partners. The drive to reduce costs is worldwide and most countries other than the United States control drug prices. The risks and the costs of developing new drugs cannot be borne by sales in any one national market. It takes as much as $500 million (if the costs are capitalized to the time of approval) to get a new drug on the market. Back in the 1960s it cost only a few million dollars to create a new drug. But since the 1970s the costs have grown much faster than inflation, the success rate has fallen, and the total development time to approval has stretched from about six years in the early 1960s to 13 years in the 1990s. The risks are greater for smaller companies than large ones because it takes them longer and costs them more to get approval.[14]

Rhône-Poulenc, which started life as a small-town pharmacy outside Paris in 1858, was a faltering giant that had been rescued from possible bankruptcy by government takeover when Jean-René Fourtou became chairman in 1986. Fourtou, a consultant until the government asked him to put some life into Rhône-Poulenc, decided his priorities were to privatize the company, decentralize management, and to concentrate on businesses where the company could be a world player. Although it was the biggest chemical and pharmaceutical company in France and it ranked 72d on *Fortune's* Global 500 list, it had no real global reach, especially in the United States and Japan. In the United States it had a small trading operation for its chemicals and had not developed a market for its drugs.

Rhône-Poulenc found an American partner in the Rorer Group, a feisty pharmaceutical company, 432d on *Fortune's* list of 500 U.S. industrials, which had little competitive potency on its own except an ability to move quickly. The two companies had come to know each other in the 1980s when both were trying unsuccessfully to acquire American Cyanamid. Instead they decided to form Rhône-Poulenc Rorer in the United States in 1990. Robert Cawthorn, the Yorkshireman who came out of Rorer to head the pharmaceutical business in the new company, says "Rhône-Poulenc was strong in Europe, but had no presence in the

U.S. Rorer was not very strong in the U.S., less strong in Europe. Neither company had a strong position in Japan. It was a good fit geographically. We at Rorer realized we were not going to be able to continue to grow by acquisition. And, we were too small to hope to spend enough on research to have a steady flow of products. Rhône-Poulenc desperately needed access to the U.S. market, and they realized they were too small overall."[15]

With the acquisition of Rorer, Rhône-Poulenc now had a global pharmaceutical business, run out of Rorer headquarters in Collegeville, Pennsylvania. While the Rorer acquisition put Rhône-Poulenc on the global map for pharmaceuticals, the French company also needed to internationalize its chemicals business. First, Fourtou took the company out of two unpromising areas, textiles, where the competition from Asia was too stiff, and electronic tapes and disks, which had become low-return commodity businesses. Then he set about becoming a force in North America, where the company had only a small trading business in chemicals. Rhône-Poulenc bought 18 U.S. companies over the next ten years, including Union Carbide's agricultural products division and Stauffer Chemicals' basic chemical business. This massive invasion of North America, at a total cost of $4.5 billion (including a 68% share of RPR), raised Rhône-Poulenc's revenues in North America from a mere 3% of its total sales in the mid-1980s to 26% by 1995.

Whether the enormous expense and effort of the last decade to play the international game has been worthwhile remains to be seen. The shares of the parent company in France went nowhere from 1992 to 1996, and then finally did pick up, while the Rorer partner performed very well on the stock market in 1995 and 1996. But both are now important players in the world markets. They are not destined to disappear, as seemed possible in the mid-1980s.

WHO WILL COMPETE WITH AT&T?

International markets set the pace, but other powerful forces are also heightening competition. Domestic markets have been freed up by deregulation and privatization. The United States deregulated its airlines and, although passengers might have some doubts about how they benefited, fares have dropped and the bedlam of competition set off by deregulation continues now, two decades later. The electric power industry, the model of consistently profitable, regulated monopoly, now faces competition.

All of the major drivers of competition—new technology, deregulation, and growing global markets—come together in the communications industry. Before the breakup of AT&T by consent decree in 1984, a telephone was just a telephone and most people used Ma Bell to make their local and long distance calls. Today you have to ask: Who will be AT&T's chief competitors? The cable TV companies with their high-capacity communications lines? The Internet connections, which can already provide rudimentary phone service anywhere in the world virtually free through local lines? The providers of wireless cellular service? Or will the competition come from the seven regional Bell companies? They were freed by the Telecommunications Act of 1996 to compete with AT&T's long-distance service, as AT&T was freed to compete with them in local service. What about companies in the adjacent communications industries, such as business information providers and systems integrators? The other long distance providers? Foreign telecommunications companies, such as Nippon Telegraph and Telephone? All of them can compete with AT&T and any of them could emerge as major competitors.

AT&T and other telecoms face a bewildering set of choices, which is one reason why AT&T has gone through so much upheaval since the days when it was a regulated monopoly. The same conditions of technological upheaval and deregulation give AT&T the opportunity to expand into new businesses. Whatever the choices may be, the customer—at least the business customer—will want one-stop shopping around the world. The communications world is a lot more complicated, but the customer wants it simple, just as when a telephone was only a telephone. For AT&T there's no choice about going global. Before divestiture, in 1983, AT&T was in five countries and had 1,000 employees overseas. By 1995, AT&T had 52,000 employees in more than 100 countries.[16] (Most of them went with Lucent and NCR when AT&T split again, but 6,000 remained as overseas AT&T employees.)

With its strong brand name and its heft as the world's largest telecommunications company, AT&T can be handicapped only by poor management. The acquisition of McCaw Cellular Communications in 1994 put AT&T in a strong position to compete for cellular customers around the world. But other decisions and acquisitions hurt AT&T badly. The rewards for the best global performers will be enormous. AT&T estimates that the "global communications and information market" will grow from $1 trillion in 1995 to $2 trillion either in 2000 or 2005 (depending on which page of the company's 1995 annual report you read).[17] Whatever the number, no one will deny that the growth will be vast.

TRYING TO ACT LIKE AN ISLAND

Reports from Japan indicate the competitive spirit there is even breaking into its cartel- and regulation-ridden business culture. Japan's tigerish competitiveness is confined, of course, to a few major exporting companies in a few major industries. Cartels smother the domestic economy, fixing high prices for everything from haircuts to steel. The government regulates and subsidizes much of the economy, forcing travelers to pay exorbitant domestic airfares, for example, and preserving so much farmland around Tokyo that the unfortunate "sarariman" has to commute two hours each way to find housing he can afford.

Kenichi Ohmae, formerly managing partner for McKinsey & Company in Tokyo, writes that younger Japanese, the "Nintendo" generation, are rebelling against these constraints on enjoying the fruits of Japanese economic success. They resent the high prices they have to pay for goods and services, and they get around them where they can. Foreign travel is a bargain and 97% of the newlyweds in Japan honeymoon abroad (which is the exact reverse of what the previous generation did). They can use phone, fax, or computer to order clothing from Land's End or L.L. Bean, or get software support from Singapore, or earn higher interest on their money in Great Britain than they can get from a Japanese bank.[18]

Business and the government are moving, if sluggishly, to make Japan's economy more competitive. Just like many American companies, Japanese companies move operations overseas when they find costs at home too high. Rather than go on buying high-priced Japanese steel, the automakers are buying some of their steel from South Korea. In 1991, the Japanese Fair Trade Commission fined the cement makers $110 million for price fixing and then, with a beefed-up staff, moved against a half-dozen other industries.[19] After privatizing Nippon Telegraph and Telephone, second only in the world to AT&T, in 1985, the Japanese government backed off two opportunities to deregulate the phone company. But in 1996 it announced plans to divide NTT into a long distance company and two domestic companies.

Japan has a long way to go. "No industrialized nation can be an economic island," writes Ohmae, "yet Japan continues to behave like one." The government still acts "as though it can continue to control its own national economic destiny entirely by itself—that is, as though borders still fundamentally matter in the global economy."

Even though Ohmae writes off the importance of national borders, he does recognize that national differences in tastes, laws, and customs are important considerations for the transnational corporation.[20] The world is not one homogenous market or workplace, not yet at least. Coca Cola, Kleenex, Panasonic, and Rolex are worldwide brands that sell the same products everywhere for pretty much the same reasons. However, other products don't travel so well. Chinese like their rice rather dry while Japanese like it sticky; Americans like furniture and appliances that are bigger than what Japanese and Europeans prefer. Therefore some things are best organized on a regional or national basis. Credit cards seem to travel well, but insurance policies don't.

The auto companies have made some obvious international gaffes. For a long time, Detroit complained that Japan wouldn't buy its cars, but the Big Three were not producing any with the steering wheel on the right. When Chevrolet introduced the Nova the name had a nice futuristic ring for English-speaking people, but for Hispanics GM might as well have called it "Lemon." In Spanish "no va" means it doesn't work. Obviously advertising needs to have a strong local content. Local managers also need considerable autonomy in accounting, labor, legal, and tax matters. But certainly the transnational company headquarters should decide strategy and set policy on such matters as brands, sourcing, and exports.

Nor should global corporations ignore the significance of regionalism. While the overall trend of the world economy is certainly towards a global economy, regionalism and factionalism have become stronger in some respects. Several trade agreements in the Western Hemisphere, notably the North American Free Trade Agreement, have set up groups that to some extent rival each other and the European Community. They create some barriers, but they also create opportunities because the transnational company that gets a foothold in one part of a regional group, gets entry into the rest of the group. An American company in France has equal access to the whole EC.

DEMOTING THE GOVERNMENT

Some politicians, labor leaders, and even businessmen in the United States also have the illusion that they have sovereign powers over the global marketplace, that they can stop jobs or plants from moving here or there, that they can protect inefficient industries, that they can coerce other countries into doing things they don't want to do. To the limited extent that they can, they hurt the American consumer and economy, just as cartels, restrictions, and regulations have stopped the Japanese from benefiting from Japan's economic strength. The phrase "Buy American" has gone from being plain dumb to being meaningless.

"During the cold war, government was the pace-setting player on the global stage," writes Murray Weidenbaum, director of the Center for the Study of American Business at Washington University in St. Louis. "Governments made the strategic decisions. Businesses were important, but they were responding to government orders, supplying armaments to the superpowers. In the process, of course, business created substantial economic wealth. But the shift from military to economic competition is fundamental. It means that the business firm is now the key to global economic competition. Governments, to be sure, can help or hinder, and in a major way. But they are supporting players, at best."[21] Instead of advertising their irrelevance by saying "Buy American," labor unions could follow the inevitable trend around the world, and seek foreign partners or become in fact "international," as many are in name.

For most companies, the decision whether or not to go global has probably already been made. They don't have a choice. If they have sales of $500 million or more and are not transnational, they probably don't exist, or aren't likely to last much longer. By the same token, companies that do not already realize that their markets are more competitive are probably rare.

Even companies that can honestly say their business is still local should realize they are part of the world market in the sense that customers everywhere have come to expect better quality and speedier responses, that their markets are more vulnerable to international competition, that information about products and services is universal, and that innovation can suddenly turn a business upside down. For those still hesitating to internationalize or wondering whether their business has become more competitive, some clear signals should tell them their world is changing.

Pointers

- Are their customers global and do they want global services or solutions to their needs?
- Are the products or services they provide the same or largely similar around the world?
- Are they in a high-tech business?
- Is the market consolidating down to a few powerful players?
- Are there important research centers around the world in this business?
- Are there promising manufacturing centers in their industry to be found elsewhere? Good sources of materials, supplies, and people?
- Is the business capital intensive?
- Has the business been deregulated or privatized?

4

SOCIETY'S CLAIMS

"Wait a minute," I said. "You have only one constituency; the
shareholders."
—Al Dunlap, former CEO, Scott Paper Company[1]

A company which pursues only profit at the expense of
everything else cannot survive in the 21st century.
—Ryuzaburo Kaku, CEO, Canon Inc.[2]

Adam Smith wrote in *The Wealth of Nations* in 1776 that an "invisible hand" guides the entrepreneur when he is looking out solely for himself, without any concern for the public interest, so that "by pursuing his own interest he frequently promotes that of society more effectually than when he really intends to promote it." Smith turned out to be essentially right. A business has to make a profit, and if it fails to do so, nothing else it does really matters because it will disappear. Businesses, on a scale unimagined by Smith, became the great engine of economic progress in the developed world, creating products, services, jobs, and the whole paraphernalia of the market economy, and improving the quality of life.

However, it was just as well Smith used the qualifier "frequently" because the behavior of the entrepreneur has been hotly debated ever since, perhaps as much today as 100 years ago when robber barons, market manipulators, and other rascals made the public ownership of the means of production seem like a good idea. Pure laissez-faire capitalism died in the 19th century and new laws brought the worst excesses of capitalism more or less under control. In the United States, the Sherman Antitrust Act (1890), the Federal Trade Commission Act (1914), the Clayton Act (1914), and the Securities and Exchange Act (1934), among others, reflected the growing public conviction that some standards and limits had to be applied to the exercise of greed.

That we have not reached the millennium of corporate behavior is amply evident today. A recitation of recent frauds, swindles, thefts, bribes, rackets, and other forms of corruption even in the most solid and respected institutions is breathtaking. A rogue trader brings down the venerable Baring's Bank, a copper trader runs up losses of $2.6 billion at Sumitomo Corporation, and a bond trader at Daiwa Bank loses $1.1 billion on illegal deals. (Talk about employee empowerment!) Three banks turn out to be fronting for criminal activities: BCCI, Franklin National, and Banco Ambrosiano. In the 1980s the savings bank industry in the United States is revealed to be riddled with corruption. An Italian swindler takes over MGM and, with the help of bribes, gets France's second-largest bank, Crédit Lyonnais, to finance a brief, wild ride through Hollywood. That, and other misadventures, left Crédit Lyonnais with $25 billion in bad debts. The heads of one out of four of France's 40 biggest companies have been *mis en examen* (placed under investigation) in recent years.[3] The heads of eight of South Korea's *chaebol* are sentenced to jail terms for bribing a former president (although none are likely actually to serve time). The tobacco industry in the United States stonewalls and lies for years about what it knows about the effects of smoking. Little wonder that the man in the street regards business ethics as an oxymoron, a subject fit for discussion only by the terminally naive.

SEI Survey	
Ensuring ethical behavior is critical	55%
We are doing that	45%

AN ISSUE OF EQUITY

Yet the whole issue of the role of business in society, including business ethics, is very much alive. The issue grips corporations, business schools, politicians, employees, shareholders, and even self-styled public interest groups—the whole community of what has come to be known as the stakeholders. What really hit the public gut is not so much the ethical lapses, which were shocking enough, but the issues of equity—issues of pay, privilege, and security. It's not just a matter of layoffs (which will be discussed more in Chapter 8), but of layoffs plus stagnant pay for workers, plus huge increases in the rewards for top executives (see Chapter 7), plus record gains for stockholders.

Business Week reports that the CEO of a large company earned on average 42 times as much as the ordinary factory worker in 1980, but by 1995 the multiple had reached 141, and in 1996 it leaped to 209 times the factory wage. In 1995, average CEO pay in large corporations gained 18% (30% when long-term compensation is included) over the previous year, while white-collar professionals earned 4.2% more and blue-collar workers just 1% more. The CEO's total compensation rose 54% in 1996, compared to a 3% pay increase for the factory worker.[4] Of course, the huge rewards for CEOs were partly the result of reformist demands that pay be tied more to performance. Since business performed extremely well in 1995 and 1996, the CEOs got their performance-based rewards. But the results were excessive, especially when corporations laid off 439,000 employees in 1995, while profits increased 15% and the Dow-Jones index rose by 33.5%. The belt-tightening inflicted on employees might have been acceptable had there been some appearance of equity, some gesture by the fortunate toward the less fortunate. But there was none, except in a few instances, and the resulting outrage contributed to the sense that the corporation must do more for society.

SEI Survey	
The corporation is responsible to society, not just the shareholders	53%
We have achieved this posture	47%

Just what is the responsibility of the corporation? Does it answer solely to the shareholder? Or does it answer to a whole collection of stakeholders, and if so, who has priority? What does it owe its employees? The customers? The suppliers? The community? To what extent, if any, should the corporation deal with social problems that government, schools, and other organizations seem to be handling so poorly? Should the corporation help stop the growing division between poor and affluent in the United States? Is the greater pay of the CEO justified if he is paid more according to performance and more likely to be fired if he fails? Has competition in business become so ferocious that executives are bound to act ruthlessly, stomping on ethics and society itself if need be? Has Wall Street's demand for performance *right now* made them immune to other demands?

Many of these are old questions, and they have been long debated. But the clash today between business interests as narrowly interpreted and the demands of society has intensified. The successful 21st century enterprise will have to resolve the conflict in a way that satisfies both corporate and society's interests. Not many CEOs today would say, as did Al Dunlap when he ran Scott Paper, that "I respect predators." He recalls that soon after he had taken over Scott and had started shredding the company, he heard one of his executives "talk about constituencies like the community, like employees—I think he went through six constituencies. Wait a minute, I said. You have only one constituency: the shareholders."[5]

OWNERS WITHOUT CONTROL

The idea of the supremacy of the shareholder's interests began to weaken with the publication of *The Modern Corporation and Private Property* by Adolf Berle and Gardiner Means in 1932. Until then economists and lawyers had pretty well followed the Adam Smith argument that all the benefits of an enterprise should accrue to the owners of a business, who would achieve the greatest good for all by maximizing their profits. But Berle and Means pointed out this argument came from a time when ownership and control were unified. Businesses were small, owned by an individual or a few partners, and the owners provided the capital, took the risks, ran the business, and enjoyed the profits. But the large corporation , Berle and Means argued, has broken that unity. The stockholder becomes passive, surrenders control of his wealth and becomes simply a risk taker. Managers take over responsibility for running the company and for its success. The split results in "the owners without appreciable control and the control without appreciable ownership," the authors wrote. "There is no longer any certainty that a corporation will in fact be run primarily in the interests of the stockholders." The modern corporation had become a quasi-public institution.[6]

In a business classic published in 1946, Peter Drucker described the role of the corporation in modern American society.

> The corporation as a representative institution of American society must hold out the promise of adequately fulfilling the aspirations and beliefs of the American people. A conflict between the requirements of corporate life and the basic beliefs and promises of American society would ultimately destroy the allegiance to our form of government and society. Hence, we must analyze whether the corporation is satisfying these basic demands: the promise that opportunities be equal and that rewards be commensurate to abilities and efforts; the promise that each member of society, however humble, be a citizen with the status, function and dignity of a member of society and with a chance of individual fulfillment in his social life; finally, the promise that big and small, rich and poor, powerful and weak be partners in a joint enterprise rather than opponents benefitting by each other's loss. . . . The old crude fiction still lingers on which regards the corporation as nothing but the sum of the property rights of the individual shareholders. . . . In the social reality of today, however, shareholders are but one of several groups of people who stand in a special relationship to the corporation. The corporation is permanent, the shareholder is transient.[7]

Drucker said we often make the mistake of thinking of the corporation as a collection of machines and raw materials, of gadgets and tools, when in fact it is essentially an organization of human beings, a social organization.

Over the years, the different view of the corporation has taken hold. Donald S. MacNaughton, then chairman of the Prudential Insurance Company, said in 1971 that the "corporation is really not private property in the traditional sense." The stockholder is no longer involved directly in the fate of the company. He is not even the primary source of capital.

His risk depends as much on the behavior of the market as on the success of the particular business. The corporation has become a private enterprise organization "whose managers act as trustees for *all* who have an interest in the enterprise—the stockholders, employees, suppliers, consumers and the public." MacNaughton said that business operates under a franchise granted by the people which can be withdrawn if the people think they are not benefiting. Thus business is faced with "the disorganized, imprecise, chaotic social demands currently being made of us by the public."[8]

SOCIALLY RESPONSIBLE GLADIATORS?

The chaotic demands MacNaughton spoke of 25 years ago are even more intense today. Human rights groups and advocates for women, not to mention government agencies, are ready to beat up any company that appears to exploit its labor or condone the sexual harassment of its employees. The press and politicians from both ends of the political spectrum, from former labor secretary Robert Reich to the right-wing politician Pat Buchanan, jump on companies that lay off workers by the hundreds or thousands. The word "stakeholder" has become fashionably correct. Reich went so far as to suggest in 1996 that perhaps the benefits of incorporation should be reserved for socially responsible companies, or that responsible corporations' taxes should be reduced or eliminated.[9] (It should be added that he did not pursue the theme.) That same year President Clinton lectured businessmen on five ways to show "good citizenship" toward their employees. His proposals were decidedly modest in the current context: (1) Be "family-friendly," by promoting flexible schedules, for example. (2) Give employees health and pension benefits. (3) Help workers with their education and training. (4) Make employees more like partners in the business. (5) Provide a safe workplace.[10] The president subsequently convened a meeting of more than 100 chief executives at Georgetown University to tell stories about their acts of good corporate citizenship.

To get businessmen to do all the good things they should do is not easy today. First of all, the market makes them more competitive. Reich himself says that "American businesses have been transformed from comfortable and stable rivals into bloodletting gladiators."[11] Second, top executives are being held accountable for their performance more closely than before by boards and by shareholders, especially institutional owners. Pension fund administrators may be patient, but mutual fund managers tend to want performance now and have little patience for good works. While institutional investors have certainly become more active, their influence is limited by their very growth. They have become so big that they can't readily move in and out of investments.

The "Chicago school" predictably can be found in the lead of the resistance to the stakeholder idea. Just as Vince Lombardi said that winning was the only thing, Milton Friedman believes that maximizing shareholder returns is the only thing for a corporation. Like Adam Smith, he believes that is how a corporation can contribute the greatest public good.* Another Chicago school economist, Herbert Stein, has attacked the current stakeholder movement. He argues that "to rely on corporations' responsibility to solve major social problems—other than the problem of how to put our people and other resources to work most efficiently—would be a wasteful diversion from their most important function." When corporations try to do more than maximize profits they will not only lose efficiency, but get on a slippery slope where they might find themselves doing things they would not want to do just to prevent the government from doing them.[12] William Safire, the *New York Times* conservative essayist, writes that the "stakeholder" has "replaced 'proletariat' in the lexicon of the left." Now that socialism has failed, the left is introducing the "new socialism" under the guise of protecting the stakeholder.[13]

A cooler and perhaps more realistic reaction comes from Jacob Wallenberg, a Swedish banker and a member of Sweden's famous business family. He believes the stakeholder approach is useful and alerts corporations to the need to play well in many arenas today. But he is concerned about the temptation "to accept as legitimate a notion of equal

---

*Friedman does, however, recognize that corporations have to act within the law. And although Adam Smith is more famous for his statement that the businessman "by pursuing his own interest . . . frequently promoted that of society," Smith was primarily concerned with society. For that matter, Lombardi later said he wished he'd never said that winning is everything, because "I meant the effort. I meant having a goal. . . . I sure as hell didn't mean for people to crush human values and morality." (Gordon Carruth and Eugene Ehrlich, *American Quotations,* Avenel, N.J.: Wing Books, 1992, p. 235).

weight and equal rights for all interest groups in society to share the power over private corporations. It just ain't so. Some holders have more stake than others, mainly those who risk their money on a long-term basis." He asks, "What is more social than a profitable company, satisfying human needs and creating work? And what is less social than an unprofitable business wasting human and financial resources?" He points to the difference between the energetic United States and the booming Asian tigers, on the one hand, little encumbered by stakeholder ideas, and on the other hand the old world of Europe, "plagued by unemployment and rigid structures."[14] (See Figure 4.1 for contrasting national views on who should come first in a company's priorities.)

While Americans are beginning to worry about the other stakeholders, in other nations, by contrast, it is the shareholder who is beginning to get the sympathy. In Europe and Japan, shareholders have traditionally been treated as a nuisance—except of course those large banks that have held big pieces of big companies. They are part of the club. Other shareholders are outsiders, given modest dividends and murky financial reports, not allowed to shake up managements that performed poorly. Other stakeholders got more respect. In Japan, the workers' interest has traditionally stood out above the rest and the big companies endorsed their interest with guaranteed life-time employment. That guarantee is weakening, if only slightly. Germany had a full-fledged stakeholder economy. Companies have two boards, a supervisory board made up of bank, business, and labor representatives who appoint the chief executive and loosely supervise the company's major decisions, and a management board, responsible for running the company. But the poor performance and lax oversight of companies in Germany and elsewhere in Europe are changing the balance. Not only are those friendly banks turning nasty to their favorite companies (see Chapter 1), but regular investors are restive too. That may be partly because of American influence. The California Public Employees' Retirement System, which aggressively challenges management in the United States, raised its investment in European equities from $11 billion to $18 billion. American institutions have invested heavily in privatized European companies. However, the European investors themselves are more assertive than they used to be, forming associations, backing activists, demanding a better return, going after the CEOs they think are performing poorly. In Japan, a group

FIGURE 4.1

When the Institute of Fiscal and Monetary Policy in Japan's Ministry of Finance surveyed executives in five countries to learn how they viewed a company's responsibilities, it got some highly contrasting responses. American and British executives think alike, and disagree radically with their colleagues in France, Germany, and Japan.

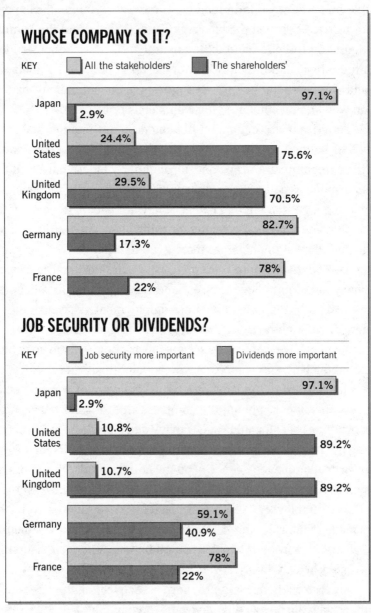

WHOSE COMPANY IS IT?

KEY ☐ All the stakeholders'   ■ The shareholders'

	All the stakeholders'	The shareholders'
Japan	97.1%	2.9%
United States	24.4%	75.6%
United Kingdom	29.5%	70.5%
Germany	82.7%	17.3%
France	78%	22%

JOB SECURITY OR DIVIDENDS?

KEY ☐ Job security more important   ■ Dividends more important

	Job security more important	Dividends more important
Japan	97.1%	2.9%
United States	10.8%	89.2%
United Kingdom	10.7%	89.2%
Germany	59.1%	40.9%
France	78%	22%

Source: Ministry of Finance (Study Group of the Institute of Fiscal and Monetary Policy), *Socio-Economic Systems of Japan, the United States, the United Kingdom, Germany and France.* Tokyo, February 1996.

of shareholders took the unprecedented step of suing directors of Sumitomo in 1997 over the copper trading scandal. Japanese law was amended in 1993 to make it easier for shareholders to file suit against the corporation—unthinkable in Japan until recently—and they have filed several suits in fraud and extortion cases. But this marked the first time the directors had been sued.

Presumably we are seeing a convergence of thinking about the purpose of the corporation, with Europeans and Japanese giving more weight than they have in the past to the rights of shareholders, and Americans more weight to the other parties. The need to make a profit remains absolute. Without it, you have no company. With it, you can create jobs, products, and services. What could be more socially useful, as Wallenberg asks? And, as Wallenberg suggests, you need to balance the different interests. You don't equate a "public interest group" consisting of three teenagers and their teacher with the stockholders—but you might pay attention to them.

There are new limits to the quest for profits which even the unrepentant Chicago school economist would have to recognize because they are economic and they impact profits. For example, it is socially desirable to treat the environment kindly and make safe products—and it can be very costly if you don't. Producing high-quality products and services is admirable, and it is also good business, because customers expect that today. Creating a good environment for employees is socially responsible, and if this is the age of the knowledge worker, then employees are a company's key asset and treating them well becomes a sound business strategy. Employing a diverse work force is an act of good citizenship. But as the work force itself becomes more diverse, it becomes essential to running the business. Jamie Houghton, who retired as CEO of Corning Inc., says that diversity was one of the three things he concentrated on during his 13-year reign as chairman (the others being performance and quality). He adds, "it may make us all feel good if we give blacks jobs, but if you take the demographics of the 21st century, you know, there are some people who say that after the year 2000 only 15% to 20% of the people entering the work force are going to be white male. What that says to me is, forget the ethics of it. Unless you want to avail yourself of only 15% to 20% of the available talent out there, you better learn to get diverse real quick."[15]

C. K. Prahalad, professor of business administration at the business school at the University of Michigan, offers yet another sound business reason for paying more attention to other stakeholders. Putting the shareholder first made sense when the scarce resource was capital, he writes. "There was a plentiful, undifferentiated supply of labor, customers, and suppliers; capital was the resource in relatively short supply." This priority may be weakening as we approach the 21st century. "What is relatively new . . . is the intensity of the global competition for other key stakeholders," he continues. "While capital remains a necessary ingredient, access to specialized talent (labor) and to a specialized supplier infrastructure (including technology) have become much more important factors in corporations' ability to compete in increasingly sophisticated and global consumer markets." Companies will have to compete in these markets—for employees, suppliers, consumers—as they have always competed for capital and these markets will impose new internal disciplines on them.[16] Two corporate chief executives interviewed during the research for this book, both heads of consulting firms, agreed that competition among them in the future will focus on getting the best people. That need will overshadow even the competition for clients.

HONORABLE PROFITS

Corporate ethics emerge as another large, fundamental, and complex issue that businessmen, academics, and ethicists around the world are trying to elucidate—sometimes at stupefying length. Business ethics clearly has become one of the issues of the day. Business ethics journals proliferate (even Italy has one) and resource or study centers on business ethics spring up around the world. No business school would be caught without its ethics program in place today—perhaps topped off with a required stay in a monastery or volunteer work in the inner city. The statesmen of business gather from around the world in splendid surroundings to establish the high moral ground for the next century. It would be hard today to find a major American company without a code of ethics, or some equivalent, although not so difficult in Europe or Asia.

The reasons for so much concern with the morals of business are not hard to find. All those business transgressions mentioned early in this chapter have made the need for better ethics clearer. But at the same time, the pressures to perform, the new competitiveness, the greater discretion allowed managers, make it tempting and easier to cut corners. We have a more litigious society and more people ready to take up arms against offenses, imagined or real, committed by business—whether it be the high prices charged for drugs, the sexual harassment of employees, or the exploitation of third-world laborers. Investigative journalists rummage through SEC filings, proxy statements, and court records seeking fresh scandals, without much concern for the subtleties. Downsizings raise basic issues about the ethics of handling employees. Washington has also decreed better ethical behavior. The Foreign Corrupt Practices Act has perhaps made shady actions like paying bribes less common, and the U.S. Sentencing Commission guidelines laid down lighter penalties for corporations whose employees are caught in illegal acts if they had a working code of ethics. All of these reasons, combined with the general increase in interest in business ethics, force companies to be more serious about their ethics today.

The general principles that should govern the ethical behavior of a corporation are fairly obvious. Companies should obey the law, honor contracts, respect the individual, assure the quality of their goods and services, deal kindly with the environment, and so forth. Managers should refrain from cooking the books or otherwise misinforming superiors, regulators, investors, and the public. These principles are pretty well acceptable around the world.

Ethics become a lot more complicated when you start to apply them to specific situations. You can argue plausibly that closing an unprofitable plant to save a company is not only good business but morally justifiable since you are cutting a few jobs to save a lot of jobs. But how do you deal with the people who lose their jobs? American executives clearly have not found the ethical answer to that dilemma. If you discover that a colleague is colluding with competitors to fix prices, good ethics require you to report him. But experience tells you that as a whistle-blower, you will become a pariah in your own company and elsewhere. Does ethics demand that you wreck your career?

Andrew Stark, a professor of management at the University of Toronto and a researcher on business ethics, has argued that most managers find discussions of ethics irrelevant not because they don't want to be ethical but because the discussions they hear don't give them much practical guidance. "Too many business ethicists have occupied a rarified moral ground, removed from the real concerns and real-world problems of the vast majority of managers," Stark writes. They tend to be absolutist, to regard profits as immoral, to require businesses to hurt themselves as proof of their virtue.[17] A more practical approach accepts as perfectly honorable selling a good product at a decent profit. As Joanne Ciulla, previously a research fellow at Wharton and now a professor of leadership and ethics at the University of Richmond, put it, a manager needs to know what to do that "is morally right and socially responsible, without ruining your career and company."[18]

While we still wrestle with what is ethical behavior in the United States, the issue has become considerably more complex because it has gone global, along with business itself. The ethics-in-business movement clearly got going in the United States in the 1980s. By 1991, according to a survey by the Conference Board, 84% of companies in the United States had codes of ethics, while 50% of the companies in Europe had them. (The survey covered 264 companies, mostly American, with median sales of $1 billion.) While the increase in the number of companies that had codes over a previous survey in 1987 was not great, more than half of the codes had been written since 1987, indicating a burst of revisions after the 1991 sentencing guidelines came out.[19]

The idea of codifying corporate ethics was carried overseas principally by American multinationals, and causes some puzzlement and dismay in other countries. It has been described as a form of cultural imperialism. The worldly European executive may wonder bemusedly why American executives would waste valuable time elaborating a code that good people will obey anyhow and the bad guys will ignore. But a code is necessary because even the good people today don't know what they are supposed to do.

An international code of behavior has to span a wide reach of attitudes towards ethics. Americans have a legalistic approach. But as Joanne Ciulla points out, Italians might be described as practicing "amoral familism": they behave ethically towards their families or group, but have no sense of responsibility towards strangers or society. The Japanese could be said to practice "national amoralism": they have a strong sense of needing to advance their country and society, but less sense of responsibility for their behavior in the world.[20]

When it comes to applying ethics, being global adds several levels of complexity. A company that is serious about ending sex discrimination will presumably hire a qualified woman for any job in the United States. That same company would presumably not insist on using a female truck driver in Saudi Arabia. But what if a German client makes it clear that if your team is headed by a woman, you won't get the contract? What do you do if you are being hammered by the press for hiring workers in Central America at wages that are pitiful by American standards, but happen to be better than the local wages—and jobs there are scarce?

Studies sponsored by the SEI Center at Wharton find that standards are even more important in global business than local business because international transactions can fall through the gaps between different national legal systems and moral codes. Robert Holland, former president of the Committee for Economic Development and now a Wharton senior fellow, sees a "global market for morality gradually emerging. . . . The more homogeneous access to information, capital, technology and even talent pools may gradually lead the major stakeholders of global firms to have more similar interests in ethical values."[21] Two Wharton professors, Tom Donaldson and Tom Dunfee, who have been working on corporate ethics theory, propose that corporations develop series of formal and informal contracts with various stakeholders that would create a framework for what constitutes acceptable behavior by the corporation. The ethics embedded in these contracts would evolve gradually and become more important as they evolve. Stakeholders who felt that a contract was being violated would have a whole range of options, from complaining to management to seeking government action.[22] Right now there are plenty of contradictions and anomalies in ethical behavior, but they should slowly wear away.

The complexities, the contradictions, the ambiguousness, all make it difficult for a company to find the right ethical path, just as it is difficult to find the right balance among the constituencies of a corporation. But there is no question that companies are being held to higher standards of behavior and responsibility. Business is being driven to behave better. That will be a reality of the 21st century. Many companies are highly ethical and do very well. Du Pont, Levi Strauss, Johnson & Johnson come to mind. But there is no guarantee that good behavior will be rewarded. It may even be costly. The mutual funds that specialize in what they consider ethical companies are, at this writing, substantially underperforming the Standard & Poor 500 index.[23]

Free enterprise and market economics stand triumphant today. They have no competitors. However, much is expected of them. To meet those expectations, corporations have to show they can behave ethically and equitably, that they can serve society's needs, that they can still improve the lot of ordinary people. So much of the world has only lately embraced market economics that unless corporations can show they can meet society's needs, those new converts could rapidly turn away. The argument pitting shareholder interests against stakeholder interests is losing force simply because the two interests are merging. Unless the corporation does behave ethically, unless it treats workers reasonably well, unless it is careful of the environment, the more likely it becomes that its behavior will hurt the bottom line and therefore the shareholder. Good citizenship is becoming good business.

Pointers

Almost any company may find itself today pilloried for its real or concocted abuses, but there are some danger signals to watch for:

- Doing business in countries ruled by dictators, or in developing countries with low wages.
- Lacking an ethics code that is visibly supported by the CEO and by other means, such as training and the appointment of a relatively independent ethics officer.
- Failing to plan for dealing with emergencies which, badly handled, can turn a bad break into a disaster.
- Making products that can injure or affect the health of the customers.
- Using processes or making products that can damage the environment.
- Reengineering, reorganizing, downsizing, rightsizing, or whatever you want to call it, on a large scale, especially if departing employees are not given a lot of support.
- Rewarding CEOs excessively.

Cautions

- Ethical issues will not always present clear-cut, unambiguous choices. It is almost impossible for a business to have no impact on the environment, or to produce a totally safe product. Is a product that may harm one customer in 10,000 safe, or should the odds be one in a million? These dilemmas have to be sorted out with a sense of balance.

- However ethical a company may be, it should be prepared to be cast as a villain because the mind-set of the media, and perhaps the public as a whole, sees business that way.

5

THE CUSTOMER'S
DEMANDS

There is one valid definition of business purpose:
to create a customer.
—Peter Drucker[1]

The idea of serving the customer well is hardly new. To cite a favorite legend, L.L. Bean founded his outdoor outfitting company in 1912 on this principle: "Sell good merchandise at reasonable profit, treat your customers like human beings, and they'll always come back for more." When his first batch of 100 pairs of hunting shoes came unstitched, he redesigned the shoe and sent out free replacements. Thus was the Bean legend born. Other companies have their legends about feats of heroism to serve the customer. Saturn advertised how one of its representatives flew with a new car seat strapped in beside him to replace one that failed a customer in Alaska.

Thomas J. Watson Sr. believed that IBM should excel in everything it did, especially in how it treated the customer. One of the three simple precepts he laid down for IBM during his three decades at the helm was: "Spend a lot of time making customers happy." IBM was good to its customers. Not only did it sell or lease them excellent products, but it provided good service, listened to what they had to say, and helped them solve their problems. But then, like many other companies, IBM became so big and rich and successful that it began to forget the customer. IBM produced what it thought was best, fixed a price, pushed it out the door, and in effect told the customer to take it or leave it. Why would anyone be dumb enough not to deal with IBM? So far did IBM stray from Watson's precept that 30 years after his death CEO John Akers had to declare 1987 to be "The Year of the Customer." What were all those other years? And in any case 1987 turned out not to be the year of the customer but the year IBM tried to push PCs, whether the customers wanted them or not (on the whole, they didn't).

Under any circumstances, the cavalier treatment of the customer by IBM, by General Motors, by Ford, and by many other companies would eventually have proven disastrous. But just when the callous treatment of the customer began to hurt, the customer started to have more choices and became more demanding. Businesses had to make a huge adjustment. The whole relationship between customer and company became far more complex. First came improvements in the quality of products and services, which whetted the appetites of customers for more improvements. Then came an effort to find out what satisfied the customer, which drew corporations into a deeper understanding of what the customer wanted. That resulted in a different approach to the customer, "relationship marketing," which moved well beyond the old "transaction marketing," with its shotgun techniques of mass-media advertising, coupons, and point-of-sale promotions. Instead of nailing down the one-time sale the goal became to capture the long-term loyalty of the customer. Information technology helps enormously because the corporation can capture usable information about preferences and behavior not only of segments of the market but of individual customers—by the millions. New manufacturing technology helps too because production can be made to fit the quantity and schedule demanded by the customer, to the point of reducing a production run to one item—for delivery tomorrow if necessary. As Alvin Toffler predicted, the market becomes "demassified."

Fundamental changes in the way customers are treated can't be accomplished by some rework in the sales and marketing departments. They involve the whole company, the way it is organized, the way it is managed, the way people are trained, evaluated, and compensated. Deeds of heroism to serve the customer are all very well (although in fact they are often expensive solutions to mistakes that shouldn't have been made in the first place), but the market today demands a more systematic, sophisticated, long-range approach to the customer. As Jack Welch said, a corporation has to stand facing the customer, and not with its face to the CEO and its rear to the customer.

WHEN THINGS GOT BETTER

Imagine taking home today a VCR, or a television set, or a personal computer and finding that it did not work, or that it needed servicing after a few months. We would consider that intolerable. Or imagine owning a car that needed a grease job every 1,000 miles, whose tires kept going flat and needed replacement at 20,000 miles, and which needed a valve job if not a whole new engine by 40,000 miles! It would be intolerable. But that was the normal experience for car owners up to the 1960s. Or imagine standing in line for 45 minutes to get some of your own money from a teller at your own bank! That happened at big city banks a decade ago. Intolerable quality failures still happen all too frequently. We see them all the time, in the construction industry, in many government services, in the accuracy of medical bills (not to mention in the operating theater), in the insurance business, obviously in the way airlines treat their passengers, and not so obviously in the caliber of newspapers and network news.[2] (See Figure 5.1.)

The customer began to realize that things could be made a lot better, without raising prices to the levels of luxury goods, when Japanese cars started to capture a big share of the American market in the late 1970s. They were very good cars and the prices were reasonable. They had fewer problems than American cars. The same levels of quality at good prices became evident in TV sets, computer chips, and copiers. But American-made Xerox machines of that period, for example, scorched documents, jammed papers, and gave off bad smells, and the Xerox Corporation's share of the U.S. market plummeted from 90% to 13%.

It took all of the 1980s and some of the 1990s, and it was a traumatic struggle, but many American firms, at least those challenged by foreign competition, did dramatically improve their quality. Quality improvements spread from one sector to another as consumers became more demanding. They wanted things better and they wanted them faster. If a PC manufacturer can get an order out overnight, why can't a book publisher do the same? Exposure to foreign markets forced many American companies to tighten their standards everywhere. Labconco, a $32-million-a-

FIGURE 5.1

Customer Dissatisfaction

Americans would seem to be getting somewhat less satisfied with most of the goods and services they pay for, which could well reflect greater expectations rather than declining quality. Americans would seem to be particularly displeased with their newspapers, airlines, and fast-food dispensers, and even more so with their police and the IRS. Judging by these ratings, the U.S. Postal Service has improved markedly, more than any other business or service, but has not reached the levels of the express delivery services. The National Quality Research Center at the University of Michigan Business School surveys samples of consumers every quarter to come up with a national satisfaction index. The index is based on what consumers think of specific organizations. Their responses are not used directly but fed into a model that calculates the index. Here are the ratings for the seven major sectors surveyed and for some of the industries within the sectors:

Sector (Industry)	*1994*	*1995*	*1996*
Manufacturing/Nondurables	**81.6**	**81.2**	**79**
Soft drinks	86	86	86
Beer	83	81	79
Apparel (nonathletic)	82	81	78
Newspapers, publishing	72	68	69
Manufacturing/Durables	**79.2**	**79.8**	**78.8**
Appliances	85	82	82
TVs & VCRs	83	81	81
Vehicles	79	80	79
PCs	78	75	73
Transportation/Communications/Utilities	**75.5**	**75.1**	**75.5**
Parcel/express mail	81	81	85
Long distance phone	82	82	81
U.S. Postal Service	61	69	74
Network news	77	76	70
Scheduled airlines	72	69	69
Retail	**73.6**	**74.6**	**73.2**
Supermarkets	74	75	74
Fast food/pizza	70	70	66
Finance/Insurance	**74.8**	**74.1**	**74.5**
Property, home, auto insurance	76	75	77
Services	**74.4**	**74.2**	**71.2**
Hotels, motels	75	73	72
Hospitals	74	74	71
Public Administration/Government	**64.3**	**61.9**	**59.2**
Police (central city)	61	59	59
Internal Revenue Service	55	54	50
National Index (4th quarter of each year)	**74.2**	**73.7**	**72**

Source: National Quality Research Center, *American Customer Satisfaction Index Quarterly Updates* for February, May, August, November 1996, and January 1997 (Ann Arbor, Michigan, University of Michigan Business School, 1996 and 1997).

year manufacturer of lab test equipment, used to measure the sheet metal it turned into cases for the equipment with an ordinary tape measure. Measurements were accurate to 1/16th of an inch. But then Labconco began selling to Japanese customers, who complained that the measurements might be acceptable to unsophisticated American clients but not to them. Labconco now measures the metal with calipers accurate to 1/1,000 of an inch. And it tries to get deliveries out in 48 hours, rather than the eight to 12 weeks that customers used to accept.[3]

A MEASURE OF SATISFACTION

As corporations began to try to serve customers better they realized they didn't know them very well. Executives in fact had grown so immersed in their own affairs and so overconfident that they made little effort to understand customers. To be sure, the marketing people and the salespeople could report what the customers said, but they didn't try to understand them systematically and they couldn't find much of an audience at home to listen to the complaints they had picked up. Senior managers, isolated with their financial officers and analyses and strategic plans, lost touch with the clients. The aloofness had to disappear.

To the extent that they studied the customer in the past, companies looked at "customer satisfaction." Satisfaction ratings provide a rough measure of the quality of the product or service, especially if the quality is terrible, as is the case with airlines services, newspapers, or government services, in the view of the public. But for the companies that have improved in order to remain or become competitive, the satisfaction measure ceases to have much meaning, except as a negative check. "Customers start to see things as defect-free," says Blanton Godfrey, CEO of the Juran Institute Inc. He pointed out that when cellular phones first came out people treated them carefully and carried them around in padded cases. "Now, people toss them around and leave them in the glove compartment when it's 150 degrees. It becomes a commodity and you have so few problems, you don't think about it."[4] At this point the quality of the product becomes a given, almost a precondition for surviving in the market. The customer's satisfaction—with the product itself, at least—can be assumed.

"Customer satisfaction measures only really give you a reading on the surface of the customer's experience," says Richard LeVitt, director of corporate quality at Hewlett-Packard. "They don't give you the kind of richness of understanding of a day in the life of the customer that you need. What happens when, say, they first try to use your product? They take it out of the box, and they try to set it up and use it. And, what is that experience? Satisfaction? Delight? Dismay? Anxiety? Customers may turn out to have surprisingly strong emotional reactions to things that don't seem very important to us . . . computer neophytes can have difficulty with things that experienced users find very easy to do. It's as if you bought a new car but you had never ridden in a car. You have no idea how to insert the ignition key."[5] The mistake made for so long by many companies, especially high-tech companies, was to focus on the engineering improvements that might please the customer, rather than the customer's whole experience in dealing with the company. These companies need to think more about how Disneyland pleases the crowds, and not focus so much on statistics and technology. With more ordinary consumers using high-tech products, the appeal to the senses becomes more important.

INFORMATION PROBLEMS

As they get to know their customer better, companies discover that it's not just the customer's whole experience with the product that counts, but the customer's experience with the whole company. Long after it had improved the technical quality of its products to world-class levels, Hewlett-Packard learned in the early 1990s that its order fulfillment system was a mess. There was something wrong with every order. If HP delivered a system consisting of monitors, keyboards, and workstations (all supplied from different plants, if not different countries), the connecting cables might be all wrong. HP put improving its order fulfillment at the top of its priorities.

SEI Survey	
Customer wants solutions and a good total experience	91%
We are providing that	28%

Minnesota Mining & Manufacturing, one of the best in the world at technology and innovation, has learned of a whole array of customer demands and complaints that it didn't know existed. "Over the past several years our customers have told us over and over again, 'Hey, you guys have got great products, you've got great people, you're really innovative, but you are harder to do business with than you need to be,'" says Ronald A. Mitsch, vice chairman of 3M.[6] That complaint reflects not a decline in how 3M handles its customers, but a more demanding customer. When 3M polled ex-customers to find out why they had left—which can be a lot more revealing than asking current customers if they are satisfied—it found to its surprise that half of them left because of "information problems." The 3M representative they were dealing with got the order wrong, or someone else did, or no one could answer their question, or answer it fast enough.[7]

Computer makers used to service only their own equipment. If you had a DEC work station you couldn't expect IBM to help you make it work properly—even though IBM might provide equipment linked to the DEC station. But as computers became more universal and more like commodities, the proprietary approach became increasingly irritating and irrational. It was as if buying a Buick committed you to buying only Buick gas and oil. Buick never considered selling fuel, but computer manufacturers did in effect require customers to buy only their fuel. They may have thought they were protecting their property, but customers saw themselves as being held hostage for no good reason. When IBM introduced its first PC in 1981 it offered an "open" system which, within five years, captured 70% of the *Fortune* 1,000 business market from the earlier proprietary systems, which were protected with patents and copyrights. The IBM PC could be cloned and copied and it set the industry standards.[8] Apple thrived for some more years, but then it too became a victim of its protectionism. As much as many customers liked the Apple approach, they couldn't resist joining the move to open systems, where they could find most of the new applications and equipment. Customers have clearly shown their preference for openness. Today IBM and DEC will service anybody's system.

With the demand for openness comes a demand for the "boundary-less" behavior urged by Jack Welch of GE. When a customer deals with GE, he doesn't want to deal with half a dozen different parts of the company. He doesn't want to be bounced from one part of the company to another, to get an answer to a question, or to get service, or to order a product. Many otherwise excellent companies selling good products became notorious for their inability to make life simple for the customer.

In the hierarchy of new customer demands, the most sophisticated perhaps is the demand that companies furnish solutions rather than just sell products or services. Selling solutions is not a brand new idea, though it may seem like one today. As mentioned earlier, IBM helped solve its customers' problems decades ago, at least it did if they were big customers investing in mainframes. The idea of solving problems rather than just selling things extends into many businesses—transportation, communications, banking, insurance, computer systems—and tightens the relationship with the customer. If you can bind the customer to your company by providing solutions, then you can probably count on a long-term relationship and charge a premium price for your goods or services. "Value-added marketing" is one of the current buzzwords to describe this approach.

ZERO DEFECTIONS

The value of hanging on to customers would seem to be obvious, but only in recent years has it come to be widely recognized or measured. In the magazine business the subscription renewal rate has always been a key number because it costs so much more to acquire a new subscriber than to hold on to an old one. Renewals can make or break a magazine. Other businesses, however, lacked the means or the desire to measure the cost of losing customers. In a series of articles in the *Harvard Business Review* over several years, and more recently in a book, Frederick Reichheld of Bain & Company, a consulting firm, has demonstrated how important it is to earn the loyalty of customers.[9] After the campaign for zero defects comes the campaign for zero defections. Reichheld's studies convinced him that just a 5% reduction in customer defections can increase profits by 25% (in the credit insurance business) to 85% (in branch banking).

It's not simply that getting a customer is expensive and therefore the first year is likely to show a loss. The longer the relationship continues, the more profitable it becomes. Reichheld found this to be true in a study of more than 100 companies in two dozen industries. In one company, the sales per account kept climbing for 19 years. As they get used to a company, customers tend to buy more and more from it. And as customers and company become more familiar with each other, the relationship costs the company less. The longer the customers stay, the more likely they are to recommend the company to others and the more willing they are to pay a premium for the goods or services. Employees enjoy dealing with long-term, happy customers, so they are likely to remain longer too. But the average American company loses half its customers every five years.

A customer who defects is worse than scrap in a factory. When you throw out scrap, it costs you the price of the part, but when an unhappy customer stalks out the door, that costs you a stream of profits for years—say, $5,000 in the next ten years in the case of a retail bank. Worse, a defective part can be picked up and examined so you know what went wrong, but the steaming customer may not even mention the reason for defecting and unless you make an effort to find out why, you may never know. Customer satisfaction questions are little help. The great majority of owners of American cars profess themselves satisfied these days, but the retention rate in the auto industry is only 40%. To overcome this contradiction between satisfaction and retention, more companies today survey ex-customers as well as the current ones.

Before throwing ourselves on the altar of customer retention, we should realize that under two circumstances losing a customer can be good: when the customer isn't worth having in the first place, and when the defection gives you a chance to win him back. You have only a 40% chance of retaining the unhappy customer who has a problem that you don't solve, and you have a 60% chance of retaining a customer who is completely satisfied. But if the customer has a problem and you solve it to his satisfaction, then the odds of keeping the customer go up to 80%. In other words, maybe it would be better if that Maytag man in the ads did get a call once in a while. The 40–60–80 rule of thumb is amply supported by years of work at Technical Assistance Research Program (TARP), an Arlington, Virginia, consulting firm.

SEGMENTING THE WORLD

Segmentation has been a key marketing concept since the early 1960s, but the recent "revolution in information technology and strategy makes possible the creation of data bases on the entire universe and enormous advances in database marketing and innovative distribution approaches."[10]

The new data bases can chop up the population by region, by lifestyles, by generation, by incomes, by values. They can take the segment of people who work at home and then slice it into subgroups. They can segment six types of people according to their attitude toward high technology (from "enthusiasts" to "old liners") and the dog food market into eight groups according to how the owners treat their pets. A more diverse population makes the market more complex. Only one-quarter of the households in America consist of the traditional family of mother, father, and children. Market analysts have to deal with more working women, more singles, more elderly, more people working at home, more racial mixes, not to mention Generation X. Segmentation follows business abroad because corporations need to know more about the millions of new customers they can acquire. The 25 million Hispanics in the United States open a window to the huge market of nearly 500 million in Latin America and the Caribbean. New customers are appearing all over the world, in the former Soviet territories and, for example, in India. India may be poor, but its middle class numbers 200 million people with growing buying power. CNN and MTV can spread the appeal of new products to these hundreds of millions around the world in a matter of hours.

John Sculley, the former head of Apple Computer, aptly described the difference between the old way of selling and the new way. He was speaking of the computer business, but what he said could apply to business in general.

In the U.S., we set up data-base marketing because in the old way of selling software it was about selling something to someone. You measured your success on the return on sales and your market share and the number of units that you shift in a particular quarter. The whole dynamics of how the business model and software works has changed and now you essentially have almost to give something away for free in order to sample future customers who you hope will become loyal customers in your data base. Then you can sell them upgrades to the software that you sample to them, and you can sell them enhancements and add-on products and other things. The measurement of success is not how much did you sell to the customer that you just met, it is how you get that new customer into your data base to build a long-term relationship with them and make sure you are doing the things to retain them. The return on the customer base can have a major impact on the profitability. So, it is a completely different kind of marketing. It is managing and valuing the business about a customer relationship and the annuity streams that derive from it as opposed to selling something to someone.[11]

It takes a different kind of company, even a different concept of business, to put the customer at the heart of the business. Production is determined by "pull," not "push." Or, to put it another way, you replace the "market-out" approach with the "market-in" approach. The whole idea, first implemented by Taiichi Ohno when he designed the Toyota production system in the 1950s, is that instead of planning what you intend to produce and then pushing the product onto the market, you produce what the market tells you it wants.[12]

Pointers

- The customer is more demanding than ever.
- The demanding customer wants more than high-quality products and services.
- To create real value for the customer, you should try to solve his problems.
- The most profit comes from the long-term, closely tied customer.
- A detailed knowledge of the customer and an accurate segmentation of the market are more important than market share and productivity.
- The demanding customer wants a simple, direct, and easy relationship.

Links

- Speed and flexibility are critical in serving the demanding customer well.
- Satisfied, long-term employees and satisfied, long-term customers reinforce each other.
- Compensation, promotions, and training need to aim at creating employees who serve customers well.
- Understanding customers and working closely with them demands the intelligent and large-scale use of information technology.

• Intimately connected customers can contribute to developing new products.

Cautions

• Not all customers are created equal—some may even be a handicap.
• Trying to satisfy the customer totally would be prohibitively expensive and in any case would be defeated by rising expectations.
• Serving internal customers doesn't necessarily add value to the external customers, the ones who really count.
• Mass customization and data-base marketing are fine, but soft drinks, sausages, soap, and sandpaper still have to be mass-produced the old-fashioned way.

II
THE RESPONSE—
THE PLAYERS

6

ABSORBING THE CUSTOMER

The quickest way to profits is to serve the customer in ways
in which the customer wants to be served.
—Alfred Sloan, 1927[1]

When VeriFone was founded in 1983, the business world was
changing so much that the founders could make a choice that
might not have occurred to entrepreneurs in earlier years. The company
would be organized so that it faced the customer. The internal organization, headquarters, offices, staff meetings, agendas, memos, and all the
other paraphernalia of corporate life would be secondary to getting out
and spending time with customers.

Contrast that with the way 3M, an otherwise exemplary company, created "quality" time to be with its customers. Its top executives would fill
out their calendars with staff meetings and other internal obligations and
then use the blanks left in the calendar for visits to customers, distributors, and others in the outside world.

Will Pape, a former senior vice president and one of VeriFone's
founders, says "You can organize to optimize the internal relationships
or the external relationships. We chose the latter knowing it would make
it harder to work with each other than with our clients. Our travel costs
would be higher, but we would get there first and get control." VeriFone,
which agreed early in 1997 to a friendly takeover by Hewlett-Packard, is
number one in a growing niche of the global market known as "transac-

SEI Survey	
Organizing the company around the customer, not the boss, is critical	74%
We are achieving that	26%

tion automation," the networks that verify your credit cards when you use them in a store or restaurant. Sales in 1996 grew 22% to $472.4 million.

VeriFone's CEO, Hatim Tyabji, maintains that his company has no corporate headquarters. Well, its Redwood City corporate offices in California's Silicon Valley bear a suspicious resemblance to a headquarters. But the offices contain only 120 of the company's 3,000 employees. Tyabji and Pape are seldom there. When he is not traveling, Pape, a big, burly information technology whizz, works out of homes in Hawaii and Santa Fe. Tyabji, a dapper engineer born in Bombay, flies 400,000 miles and visits 200 customers a year. Life at VeriFone is not easy. Tyabji sustains a constant sense of urgency. Senior managers do need to meet face to face sometimes, so Tyabji gets them together somewhere in the world for a few days every six or seven weeks.

What justifies and governs VeriFone's behavior is the need to stay close to the customer. Tyabji spends about 70% of his time with customers. Not only does he need the personal contact with customers, he says, but "the velocity of change in the market place is significantly greater than it was in the eighties . . . so that it becomes imperative to be constantly outside in the real world. You have to understand what people are thinking about, and then move with alacrity." When a hacker's idea can turn into a major industry in 18 months you can't spend too much time in the home office perusing ledgers.[2] VeriFone has to watch for the latest thing in smart cards or computer security in Paris, for instance, because France has been a leader in these matters.

The traditional CEO would more likely spend time with his accountants, lawyers, and strategic planners than with customers, although he might visit customers on state occasions. Alfred Sloan set the right example, as he did in so many matters relating to management, by visiting GM dealerships in the 1920s and 1930s in most of the cities in the United

States. How close he got to the dealers and customers is questionable, however, since he traveled in a specially fitted private railroad car with an entourage of advisers.[3]

The idea that the CEO should get to know the customer personally has gained some ground lately. When he was CEO of Motorola in the mid-1980s, Robert Galvin was urged to spend one day a month with a client—not the top executives but the people who actually dealt with Motorola—and he got an earful every time about Motorola's failings. Other companies have various ways of getting their top people closer to the customer. At Hewlett-Packard, senior executives each take lead roles in dealing with particular customers. Chairman Lewis Platt takes care of problems that may arise at Alcoa, Boeing, GE, and GM. Other companies send their top people out on sales calls, or put them to work on the road or in the store.

GREAT PRODUCTS, BAD PROCESSES

Getting the top executives to face the customer is good and necessary, but the whole company needs to get aligned with the customer too. This need lies behind some recent and major corporate reorganizations, at 3M, at Hewlett-Packard, at KPMG Peat Marwick, and Xerox, to name four examples encountered by the authors in the research for this book (See Figure 6.1).

The restructuring of Minnesota Mining & Manufacturing Company in the fall of 1995 was not devastating as those things go, but it was surprising in a company so successful and so admired, and it was the most drastic in 3M's history. The company announced a reduction of 5,000 in its work force of 85,000 and spun off most of its information, imaging, and electronic sector. The disks and tapes sold by that sector had become commodity products under too much price pressure to help 3M meet its financial targets of a 27% return on capital and a 20% to 25% return on equity. The sector spun off, now known as Imation Corporation, could earn perhaps 10% on its capital.

The other part of 3M's restructuring changed the company to face the customer in order to resolve the problem (mentioned in Chapter 5) of being too hard to deal with. In terms of successfully filling orders, on-time deliveries, cost of acquisitions, answering questions, and just work-

FIGURE 6.1

FOCUS ON MARKET DRIVEN STRATEGY

1
Who are the customers
and what do they
need?

2
What product or service offerings will meet
the target segment's needs and offer us
a sustainable competitive
advantage?

3
What strategies and programs, resources, capabilities,
and processes are required to develop and
implement effectively the product
or service solutions?

ing on the phone, 3M was failing to meet the customers' increasingly ex-
acting demands.

The company's very success at innovation created part of its problem
because the profusion of products spawned organizational complexity—
some 50 divisions selling 50,000 products. It was no longer enough to
want to be the most innovative company. So when 3M restructured itself—with some guidance from the 13 characteristics of the 21st century
enterprise developed by the SEI Center at Wharton and listed in the Introduction—it added a second part to its corporate vision. As well as

being the most innovative, 3M would try to become the customers' "preferred supplier" by improving the whole supply chain, from raw materials to the consumption of the product, and by reducing mistakes and delays, and treating the customers better.

Being technology-driven, 3M had previously organized itself by technologies—a division for each technology. And each division had its own business practices, its own terms and conditions, its own distribution system, and its own information technology. Therefore, if an auto company wanted to buy both abrasives and electric insulation from 3M it would have to deal essentially with two different companies: different salespeople, different processes, different distribution systems, different schedules for price increases.

The 1995 reorganization turned around 3M's industrial and consumer sector, the company's largest, to organize it by markets instead of technologies. The sector's 44 technology divisions were reorganized into five groups, one for the auto industry, one for the pharmaceutical and related industries, and so forth. Now when an auto sales team calls on Ford, for example, the team can sell abrasives and insulators, and masking tape, adhesives, and static protectors, and whatever else 3M makes that Ford may need. The different products are sold under common terms of sale, and price increases are bunched together, twice a year, instead of trickling out. 3M also plans to sign up common distributors for each group.

The regrouping of 3M reflects changing markets as well as the demands of customers that 3M be easier to deal with. The traditional small stationery store, which might stock hundreds of 3M items, has lost half the business to office superstores, which do not want to deal with five different 3M salespeople selling different products under different policies. Therefore 3M now has an office supply group for the superstores. The company reduced the size of the sales force, and since the retrofitted salespeople, or "transaction managers," have to cover more products than they did before, specialists stand behind them on call in case the customer needs greater expertise. If a customer finds a mistake in an order, the transaction manager handles it. But if a customer needs to know more about the coating for a satellite, the specialist gets a call. The pattern of having one salesperson or team deal with a customer backed by product specialists has emerged as companies tried to please their customers.[4]

THE END OF GEOGRAPHY

While 3M quit being product-based to face its markets, KPMG Peat Marwick, the second largest of the so-called Big Six accounting and consulting firms, quit its traditional geographic organization to face its markets. Like the other Big Six firms, KPMG delivered services to its United States clients through 100-plus local offices. That was partly a legacy from the time when it expanded through local franchises. Clients in New Jersey did not want to deal with KPMG people in New York and clients in Manhattan certainly wouldn't talk to an auditor or consultant in New Jersey. If a client in Des Moines needed some specialized service in the health field, the client got whatever expertise was available in Des Moines. Consultants and accountants did not trespass on each other's territory. "None of these things means anything today," says the international chairman of KPMG, Jon Madonna. "Nobody cares. People are flying all over the place or talking to each other through technology. . . . Geography is far less important today than it was ten years ago and in another ten or 20 years, it's going to be irrelevant. Clients in Des Moines have every service available to them that clients in Manhattan do. In the 21st century you are going to be able to get in Rome anything you get in Manhattan. That's a totally different paradigm than what existed ten years ago."[5]

Madonna became CEO in 1990 and since 1991 has been leading KPMG through what he describes as hard and destructive change, realigning the firm into five market segments according to the clients' businesses: financial services; manufacturing, retailing, and distribution; health care; information, communications, and entertainment; and public services. The Des Moines client who needs help in the health field can get it from that health care segment of KPMG anywhere in the system. The new organization, backed by new information technology, makes the help accessible to any client from any part of the company.

Now KPMG needs to roll out its approach and its products globally. The firm has offices in 131 countries all organized under a loose system that gives each unit a freedom to develop its own products and style. That suited clients in the past. When a client was going to open a business in India, for example, it wanted to know if KPMG had an office in India to serve it. Now the client wants to know if KPMG has the right resources to help it, says Madonna, who became international chairman of the firm after stepping down as CEO in 1996. He adds, "they don't care where they come from." He wants to create global market practices just as he has created North American market groups, and to tie the firm together globally with the same information technology, offering the same products around the world.

THE SINGLE BIGGEST WASTE OF TIME

When Hewlett-Packard, another of America's exemplary companies, turned around to face the customer it ran into several complications. In addition to having the classic geographic organization, it was (and is) a loose organization, more a federation of some 60 businesses than a top-down hierarchy. Sales people could choose whatever computer they fancied, so they couldn't be linked to a common data base. The company carried the burden of damaging legacies, especially the poor quality of order fulfillment. HP's increasing sales of consumer-market PCs, printers, and fax machines pushed the company into retail distribution channels where it had little experience.

Manuel Diaz, who created a successful market-focused sales structure when he ran HP's operations in Mexico in the 1980s, believed the same system would work for large accounts worldwide. He had moved up through several positions in the Americas to become worldwide chief of computer sales. Beginning in 1992, he began to change the sales structure. He created four national business units in computer sales, each responsible for major accounts in a different industry group—manufacturing, financial services, communications, and the federal government. The regional offices remained to handle retail businesses, local governments, and other smaller accounts.

At the same time, HP had to improve the productivity and effectiveness of its sales force. Because of the legacy of patchwork information systems, "the tracking of sales was the single biggest waste of time for our salespeople," says Dick Knudtsen, who helped Diaz reform HP's computer sales. Improving productivity was particularly important as HP had cut its sales support force by 40% without reducing the work load. The information system had to be made seamless so that salespeople could not only track orders, but enter them correctly in the first place, get technical help quickly, and present attractive multimedia sales material. Instead of driving around with a trunkful of documents, probably outdated and unread, salespeople now use a computerized "electronic sales partner" that gives them access on the road to 18,000 documents. They can produce data sheets, training manuals, organization charts, or whatever else they may need. The data base is updated at the rate of 50 documents a day. The whole corporation adopted SAP's unifying software which puts all of a company's operations into a single information system. The popular SAP system, developed by a team of four young engineers who broke away from IBM's German operation, will take years to install fully at HP because of its complexity, but it is successfully replacing the old patchwork system. At the same time HP replaced the random mix of computers used by its salespeople with 3.5-pound HP Omnibooks.

To make the sales offices more efficient, the computer sales operation appointed senior administrative officers to perform the office work required of the salespeople, and began testing different types of office configurations. "The sales office is a very unproductive place," says Knudtsen, because when they are in their offices salespeople tend to do office things rather than selling. The salespeople were encouraged to work at home if they wanted to and work the hours they preferred. In one experiment at the HP London office, the sales reps have no space of their own in the office. If they need to work there, they simply sit down at an empty desk, plug in their computers, and program the phone to pick up calls to their number. This arrangement allows 200 people to share 40 desks.

Not only do sales reps have on-line and automated sales material and systems for configuring orders and quoting prices, but clients themselves can run some of the same processes. Some one dozen "channel partners," such as retailers and distributors, can configure a system themselves through CompuServe and place the order. Customers can also use the Internet to browse through the HP "catalog" on the company's home page, configure an order, place it, and later track its status—all on-line.

Should the sales reps feel threatened that the new system will undermine what used to be their exclusive relationships with clients, they have the opportunity to earn more. Instead of a single commission rate, the rate goes up once they have achieved 60% of their annual target, and it accelerates again if they pass 100%. Like other employees, the sales reps are also rated on customer satisfaction. By late 1995, halfway through HP's turn to face the customer. the cost of computer sales had dropped from 30 cents per dollar of orders in 1992 to 15 cents, the orders per sales rep had jumped from $1.5 million to nearly $4 million, and the numbers continued to improve.[6] In May 1997, HP reorganized its sales force again to consolidate three groups—for systems, for PCs and peripherals, and for services—so that the customer could deal with only one HP team.

DEFINING THE CUSTOMERS' NEEDS

The examples of VeriFone, Hewlett-Packard, and KPMG Peat Marwick demonstrate that corporations are going to extraordinary lengths today to restructure their organizations to the point of absorbing their customers. The means of catching those customers—finding them, understanding them, defining their needs, suiting the product to those needs, and providing a degree of satisfaction consistent with making healthy profits (and maybe knowing and dumping marginal customers)—have become radically more sophisticated and effective. Mainly because of new information technology, business now has the means to segment the market, mine data, mass customize, promote brands, and create new channels with more knowledge and precision than before.

The basic ideas of serving a segment are not new. The retired army officers who founded United Services Automobile Association (now the USAA Group) in 1922 saw opportunity in what looked like an unpromising market segment—their fellow officers.

By serving the military market segment efficiently and economically, and leading the way with new information systems, USAA became a major insurer with a large body of loyal members (much enlarged by veterans of subsequent wars). Its strength lies not in its services, which others can duplicate, but in "its knowledge of its customers' needs and its ability to fulfill these needs efficiently and profitably," according to a study by Mercer Management Consulting.[7]

AMERICAN EXPRESS: A BACK ROOM IN BRIGHTON

American Express still has its 100-year-old offices on the Rue Scribe in Paris where lost tourists can go for help and reassurance, as well as 1,700 other offices around the world for the traveler. However, the way American Express handles, bills, and sells to that traveler is changing radically, mostly because information technology makes it possible. In Western Europe, which in some respects is the company's test lab, American Express broke its business down into three customer groups: the ordinary traveler or consumer, the corporate customer, and the merchant. For the consumer sector, the front offices remain open in 16 countries, but the back office operations have been centralized in Brighton, England. The bills and correspondence for all of Europe are handled there. Multinational teams in London develop new consumer products for all of Europe, look at how to retain customers, how to get new customers, how to take advantage of Europe-wide TV advertising rates and mailing lists. Now, instead of being a relatively small player in 16 different countries with separate operations for each, American Express can be a big regional player—and get the economies of consolidating all those national operations.

American Express is also using its regional information systems to mine for data to segment the market more finely and focus more clearly on particular types of customers. "We're one of the few card companies that has data on both the merchant relationship and the card member," says John Crewe, president of international marketing and product development. "We're able therefore to model card members' behaviors. We can pick out people who eat in Italian restaurants in London more than three times a month." Therefore, when those members get their monthly bill it won't be stuffed with a random collection of advertising blurbs, but it might have a message on the bill notifying them of the opening of a new Italian restaurant in London.[8]

GENERAL MOTORS: REVIVING OLD BRANDS

American Express also enjoys the enduring strength of its brand name. It may not have the mass popular appeal of Coca-Cola or Nike. Michael Jordan and Nike together can give youngsters from Madras to Muncie an instant craving for a new basketball shoe. American Express can't do that, but its green card, along with its variants in gold and other colors, is still esteemed as the right sort of companion for the well-heeled traveler. Good brands have extraordinary staying power. They can slip, however, if the owner doesn't maintain their particularities and match them to defined and reachable groups of consumers. Alfred Sloan—to refer yet again to the Father of GM—understood well the importance of brands and market segments when he declared GM would have "a car for every purse and purpose." This was the weapon he used to overtake Ford with its one-version black Model T. Out of a hodgepodge of overlapping models, Sloan created in 1921 an orderly progression of models, each with its own price range which touched but didn't overlap the next model up the scale. The range began with a Chevrolet selling for $525, somewhat more than the Model T, and going up through six grades to the most expensive Cadillac, which cost over $3,000.[9]

By the 1980s, GM's nameplates, mostly the same as they were in Sloan's time, had become hopelessly muddled. The brands overlapped, competed with each other, and lost whatever distinction they had enjoyed. The cars looked alike. Some Cadillac models, for example, were hard to tell from Chevrolets and suffered major quality failures. Tell a yuppie of the 1980s that something was "the Cadillac of its class," and the yuppie, unaware of the old connotation, might answer, "So what's wrong with it?" A disastrous reorganization of GM in 1984, lumping Chevrolet and Pontiac into one division, and Buick, Oldsmobile, and Cadillac into another, further weakened the brands. As *Fortune* observed, "Not even a junior brand manager at Procter & Gamble would have mismanaged GM's product line as badly as GM did in the 1980s. It allowed divisions to market nearly identical cars to nearly identical customers. Thus, Pontiac and Chevrolet went wheel-to-wheel for younger buyers, while Buick and Oldsmobile dueled for the sixtysomething crowd."[10]

GM's attempt to recover has three elements: (1) cost reduction, (2) better innovation, and (3) brand management. The third is the gift of John G. Smale, who led the board forces that ousted Robert Stempel as chairman of GM in 1992, a year of record losses, and then served as chairman himself while John Smith became president and CEO. Smale is a former CEO of P&G and he persuaded GM to return to disciplined brand management. GM brought in a new team of outsiders to run its marketing. Ronald Zarrella left his job as president of Bausch & Lomb to head the effort and Vincent Barabba, a former head of marketing intelligence at Eastman Kodak and director of the Bureau of the Census, came in to run strategic planning and market information.

GM's management imposed brand discipline to stop one nameplate from fighting another for the same customer. The company's orientation changed. Instead of being fixated on products—which had really meant that it shoved out the cars the engineers thought the customers should have—or trying to beat the competition, GM tried to focus on what the customer wanted. Back in 1988 GM had begun developing a huge data base of customer preferences and now the information was used to define 19 distinct market segments for cars and 14 for light trucks. Back in Sloan's time, segmenting the market didn't amount to much more than setting price brackets based on hunches about the market.

If you look through the adman's blarney, you can see how GM situates its four midsize cars to fit the market segments it has picked out. Pontiac appeals to young, unencumbered show-offs, Chevrolet is for young families on a tight budget, Oldsmobile is for the family that is a little older and more affluent, and Buick appeals to stodgy old codgers.

WHAT THE CUSTOMER CAN'T SEE

GM's research goes far beyond this simple segmentation, of course, to find out more about what customers want. The idea is to emphasize the things that matter to drivers and differentiate one model from another in the customer's mind and to worry less about the things that don't matter to the customer. That way GM can cut costs by avoiding what one executive calls "customer transparent proliferation." In other words, it wouldn't matter in the slightest if all GM cars had the same wheel bearings and transmission cases because the customer can't see them and doesn't care. The proliferation of radios in GM vehicles benefited nobody. In 1993, GM offered 160 different radios in its whole vehicle line. By using common components that the customer doesn't see, GM planned to cut that number in half by 1998 and wind up with 35 radios eventually. That would save $150 million on the nine million radios that GM sells annually.[11] GM has reduced the number of ignition systems from 17 to three.

General Motors reorganized its North American Operations (NOA) to make the new approach work. The reorganization is complex and GM executives have trouble explaining it lucidly. The old division structure is gone and Smith has lifted corporate headquarters off the backs of the line executives. The new organization is meant to make sure NOA develops, makes, and sells cars in a coordinated, disciplined way. Three vehicle centers (for small cars, regular and luxury cars, and for trucks) develop new vehicle platforms and the processes to make cars more efficiently. The 14 "vehicle launch executives" and their teams each work to design and develop a specific new model, focusing on everything from manufacturing to marketing. Finally, brand managers are responsible for presenting the vehicles to the market. A NOA strategy board supervises all three levels of operations.

Although GM's share of the U.S. car and light-truck market dropped from 44% in 1980 to 31% in 1996 and went on down to 30.2% in 1997, GM has had successes, particularly with the Chevrolet Lumina and Cavalier, and it has improved as an organization. David Cole, director of the Office for the Study of Automotive Transportation at the University of Michigan, believes that a company that was a "bureaucratic quagmire" has cut costs and gained competitive advantages. "GM was bureaucratic and inefficient without enjoying the advantages of size," says Cole. "Now it is maximizing the advantages of size. It's all falling into place very quickly. GM is a completely different company."[12]

TOO MUCH OF A GOOD THING

As companies turn to face the markets of the 21st century—many, many more than the examples cited in this chapter—they have to deal not only with intensified competition for the customers but also with new and rapidly changing means of finding and securing those customers. Hewlett-Packard and 3M have to learn more about selling in consumer markets. New marketing channels are changing the nature of some businesses. Applying the methods of supermarkets to hardware and to office supplies led to the creation of Home Depot, Staples, and Office Max, offering bargains to the shopper. Managed health care changes the nature of selling prescription drugs because organizations rather than individual doctors make the purchasing decisions. Flexible manufacturing technology creates the ability to produce to order for small market segments, even segments of only one buyer, and to do so almost instantly.

The power of information technology changes the nature of marketing. Market segmenting and "data mining" today depend totally on computers. If mass marketing belonged to the age of mass production, then data mining belongs to the information age. Data mining begins with the acquisition of the purchasing histories available on tens of millions of consumers from credit card data, frequent shopper club data, and similar sources. A first cut on the data might be what IBM calls "neural segmentation" in a description of the data mining services it offers. This might identify the preferences of, say, retired couples living in the Midwest. At a more sophisticated level, data mining reveals associations. To take an obvious example, if you buy paint, there's a 20% likelihood you will also buy a brush, and if you buy both of those there's a 40% chance you will buy paint thinner. (But a similar relationship between paint and hair rollers would be discarded because both were on sale at the same time.) Then there is the sequential association: There's a 30% chance that someone who buys a canteen from the January catalog will buy a sleeping bag from the March catalog. These and other far more sophisticated forms of data mining make it possible for companies to know their customers better and focus their marketing.[13]

Entirely new markets, such as electronic trading, shopping channels on TV, sales through the Internet, are arising out of information technology. The effect of electronic knowledge is profound, write two Harvard Business School professors, because "information about a product or service can be separated from the product or service itself. In some cases it can become as critical as the actual product itself. . . ." They cite how used cars are auctioned to wholesalers in Japan. The cars used to be brought physically to a lot and sold there to wholesalers. That system was replaced by a weekly live auction on a closed circuit TV system, which makes it unnecessary for the cars or the dealers to gather in one place. *Marketspace* replaces *marketplace*.[14] Automatic teller machines have changed the nature of retail banking—and weakened customer loyalty because networks of the popular ATMs mean you can transact some banking business anywhere without going to a particular bank. The voice-mail service provided by the phone companies replaces a physical product, the answering machine, and, in contrast to the ATM, ties the customer more closely to the company.

The new marketspace created by cable TV and the Internet has generated more excitement than revenue, at least as of the close of 1996. Home shoppers still favored, by a huge margin, the classic type of catalog first mailed out by Sears Roebuck more than 100 years ago (and recently abandoned by Sears while other companies thrive on it). Sales through catalogs amounted to 27 times sales through home-shopping TV channels, and on-line sales through Internet were barely a blip in the market in 1995.[15] Big companies such as Time Warner, AT&T, and MCI Communications Corporation discovered that money pours out through the Net easily but doesn't necessarily come back. The latter two companies pulled out quickly and Time Warner foresaw profits coming in only after heavy losses. Some smaller companies, notably Amazon.com, an on-line bookstore with quick access to more than one million books, have found a profitable place on the Net. These are low-budget operations focused on providing customers with a particular product or service in a way that provides a perceived advantage. With 15 million homes in the United States connected to the Internet, and the number growing phenomenally, the potential market in cyberspace is enormous, but just how it will work out is one of those predictions about technology that entrepreneurs are finding so devilishly difficult to make.

As we have seen in this chapter, turning to face the customer has profound effects on the whole company, beyond the restructuring of the company itself. For example, if the company is reorganized into divisions corresponding to market segments, then the pay structure, or at least the bonus structure, may have to be realigned to reward executives for their "customer satisfaction" ratings. To improve service for customers, companies may take people out of their specialties and put them in teams that can deal with any type of question or problem customers may raise, whether it relates to technology or an invoice.

The customer becomes in a sense an extension of the company because the company gets close to him and responsive to his needs. When the auto companies use customers to help them design cars, when FedEx gives a customer direct access to its computers to order a pickup or track a package, when Boeing invites airlines to sit on the teams designing a new aircraft, then the customer is almost absorbed into the company. The company that can find a way of creating real added value for the customer at an acceptable cost will always have an advantage. Even in a business as brutally competitive as the airline industry, some companies can make money by treating the customers better. U.S. airlines sell on the basis of low prices and frequent flier awards while inflicting truly dreadful service on their passengers; the privatized British

Airways makes a profit by charging a premium for a little extra service. U.S. lines worry about how to save pennies on pretzels (which long ago replaced real if unattractive meals on most domestic flights); British Airways maintains the quality of the wines it serves. As one of the authors discovered, British Airways has found a delightful way to help travelers recuperate from that early morning, red-eyed arrival in London, too early in the day for the hotels to honor reservations. The lounge for first-class and business-class passengers at Heathrow offers breakfast, showers, haircuts, clothes pressing, and other amenities, all free.

Here are some of the things a corporation should ask itself about the way it treats customers:

Pointers

- Does the company face the customer, that is, is it organized to handle its markets, or does the organization follow some internal rationale based on divisions or technology or geography?
- Do the top executives really know the customers and deal with them regularly?
- Does the company look towards achieving a dominant position in key markets by meeting the customer's requirements?
- Does the company have the right information technology to know the market and serve the customer?
- Does it know what the customer really values?
- Does it examine the entire relationship with the customer and not just the quality of the product and service?
- Are there new channels to be exploited or invented? New segments?
- Does the company make it easy for the customer to place orders, trace them, and get information about products and services, preferably all in one place?

Links

- Does the corporation have the right compensation and evaluation plans to encourage employees to serve the customer better?
- Does it have the right training to help employees serve the customer better?
- Does it extend the team approach to dealing with customers?

- Can the customer reach into the information system to give an order or check the status of an existing order?

Cautions

- Is the company making improvements that add no value in the customer's eyes?
- Is the company offering so many many updates, variants, and options as to irritate the customer?

7

REINVENTING THE LEADER

A commercial company, or for that matter any organization, is nothing but a mental construction, a concept, an idea to which people and resources are drawn in pursuit of common purpose.

—Dee Hock, founder of VISA

Americans clearly have an image of the kind of leadership they think they want: the leader is the charismatic hero, the tough guy who snaps out decisions, the loner who doesn't need help, the jut-jawed general leading the tanks. In sports we seem to admire the loudmouth coach, screaming abuse at the opposition, the officials, and of course at his own players. In business, America has had its share of abusive, bullying CEOs, people like Harold Geneen of ITT, Frank Lorenzo of Continental Airlines, and the late Armand Hammer of Occidental Petroleum.

Business has also produced fine leaders. Among the entrepreneurs there are great visionaries, sometimes greatly flawed but nevertheless people who substantially changed the world: John D. Rockefeller, Henry Ford, Thomas Watson, David Packard and William Hewlett, Sam Walton, and Bill Gates, to name a handful. In *Leading Change,* one of the best of the many books on leadership, James O'Toole, of the Aspen Institute, uses the symbol of Mt. Rushmore to make his key point about leadership. Whatever the artistic failings of this megamonument, the four presidents whose features are carved into the face of Mt. Rushmore, Washington, Jefferson, Lincoln, and Teddy Roosevelt, do share these characteristics of good leadership: "courage, authenticity, integrity, vision, passion, conviction, and persistence."[1] O'Toole nominates four chief executives to a hypothetical Mt. Rushmore of business: Max de Pree of Herman Miller, Jamie Houghton of Corning, Bob Galvin of Motorola, and Jan Carlzon of SAS. The best of these, he says, is Galvin. All four have left their jobs, but at Corning and Motorola at least, the kind of leadership they established persists.

CEOs are pretty much the same as leaders have been in every walk of life through history, probably much like the Roman officers who led their legions all over the known world, although the Romans might have had better leadership training and more rounded experience in legal, administrative, and military posts. The authoritarian, all-knowing, and preferably charismatic leader was the model, except that in business the charisma was often lacking. Instead, the CEO typically is strong on analysis, good with numbers but not with people.

However, the old model of leadership is losing ground because organizations are changing and people are changing. If people behave more like cats than sheep they are not going to be led around by a shepherd. People today don't want paternalism. They are better educated, more as-

---

Dividing Time

When he was CEO of Corning, Jamie Houghton went through what he described as an "enlightening exercise" comparing the way he spent his time with an "ideal" developed for a fitness review requested by John Marous when he was CEO of Westinghouse. These were the results.

Activity	Ideal division of time	Houghton's time
Provide strategic direction	20%	10%
Assess operations	20	15
Lead the management team	15	12
Create environment and value system	15	30
External representation; track external environment	15	18
Relationships with directors and shareholders	10	7
Personal growth and health	5	8

Houghton went through a further exercise and determined that 58% of his time was spent on "value added" activities such as board meetings, improving quality, training, and philanthropy and 42% on things that added no value, such as travel, speeches, and outside board meetings.

Source: Personal document provided by James R. Houghton.

sertive, more willing to make up their own minds. The hierarchical, stable organization, which may well have required an authoritarian boss, is giving way to the flattened, flexible organization, which evidently requires a different type of leader.

LEADING BY EXAMPLE

The fundamental shift we see today is from leadership by command to leadership by vision and example. The idea is not new. We are simply recognizing the nature of true leadership. Rather than being a remote, analytical, machine who issues commands, the CEO needs to have values and a vision, and to be seen to live and work by them. He needs to be collaborative and helpful, as much concerned with human beings as with the numbers. Real leaders, says O'Toole, win the trust of their followers by listening to them and respecting them. They do not surround themselves with yes-men, but rather with strong people, so they become leaders of leaders. They personally take charge of and live the efforts to change a company. They do not reward themselves excessively. They do what they say they are going to do. Today's leaders need to be strong on analytic and people skills, both the hard and the soft skills.

Awareness of the need for a new kind of leadership is widespread. Leading in the new way is something else. Today's crop of leaders rose to power by the old rules. They are not going to change overnight. Moreover, what is required of business leaders today is almost countercultural. In an age of celebrityhood, who wants to develop the patient, solid virtues of good leadership? At a time of enormous material rewards for CEOs, who wants to lead by good example?

The question of leadership became topical in the early 1980s when the business community began to realize just how much change it faced. Leadership had always been a focal subject at military schools, but now the business schools began to teach it too. Wharton started its first leadership course for future executives in 1987. Institutes on leadership studies and training proliferated. Books on leadership began to appear and consultants began to find a lucrative new niche. The many failed efforts at total quality management in the early 1980s drove home the need for a different kind of leadership. On confronting the need to improve quality, the natural reaction of the chief executive at the time was to announce a quality improvement drive, appoint a vice president to run it, and then turn to other less painstaking tasks. It soon became apparent that improving quality was much more than just using a new tool, that it involved a new way of managing. The cardinal rule of quality said that unless the CEO personally got engaged in the effort, it wouldn't work because no one else would take it seriously. Those who took charge personally, such as Bob Galvin of Motorola and Jamie Houghton of Corning, succeeded. Those who didn't, such as John Akers at IBM and Roger Smith of General Motors, failed.

"I'M ASTOUNDED I SURVIVED"

The degree of change demanded in leadership style can be traumatic. When Ross Perot announced the formation of Perot Systems Incorporated in 1988 he clearly had in mind something in the image of his first company, the gung-ho, spit-and-polish EDS. In classic Perotian language, he said he was recruiting "the top guns of the computer industry, the fighting generals with mud on their boots . . . guys who like to climb cliffs with ice on them."[2] But they slipped on those icy cliffs and in 1992 Perot called back Morton Meyerson, who had been the mean, tough-and-proud-of-it president of EDS, to be CEO and fix the new company. In six months, with sales stalled at around $150 million a year, a piddling amount for Perot, Meyerson came to Perot to say that it wasn't working and in fact that "everything I thought I knew about leadership is wrong." Reflecting three years later, Meyerson said, "when I look back at some of the things I did in my 20s and 30s and 40s, I'm astounded that I survived to get here, and somebody didn't assassinate me or fire me earlier. But at the time I thought I was doing fine."

Between jobs at the Perot companies, while working as a consultant, Meyerson had second thoughts about his management style. When he came to Perot Systems, he says, "my first job as a leader was to create a new understanding of myself. I had to accept the shattering of my own self-confidence. I couldn't lead any more, at least not in the way I always had. . . . I don't *have* to know everything. I don't *have* to have all the customer contacts. I don't *have* to make all the decisions. In fact, in the new world of business, it can't be me, it shouldn't be me, and my job is to prevent it from being me."

"The essence of leadership today is to make sure that the organization knows itself," Meyerson wrote in *Fast Company* magazine. "There are certain durable principles that underlie an organization. The leader should embody those values." And instead of appearing on stage once every six months to give the troops a pep talk, Meyerson made it clear that anyone in the company could talk to him directly by e-mail any time they wanted.

While Meyerson reinvented himself as a leader he was also trying to make the company reinvent itself, which made the change especially harrowing as he ran into strong opposition and sharp criticism. The top 100 people in the company met in February, 1993, to think about reinventing the company rather than simply creating an updated version of EDS. These managers were asked to fill out "greensheets" anonymously to say just what they thought of the company. As Meyerson explains it, the kind of people who work for Perot Systems are engineers, analytical, critical, Type A personalities accustomed to working on tangible problems. Ask them to critique the company, to talk about the soft side of the company, and you are likely to get an earful. After reading the first batch of greensheets, Meyerson admitted he felt like slashing his wrists because he found such a level of frustration and unhappiness. "Everybody ripped the company to shreds," he says.

Change is so tough and the rewards are so slow to come (by American expectations) that many CEOs and their boards lose faith after a year or so and go back to the old ways, says Meyerson. By June, 1994, 15 months after starting the process, Meyerson couldn't see any improvement in sales or attitudes and began to have second thoughts about the rightness of what he was doing. But sales picked up that month and "I said hey, maybe there is a flicker here." Sales grew substantially more and Meyerson stayed the course.

He thinks the Perot Systems people would still say they wasted a lot of time back in 1993 and 1994 "sucking our thumbs and talking psychological mumbo-jumbo." However, the company has changed. Compensation proved to be the tool that turned people's minds. Bonuses had been based solely on profits. The EDS legacy held that customers were suckers to be outwitted, employees were soldiers to be bullied callously, and success was individual. The reinvented Perot Systems bases bonuses not just on profits, but also on customer satisfaction, on performance ratings by subordinates as well as peers and superiors, and on teamwork. Sales reached $600 million in 1996 and, in Meyerson's view at least, "everything has changed . . . people are happier, customer service is better, customer satisfaction is up."[3] (Meyerson has stepped down as CEO of Perot Systems, but remained as chairman.)

Not many CEOs in 1996 have made the transition to the new style of leadership. Richard Hagberg of the Hagberg Consulting Group, who advises CEOs on their style and behavior, finds that the pressures of running a business today may be driving CEOs in the wrong direction. As a group, chief executives are impatient to begin with and pressures from restive boards of directors make them even more so. They try to move too quickly, pushing their vision for the company but not taking the time to get alignment behind that vision and get the execution right. In companies that have gone through the pain of downsizing, chief executives tend to protect themselves by disconnecting emotionally from the people in the company, rather than showing support and sympathy, and they fail to see how their behavior hurts the company, says Hagberg. He compiled a data base on 511 CEOs and found that those that failed could be characterized as "impatient, impulsive, manipulative, dominating, self-important, and critical."[4]

The very qualities that get executives to the top may work against them when they get there, especially today. Since they have good analytical minds, they can get to the heart of a matter quickly, but for the same reason they may be so wrapped up in their thoughts that they fail to notice the troops haven't stormed the hill with them. CEOs are aggressive and competitive, so when they create management teams they dominate them, not realizing that the consensus they think they have achieved is a false one. The people who become chief executives tend to be loners, and once at the top may tend to become more so. The pressures today may emphasize that loneliness. Hagberg says that half the CEOs in his data base could be described as loners in 1991, but by 1996 70% fit that description. Power tends to corrupt, as Lord Acton said, and once in office the CEOs listen less, act impulsively, take less time to build relationships with others, become more alienated and even paranoid, according to Hagberg.[5]

THE V-WORD

John Smale, who has some experience in such matters, having served as CEO of Procter & Gamble and then chairman of the General Motors board after it threw out the old leadership and brought in the new, has this definition of corporate leadership: "Shaping the vision and then ensuring that the organization has all the intangible as well as tangible qualities needed for everyone to pull together and attain and preserve the vision."[6]

"Vision" is an overused and abused word in business language today. But that does not mean the idea of vision should be discarded. When George Bush admitted to having trouble with "the vision thing" and when Louis Gerstner, on assuming command of IBM in 1993, said, "The last thing IBM needs right now is a vision," both men were ridiculed. IBM even made sport of the whole thing in its 1995 annual report by referring to the "V-word" and recalling the "whooping and hollering in the media about IBM wandering, visionless, through the wilderness." The report carried on its cover a cluttered, clumsy vision statement and invited readers to say it in ten words or less. In 1993 Gerstner was probably right in saying IBM didn't need a vision because the company was fighting to survive. Now, like other companies, it does need vision. Gerstner said in the 1995 report, "I don't mean a slogan. I don't mean promises and vaporware (announced products that don't exist and never will). I don't mean here's-what's-good-for-IBM-and-therefore-it's-good-for-you-too."[7]

A vision is needed to give a company the right goals and then to align the whole company behind achieving them. James Collins and Jerry Porras state in their best-seller, *Built to Last,* that the long-term success of visionary companies makes them stand out from the rest of the corporate pack. This has always been true, but vision is especially important now because empowered workers are likely to wander off in all directions unless they are aligned with one vision. As Robert Haas, the CEO of Levi Strauss, has put it, "In a more volatile and dynamic business environment, the controls have to be conceptual. They can't be human any

---

SEI Survey

It is critical for the leader to create a clear sense of vision and its accompanying culture	79%
We have that	38%

more: Bob Haas telling people what to do. It's the *ideas* of business that are controlling, not some manager with authority. Values provide a common language for aligning a company's leadership and its people."[8] Managers now seem to recognize the importance of vision. Participants in executive education courses at Wharton used to rank decisiveness as the most important characteristic of their business heroes, but some years ago they made vision the first requirement.[9]

On one practical level business is sharpening its focus. Perhaps it's only one of those pendulum swings in business strategy—in this case between diversification and simplification—but corporations are narrowing their range of activities. *Competing for the Future,* by Gary Hamel and C.K. Prahalad, urged companies to concentrate on their core competencies. They seem to be doing that. An index kept by J.P. Morgan that measures the "clarity" of American industrial companies shows two out of three becoming more focused since 1988. The shares of the companies that "clarified" outperformed the market by 14.6% in the 24 months following their action, and outperformed companies that diversified by 19.1%.[10] (See Figure 7.1.)

In a similar exercise, the Conference Board measured the number of three-digit standard industrial classification (SIC) codes spanned by the average manufacturing company. The average dropped from 4.35 in 1979 to 2.12 in 1992.[11] There are exceptions, of course. Jack Welch proudly flouts the trend of spinning off companies. General Electric remains a conglomerate, and a highly successful one, with 12 distinct businesses. However, early in his regime, in the beginning of the 1980s, CEO Welch had simplified GE by selling off 117 businesses.

STATING A DISTINCTIVE COMPETENCE

Companies and their gurus waste an extraordinary amount of executive time and verbiage elaborating gaseous statements and debating the distinctions between visions, missions, and goals. The statements are then distributed, printed, posted prominently, and promptly forgotten. A poor record, however, does not invalidate the need for the 21st century enterprise to have a vision to keep it on the right course. The statement should set a clear, specific goal, something grand and challenging but doable, something that sets the company apart from others, even some-

FIGURE 7.1

Corporate Clarity

J.P. Morgan's "corporate clarity index" followed changes in the business focus of 410 large companies over eight years. Morgan uses a complex formula that looks at the number of businesses a company is in and also takes into account the volume of sales in each business and the degree of relationship between the different businesses. In this adaptation of the index, we see that the number of "pure plays"—companies with not more than two businesses in one industry—increased from 30% to 43% of the total.

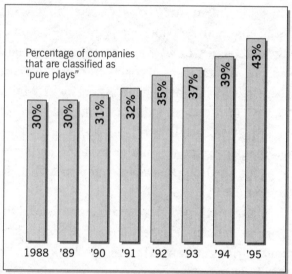

Percentage of companies
that are classified as
"pure plays"

| 1988 | '89 | '90 | '91 | '92 | '93 | '94 | '95 |
| 30% | 30% | 31% | 32% | 35% | 37% | 39% | 43% |

Source: Rick Escherich, J.P. Morgan, *Corporate Clarity Index, 1988–1995* (July 17, 1996).

thing that promises to change a business or a market. An all-purpose vision won't work. A vision requires a statement of distinctive competence, a reason for being in business and a reason for customers to buy from the company. Now that strategic planning has been declared dead—at least strategic planning of the sort concocted by large central staffs—the vision should keep the corporation pointed in the right direction.

The vision should be neither utopian nor crass. Donald Burr thought that commercial success was not good enough for People Express, so he declared that the airline's purpose was to "become the leading institution for constructive change in the world."[12] A statement at once so vague and so preposterous couldn't have helped People Express. (However, Japanese companies seem to get along fine with high-flown visions. For example, Canon, whose chairman, Ryuzaburo Kaku, calls himself an evangelist, guides itself by the *kyosei* philosophy, which it describes as "living and working together for the common good." Evidently such aspi-

FIGURE **7.2**

Creating an Appropriate Vision

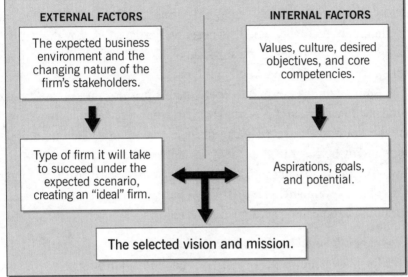

rations play better in Japan than they would in the United States because Japanese companies identify themselves more closely with national and social interests.) A purely mercenary vision would not work either in the United States. A 10% annual profit increase and a 25% return is a sound business goal, but it's not going to get anybody fired up. Nor is "Maximize shareholder value!" a battle-cry that will win much enthusiasm.

David Gaylin, a vice president of Mercer Management Consulting, which helps companies formulate visions, particularly likes the Marriott Corporation statement: "Marriott is committed to being the best lodging and food service company in the world by treating employees in ways that create extraordinary customer service and shareholder value."[13] It is comprehensive but brief, it states a clear goal, indicates how that goal is to be achieved, and has something in it for everybody.

THE HP WAY

Underlying the vision, an organization also needs an enduring set of values to guide people's behavior and corporate morals. The values may be as much ridiculed or ignored as vision statements, especially in companies where the leaders obviously don't believe their own pontifications.

However, a set of basic values, whether stated, or implicit, or built by tradition, will take hold of a company one way or another for better or worse. At Time Warner, for example, the strong journalistic values created by the founder, Henry Luce, have gradually been replaced by the entertainment mentality of his successors. Perhaps today, with so much change roiling the corporate waters, an explicit set of values is more important than it might have been in the past.

The most famous set of corporate values in the United States came from David Packard and William Hewlett, who were so gentlemanly that they did not like to hear criticism of their competitors. That kind of decency might be hard to find today in newer Silicon Valley companies. However, the values they instilled at Hewlett-Packard are still fundamental to the company. "The HP Way" has gone through various interpretations, but it can be summarized as follows:

- We have trust and respect for individuals.
- We focus on a high level of achievement and contribution.
- We conduct our business with uncompromising integrity.
- We achieve our common objectives through teamwork.
- We encourage flexibility and innovation.[14]

In most companies, people would look at the value statement, say "Yeah, right!," file it, and go on with their business. However, Hewlett-Packard keeps the HP Way alive and it counts in the company's success. For example, having trust and respect for people means that when an engineer comes in with an idea that fails to ignite the boss, the boss nevertheless lets the engineer develop the idea (up to a point). That's one reason that HP has been so successfully innovative. CEO Lewis Platt, the heir to the Hewlett and Packard philosophy, says he does not "run" the company but "I spend a lot of my time talking about values rather than trying to figure out the business strategies." He admits this is quite different from what most CEOs do.[15]

At Microsoft, CEO Bill Gates doesn't talk much about values and ethics, but the standards are there. In 1992, Gates said Microsoft people should be evaluated not only on performance but on adherence to values. After asking many employees for their views, says Mike Murray, vice president for human resources and administration, the company adopted these six core values:

- Take a long-term view, by investing heavily in R&D, hiring young people, taking time to develop markets.
- Stress results.
- Expect individual excellence.
- Rely on teamwork.
- Get customer feedback.
- Have a passion for products and technology.

People at Microsoft don't spend a whole lot of time promoting their values. "Here, you don't find slogans on coffee mugs as you do at Hewlett-Packard," says Murray. However, the values are there. They have become part of the performance appraisals that Microsoft people get every six months.[16]

LONG LIVE THE LEADER

If values-based leadership in fact is replacing autocratic and charismatic leadership, then the old argument about whether leaders are born or made loses some pertinence. The great charismatic leaders, Churchill, Martin Luther King, MacArthur, the Roosevelts, for example, were clearly born, and not the products of an executive leadership development program. However, some great world leaders have drawn their strength from an inflexible commitment to values, Gandhi and Mandela among them. Those values were learned and the commitment hardened during years of persecution.

A business leader should have enough eloquence and force of personality to sell the corporate vision across the company, and those may be innate, unteachable qualities. But values are teachable—and enforceable by pay and promotion standards. "We teach leadership by teaching GE values," says Steven Kerr, a former University of Michigan business professor who now runs the GE management school at Crotonville, New York. Business leaders tend to the dour, dry, and tongue-tied, although some—Andy Grove of Intel, Lee Iacocca of Chrysler, and Jack Welch of GE, for example—do achieve charismatic or at least celebrity status.

Values-based leadership seems to work best when the values of the leader and the values of the company are fused. That takes time, and not surprisingly, successful companies tend to have long-term leaders. In their book on 18 visionary companies, James Collins and Jerry Porras found that the average tenure of the CEO was 17.38 years, compared to 11.68 years for the tenure of the heads of 18 less successful comparison companies.[17] In his splendid book on the *Hidden Champions* about very successful smaller companies, mainly German, Hermann Simon reports that in his sample of 122 companies, the average tenure of the CEO was 20.6 years. One company, Netzsch, which builds equipment and plants for the ceramics industries, has had only three CEOs since it was established in 1873. Another, Glasbau Hahn, which makes showcases for exhibits, has had just four CEOs since 1836.[18]

The important thing about these long-lasting CEOs is not the length of tenure itself but the continuity it represents. That continuity can be achieved by long tenure, or by family ownership or a dynasty, or by careful promotion from within. It is interesting that two of O'Toole's four Rushmorean leaders come out of dynasties. Bob Galvin is the son of Motorola's founder, Paul (and the new CEO is the grandson, Christopher), while Jamie Houghton is the sixth member of his family to have run Corning in more than a century. The careful development of leadership within a company, as practiced by GE, for example, helps to assure not only a choice of qualified leaders when the time comes to pick a new CEO but also a continuity and unity of values.

ENFORCING VALUES AT GE

Jack Welch takes great pains choosing his words and he is good at metaphors, which he produces often, perhaps too often. But they have helped create the visions and values at GE. At first, when GE was worried about survival, he cut the company down to businesses that were or could be "either number one or number two in their global markets." Then he "delayered" to clear out the "stifling bureaucracy." Then, shifting from goals to values, he called for self-confidence, simplicity, and speed, the attributes, he said, of small companies. To these values he added the concept of the "work-out," a name for a gathering of people, regardless of rank or function, who meet to tackle a problem, often on an impromptu basis. Then he added "boundaryless behavior" to encourage GE people to seek and share ideas in a "fresh, open, anti-parochial environment." And he wanted GE people to stretch their goals, if not their budgets.[19] In 1996 he added the new "dream" of an effort to improve quality that would be "the most personally rewarding and, in the end, the most profitable undertaking in our history."[20]

General Electric uses appraisals as the glue to fix the values that go with the visions. Appraisals at GE were based traditionally on performance, as they are at most companies. Now the appraisals have two components, one for performance and one for adherence to the values. In the values component, GE managers are rated on their ability to communicate and create a clear vision, their openness to change, their skills at building and leading teams, their integrity, accountability, and speed. With the help of both performance and values ratings, GE has divided its managers into four types. Type I managers rate high on performance and values and are marked for great things. Type IIs neither perform nor share GE's values, and they go out the door. Type III managers have the values right but sometimes fail to perform. They get another chance. Type IV leaders get results, but often by trampling on the values. As evidence of its commitment to values, GE started to show the door to Type IVs—often the unreformed, old-style manager.[21]

From Welch on down, GE takes developing leaders very seriously, beginning with a leadership conference for new hires and going on to the advanced training at Crotonville. Welch puts in an appearance at most of the courses given at Crotonville and he spends one day a year at each of the businesses to review the potential leaders and their training needs.[22]

Companies put a lot of effort into developing leaders for a number of reasons. They need to prepare the next chief executive, and the one after that. The company of the 21st century needs leadership in depth, because if it is going to spread responsibility and power throughout, then it needs many leaders, not just one. A company must also train its leaders to cope with the change they face.

In 1990, Joseph Neubauer, chairman of Aramark, the $6-billion-a-year catering company based in Philadelphia, decided the mind-set of the company's leaders had to be changed. The company went private in 1984 and some 150 senior employees borrowed all they could, mortgaging their homes if necessary, to buy the company. In the years after the buyout, they focused mostly on operations and on cash flow to pay off the company's debt (so successfully that many of them became million-aires). By 1990, Neubauer felt he needed a more entrepreneurial type of leadership to achieve more growth. "I realized that we couldn't do it unless we changed the minds of the critical mass of people here," he says. "And it wasn't just five managers. We had the choice of firing everybody we had and bringing a new lot in, or educating what we had. We chose the latter, clearly." Aramark set up its own specially designed leadership school, with faculty from Cornell, Columbia, Harvard, Penn State, and Wharton, and over a two-year period put the 150 managers through the course in groups of 30.[23]

The whole way of looking at leadership may be changing. Dee Hock, the founder of VISA, used to ask managers what their prime responsibility was and invariably they said it was to manage the people under them. "That perception is completely wrong," says Hock. "The first and paramount responsibility is to manage one's self. . . . The second responsibility is to manage those who have authority over us. . . . The third responsibility is to manage one's peers. . . . The fourth responsibility is then obvious, for there is nothing else left. It is to manage those over whom we have authority."[24]

However, some basics of leadership never change. Regardless of what the vision or the values of a leader may be, unless the leader is seen to embody them in his own words and actions, then the ideas are worse than useless. To return to O'Toole's idea of the Rushmorean leader at the beginning of this chapter, leaders have to have integrity and courage. They have to share the pain as well as the gain. How far from the ideal are our business leaders? Look at executive compensation. Look at the corporate jets, and helicopters, and limousines. Look especially at the difference between what the top executives get, and what the rest of the employees get, not to mention those who are downsized.

Rare is the example of the top person in a company making the first sacrifice, or even a gesture. But even the smallest symbols can count. Robert N. Haidinger, CEO of JJI Lighting Group, a $100-million-a-year company based in Greenwich, Connecticut, always takes a room rather than a suite in a hotel when he travels on business and he buys his own roll of 32-cent stamps to keep in the office for personal mail. "That gets out," he says, "and you don't ever want to break those rules, because that will get out too."[25]

VeriFone has no perks for anyone. "Given our financial track record you would expect we would have country club memberships, or extra health insurance, or a company car," says the chairman, Hatim Tyabji. "We don't even have a company car. We don't want our people to say, 'These guys ask us to work hard and make sacrifices and, by the way, they're enjoying a life-style that is beyond us.' Believe me, that has an enormous effect." Everyone at VeriFone flies tourist class and stays at the Courtyard by Marriott or Holiday Inn. If they have the points from frequent traveling they can upgrade, regardless of their status in the company.[26] The corporate world rarely offers examples of that basic old Army principle of leadership: See that the troops eat first, then let the officers eat.

Pointers

- Is the corporation's style of leadership going through a basic change, from leading by command to leading by example and values?
- Is the leader articulating a believable vision and enlisting all the forces of the company toward achieving it?
- Is the CEO fully engaged in reinventing the corporation for the 21st century, and reinventing his own role?
- Does the leader's behavior embody the company's values?
- Are the leaders' human skills as well developed as their intellectual skills?
- Do the leaders manage themselves as well as they manage subordinates?
- Is there continuity at the top, if not in terms of people at least in terms of values?
- Does the corporation develop not one but many leaders?

Links

- Does the company sponsor training that can help produce executives who lead by example and by values (if not by charisma)?
- Does the company have appraisal, promotion, and compensation systems that reinforce leadership by example and by values?

Cautions

- Does the company still adhere to the fundamentals of good leadership, of character, integrity, and respect for others, that really haven't changed?
- Is there room within the new framework of values-based leadership for individual styles, even charisma and idiosyncrasy?
- When necessary, can the CEO still take rapid, decisive, and unilateral action?

8

THE DISPENSABLE EMPLOYEE

Keep interested in your career, however humble, it is a real
possession in the changing fortunes of time.
—*Desiderata,* Old St. Paul's Church, Baltimore, 1692.

If continuous "creative destruction" characterizes and strengthens
free enterprise, then during a time of restructuring we should expect
a stiff dose of creative destruction. And if business faces today the
biggest restructuring since the Industrial Revolution, then the pain is
bound to be severe. In spite of low unemployment, the continued growth
of the economy, high corporate profits, the good times on the stock market, and the creation of millions of new jobs, all of which were true in the
mid-1990s, restructuring has been painful for millions of workers since it
began in the early 1980s.

Sometimes news of the pain almost seems to have been the dominant fact of the economy. A mixture of ineptitude on the part of business
and tendentiousness on the part of the press, politicians, and unions
made a bad situation seem worse. Business got caught up in a zeal for
"reengineering," which it carried out with an extraordinary lack of feeling and common sense, and even a lack of business sense. The press,
politicians, and unions sometimes view the loss of jobs as the only thing
of importance happening in business. In a descent to the level of supermarket tabloids, *Newsweek* ran a cover story entitled "Corporate Killers,"
with a subtitle, saying, "The Public Is Scared as Hell." (The "killer" CEOs

on the cover were Robert E. Allen of AT&T, Albert J. Dunlap of Scott Paper, Louis V. Gerstner of IBM, and Robert B. Palmer of Digital Equipment).[1] In 1996, the *New York Times* ran a seven-part series entitled "The Downsizing of America"—as if the country's entire economic prospects were shrinking. While the series acknowledged that more jobs had been created than lost since 1979, the series focused on the 43 million jobs eliminated since then, and the human tragedies that resulted.* The series put forward the curious thought that technology had "undermined the bedrock notion of mass employment."[2]

This chapter will deal mostly with the mistakes business has made in handling people while reorganizing, the consequences, and what to do about them. The increasing transience of jobs and careers raises a whole lot of questions about how to deal with people decently, how to create trust and loyalty, how to manage and plan careers, how to modify benefits and training. The basic question is how do we rewrite the implicit contract between employer and employee?

"SAVING" JOBS

But first let's look briefly at the reality of job loss and job creation in the work place. Labor unions and other critics of business talk as if "saving" jobs is the important thing. Jobs can't be "saved," except at the price of holding back the economy and sacrificing general prosperity for individual security. Demand creates jobs and when the demand isn't there, then the job disappears. If it doesn't, it probably should. Jobs disappear when markets change or when technology raises productivity. As we have seen, we are going to have a lot more change in markets and technology. The 21st century enterprise will frequently change its job needs.

If you take a long view of the idea of "saving" jobs the idea soon becomes preposterous. Should we continue to employ telephone operators and ignore the improved service and efficiencies of direct dialing? Should banks have ignored the efficiencies of automated teller machines and kept the 100,000 tellers and other employees laid off since 1990? Should we have kept the jobs of Linotypists and held back, as newspapers did for a time, the use of photo-offset processes and then of desktop

---

*Happily, The *New York Times* soon recovered from its depression and a year later was able to run an article entitled, "Puffed Up by Prosperity, U.S. Struts Its Stuff" (April 27, 1997), p. 4-1.

publishing? Should the railroads have retained firemen when locomotives converted from coal to diesel fuel? What about all those butlers, cartwrights, chandlers, coopers, harnessmakers, hod carriers, longshoremen, housemaids, seamstresses, tinkers, and, of course, the proverbial buggy-whip makers? And what about farmers and farm laborers? Nearly nine million of them have been downsized since 1920. The job market is dynamic and the strength of an economy—and, ultimately, everyone's prosperity—depends largely on the ability of the work force to respond to shifts in demand. Rather than being a weakness, the flexibility of the American job market is a competitive advantage. The inflexibility of the European job market not only makes it harder for European companies to compete but contributes to unemployment rates that can be, as in the case of Spain, four times as high as in the United States.

While business has eliminated many jobs since the restructuring began, 43 million since 1979 if you accept the *New York Times* estimate, job creation has roundly outpaced job losses.* Total civilian employment in the United States grew from 98.8 million in 1979 to 126 million in June 1996, for a net gain of 27.2 million. If the figure of 43 million jobs eliminated is correct, then the total number of new jobs created in that period amounted to 70.2 million and essentially all those jobs are in businesses. So much for technology destroying jobs!

Some of the secondary assumptions put forward by the merchants of gloom turn out to be false: that the new jobs tend to be low-paid, dead-end jobs, that more people are forced to work part-time, that more people have to hold two or more jobs to make ends meet. On the contrary, the quality of the new jobs is high. The Bureau of Labor Statistics reports that 68% of the new jobs created from February 1994 to February 1996 paid wages above the median. Most of the growth occurred in management and professional jobs. The number of people slinging hamburgers and doing other work at the bottom of the economic ladder declined. The number of people working part-time and the number holding multiple jobs has changed little in years. Indeed, the whole theory that people

---

*An exact figure for the number of jobs eliminated is hard to pin down. The Bureau of Labor Statistics doesn't have figures going back to 1979, but agrees the *New York Times* estimates are roughly correct. However, for the three-year period, 1993–1995 inclusive, the BLS has a revised figure (8.4 million), that is considerably lower than the *New York Times* number (10 million). Neither figure alters the substantive point that job creation vastly exceeded job loss.

FIGURE 8.1

Since corporations began downsizing methodically in the early 1980s, the burden of pain has shifted notably. These displacement rates, based on the proportion of people 20 and over who were laid off after being employed for at least three years, show an overall decline from the period 1981–82 to 1993–94. But the burden moved away from construction and manufacturing to finance and insurance, from blue-collar workers to managers and professionals. In the earlier period, younger workers, blacks, and Hispanics were more likely to get the axe, but relative to older workers and whites, they have been faring better. (All along, the displacement rates for women have been lower than those for men.)

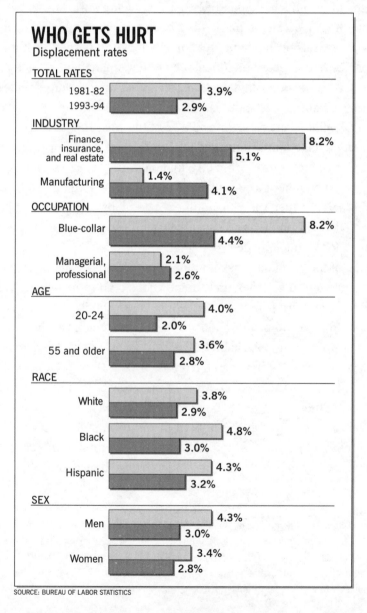

WHO GETS HURT
Displacement rates

TOTAL RATES
- 1981-82 — 3.9%
- 1993-94 — 2.9%

INDUSTRY
- Finance, insurance, and real estate — 8.2% / 5.1%
- Manufacturing — 1.4% / 4.1%

OCCUPATION
- Blue-collar — 8.2% / 4.4%
- Managerial, professional — 2.1% / 2.6%

AGE
- 20-24 — 4.0% / 2.0%
- 55 and older — 3.6% / 2.8%

RACE
- White — 3.8% / 2.9%
- Black — 4.8% / 3.0%
- Hispanic — 4.3% / 3.2%

SEX
- Men — 4.3% / 3.0%
- Women — 3.4% / 2.8%

SOURCE: BUREAU OF LABOR STATISTICS

are more likely to be displaced today is tenuous. Overall, the rate was slightly less in the early 1990s than in the early 1980s.[3]

So why has there been such an outcry of anguish in the 1990s? There are substantive differences in the nature of the cutbacks that create more pain, or, if not more pain, more noise. The people let go are more likely to be older white-collar workers. A decade earlier, the younger, blue-collar worker suffered proportionately more. (See Figure 8.1 for a comparison of the composition of layoffs.) In other words, white male managers and professionals are feeling the pain that minorities and blue-collar workers have felt all along. Moreover, employees who lose their jobs today are more likely to be dismissed permanently rather than laid off temporarily. Finally, although the economy is creating plenty of good new jobs, laid-off workers are not getting their share, perhaps because more of them are older workers with obsolete skills. On average, when they do find work they earn 10% less in their new jobs than they would have earned had they kept their old jobs.[4]

WHY REENGINEERING WENT WRONG

If job destruction and job creation are proof of a vibrant economy, then what's wrong with laying people off? It's the visible unfairness of layoffs, the downright callousness you often see, that makes "reengineering" especially hard to swallow. When the richest and biggest corporations with the highest paid CEOs make massive, abrupt reductions, that attracts unfavorable attention. When a 30-year employee gets two hours to clear out of his office, or loses his job a few months short of qualifying for a pension, then some basic humanity is missing. And when the surviving employees find that rather than benefiting from increased productivity, their own incomes stagnate while the boss's income roars ahead, then you have a deep morale problem. A lot of people pay for the mistakes of a few. Tom Urban, the former chairman of Pioneer Hi-Bred International, says that AT&T "had this overarching utility mentality and kept adding people. They finally woke up in 1995 and said, 'Oh my goodness, we have 40,000 too many people.' If Bob Allen was so good, why didn't he figure that out ten years ago? Now he is being brutal."[5]

On top of the morale problem, there is evidence that downsizing, or reengineering, or restructuring to reduce costs has, for the most part, not helped the companies that did it. The basic idea of reengineering, that you examine every process in a company and redesign it, is reasonable and had already been practiced under other labels, notably TQM, or total quality management. But the whole thing got out of hand. The revolutionary rhetoric of the leaders of reengineering, Michael Hammer and James Champy, in their book, *Reengineering the Corporation,* published in 1993, gave the CEO the choice of radical and dramatic reinvention of the corporation now or imminent extinction. Business leaders, pressured to cut costs and increase profits, grabbed that word "reengineering" and used it as a cover for any kind of activity designed to pare costs, just as TQM was used as an all-purpose label.

Even when they put out their book, Hammer and Champy estimated that 50% to 70% of the reengineering efforts would not achieve dramatic results.[6] Judging by several studies, the results of reengineering or, more often, downsizing labeled as reengineering, were more disappointing. For example, Dwight Gertz and João Baptista of Mercer Management Consulting found in a study of the *Fortune* 1,000 companies (the industrial 500 and the service 500 lists combined) from 1988 through 1993 that the stock market put a higher value on companies that increased profits by growing their revenues than companies that increased profits by cutting costs.[7]

A McKinsey & Company consulting team made a detailed analysis of reengineering efforts in 20 American, European, and Asian firms and believe they learned why most efforts failed. The six companies that achieved significant results (an average 18% reduction in business unit costs) reengineered broadly and in depth. That is, they redesigned many activities that added value for the customer rather than redesigning just one or two activities, and they looked not only at structure, or at skills, or at incentives, but at all of those elements. A company that redesigned a single process, say accounts payable, might see sizable savings in that activity but that did not translate into savings for the business unit overall. The successful efforts also had plenty of attention from top executives and were carried out by top performers.[8]

If downsizing, as practiced in the last decade or so, has not helped business results, neither has it put the remaining workers in a state of mind to contribute the work, initiative, quality, team effort, and loyalty necessary in a 21st century enterprise. Not surprisingly, surveys of employee morale and opinion reveal a serious problem. The International Survey Research Corporation, which tracks employee satisfaction for corporate clients, reports that since 1989 more employees have come to believe management does not provide clear direction, that they don't believe what management says, that they are less sure of keeping their jobs, that morale is lower, that they worry more about the company's future and about being laid off (see Figure 8.2). ISR also discovered, incidentally, in a survey of employees in 21 countries, that satisfaction with their companies was lowest among Japanese employees (31%) and highest in Switzerland (82%), with American workers in between (65%). (Job satisfaction in Japan has dropped sharply, presumably as a result of the economic slowdown in the early 1990s and resulting loss of job security, slight as that may be.)[9]

Business faces what James Champy calls "one of the central dilemmas" of our time, one that may not have a fix, certainly not an easy fix.[10] On the one hand, the 21st century enterprise needs the willing help of intelligent, motivated, collaborative, and enterprising people. On the other hand, the efficiencies of technology and new management approaches make it possible to work better with fewer people, and the pressure from investors forces executives to act with an appearance of decisiveness. Business obviously has not handled this dilemma well so far. Wholesale sackings have been a disaster. There are ways of doing it better, but before reviewing them, let's look at what Japanese and European firms are doing. They have the same problem, but approach it from different viewpoints because they regard looking after their employees as a primary responsibility, if not a sacred duty. European companies have the additional problem of a high unemployment rate.

The Japanese commitment to the worker—at least among the major companies—is weakening, ever so slightly. Here is what some Japanese executives told us in interviews:

- *Canon.* Chairman Ryuzaburo Kaku says "there are all sorts of discussions that we need to put an end to the lifetime employment system. But for now this is something we must maintain because our Japanese operations are based on lifetime employment. It gives our Japanese employees a feeling of security. . . . The solution will be through R&D."

- *Honda.* Chairman Nobuhiko Kawamoto says "by the year 2000 we want to reduce our work force by 10%" by attrition, by recruiting

FIGURE 8.2

How Employees Feel

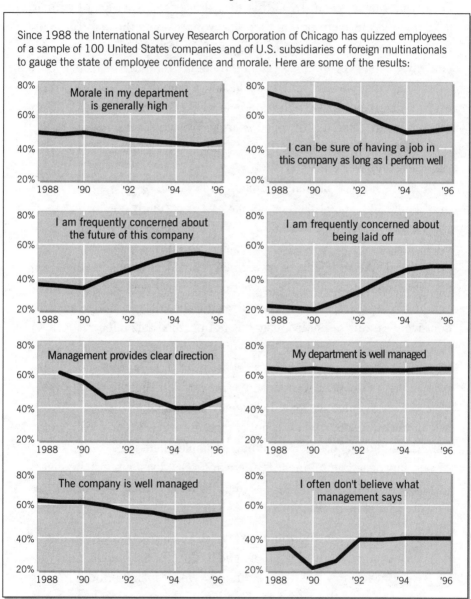

Since 1988 the International Survey Research Corporation of Chicago has quizzed employees of a sample of 100 United States companies and of U.S. subsidiaries of foreign multinationals to gauge the state of employee confidence and morale. Here are some of the results:

Source: International Survey Research Corporation.

fewer college graduates, by focusing more on recruiting engineers rather than liberal arts graduates, and hiring fewer women secretaries, but not by dismissals.

- *Kyocera*. Chairman Kazuo Inamori: "If circumstances permit, we would like to continue the lifetime employment system. Some day there may be intervening factors which prevent us from doing so. But as long as we can continue to do so, we will keep the lifetime employment system." President Kensuke Itoh: "The number of new recruits is now one-fifth of the level of five or six years ago at the time of the bubble economy."

- *Toyota*. Tokuichi Uranishi, general manager for corporate planning, says, "For professionals of the highest skills category, we are willing to pursue aggressively a new system in a very bold manner. This we call the PC or professional contract system. We now have two designers recruited from outside the company, in charge of creating a new style for a new model. In the longer term, we plan to have 80% of our labor force, excluding blue-collar workers, under lifetime employment. That means 20% of our white-collar workers will be able to consider more flexible employment schedules."[11]

The stagnation in the first half of the 1990s convinced Japanese companies they needed to be more efficient. They chose to achieve efficiencies by simplifying their products, by restructuring, by "value engineering," but not by the wholesale staff cuts that many American companies carried out. Still, Japanese executives are beginning to waffle on their commitment to lifetime employment. As we saw in Chapter 1, European companies are also reexamining their whole social contract, under the severe constraint of high unemployment rates. In Germany especially, but in France too, layoffs have become part of the restructuring of business, a small part, but still a part. The social contract, with implied lifetime employment, has become too much of a burden. With an unemployment rate exceeding 10% in 1994, 1995, and 1996, and labor costs the highest in the world, Germany had no choice but to reform its burdensome form of social capitalism. Other kinds of savings come first, but major companies such as Daimler-Benz, Siemens, and Hoechst have cut their work forces.

American corporations clearly have more freedom to rewrite the implicit contract with their employees and as a result are freer to make the changes needed to compete. But what kind of a new contract, if any, emerges from the rubble of reengineering? Where can human needs and corporate needs meet? To take the most cynical view, how can corporations get what they want out of people and still treat them as disposable assets? Presumably the wholesale layoffs of the 1980s and 1990s will not continue, but the sheer vitality of competition and change make it unlikely we can return to the "organization man" type of job security.

THE "EMPLOYABILITY" DODGE

What corporations are offering in place of security is something called "employability" which allegedly puts each person in charge of his own career. The company gives you a good job, pays well, keeps you up-to-date with training, and then you and the company part without regrets when you are no longer needed. Being well-trained and self-confident, you quickly find a new job. This philosophy not only suits the new enterprise, but it also suits the new employee, better educated, less tolerant of authority, less willing to submit to ties of loyalty, more willing to make the decisions the boss used to make. If we want more freedom, then we should be able to design our own careers, shouldn't we? But what about those who are not necessarily well-trained or self-confident, who don't have the skills or the gifts to move easily to another job, who don't really know what they want to do but really would like to be loyal to a loyal employer and stay there for many years? The fundamental human need to belong becomes harder and harder to satisfy, in families, communities, churches, schools, and now corporations. The theory of "employability" does not meet that need and has an aroma of self-serving hypocrisy. Still, the terms of the social contract have changed so the practical matter facing the 21st century corporation, and its employees, is how to make the best of it.

Employers have downsized, "riffed," "rightsized," voluntarily retired, involuntarily retired, adjusted, reengineered, "saved," discontinued, displaced, dislocated, "surplused," bumped, "rebalanced," outplaced, outsourced, and even fired their employees in more ways than there are euphemisms for the process. How it's done makes an enormous difference not only to those let go, but to the survivors and the employers.

If the downsizing is accomplished with some sense of shared pain and shared destiny, with a willingness to talk frankly about the state of a company, with support and help for victims and survivors, the damage can be contained. But the story of downsizings is littered with the wreckage of insensitive, boneheaded acts. In 1981, International Harvester (now Navistar International) forgave more than $2 million in loans to its president and CEO while cutting the work force sharply. In 1982, General Motors announced a new bonus plan for executives just as the workers prepared to ratify a new contract that included give-backs. In the mid-1980s, Motorola and Texas Instruments supplied an instructive contrast in their reactions to a slight dip in the electronic industry. Motorola cut its schedule by one day every two weeks, and resumed full-time work six months later when the market recovered. Everyone shared mild pain. Texas Instruments, then still run by Rambo-type leaders, abruptly laid off thousands of workers. When the market recovered shortly, TI had to rehire people they had fired, find new ones, and retrain them all. Unlike Motorola, most companies go straight to downsizing without attempting any imaginative alternatives.[12]

The shock of massive layoffs is hard to understate. James Irvine, a vice president of the Communications Workers of America, which had worked closely with AT&T to prepare for the future, recalls that the year he went to work for Ma Bell in Cleveland, in 1962, someone retired after working his entire career on the same floor in that building. "We used to have a covenant we lived by: come to work every day and you have a job for life, so long as you keep your hands off the cash, the copper, and the women," says Irvine. "You had one year's probation and then you were set. Now they fire readily." Even allowing for union hyperbole, the level of Irvine's hostility towards AT&T today is surprising. He says he now finds an "absolute arrogance" among AT&T executives, "transients" who can't be trusted and who want to turn the company around without the help of the employees.[13] AT&T made a big effort to help its outplaced workers, who after all are entering a market with a growing demand for telecommunications skills. No matter. What really hit hard was that in a year when CEO Bob Allen collected a record $5.2 million in salary, bonuses, and other compensation, plus options on 858,000 shares of AT&T stock, the company announced it was downsizing by 40,000 positions. AT&T pointed out that it was eliminating jobs, not necessarily people, and at the same time creating new jobs. After AT&T divested itself of Lucent and NCR, the job reduction goal at what remained of AT&T dropped to 17,000. By mid-1997, 11,000 of the 17,000 AT&T people whose positions were being eliminated had found jobs elsewhere within the company.

In total contrast to AT&T, at Microsoft the idea of a long-term social contract hardly arises. "There's no promise of a permanent job here," says Mike Murray, the vice president for human resources. "How could there be? Ninety per cent of the revenue today comes from products that were not developed two years ago. So what happens if we make the wrong decision? We hope to see you here in 20 years, but we can't promise it. If people become redundant, they get six weeks to look for a job inside and then they get outplacement service." At 33 years of age, the average Microsoft manager has not yet become overly concerned with the long-term prospects. In addition to that, 20% of Microsoft's work force is contingent, which gives the company more flexibility.[14]

REWRITING THE CONTRACT

Ideally a company would hire so judiciously that it would never be put in the position of laying people off. But that much prescience is not easy in a time of so much change and so many new products. SEI Investments, which administers and supervises pension and bank trust funds, has not been able to shield its people from the effects of turbulence.* SEI's business, organization, fortunes, and personnel needs keep changing drastically. "We've been reinventing ourselves for the last five years," said the CEO, Al West, in 1995. SEI people talk of Reinvention I and Reinvention II. The company continues to reinvent itself, but to keep the level of panic down it doesn't play up the restructuring. People move a lot at SEI. They change jobs inside the company 1.5 times a year on average, and turnover has gotten as high as 50%. Since 1990 reinvention has reduced the staff from 1,400 to 900 people, but without large layoffs. In 1992, SEI eliminated the jobs of its 90 secretaries, but retrained about 30 of them for other jobs. In 1994, SEI "blew up" the human resources department, sending some out into the divisions and others right out of the company.

---

*SEI Investments helped establish Wharton's SEI Center for Advanced Studies in Management, whose director is the co-author of this book. The SEI corporation's chairman and CEO, Alfred P. West Jr., is also chairman of the SEI Center Board of directors.

(Two HR people were set up in a new company to administer benefits in competition with other vendors.) People asked, "Who will do all those reports?" The answer: nobody. And after a few months they weren't missed.

Senior Vice President B. Scott Budge says that SEI was "rather cavalier" about hiring people in the first place and then created insecurity with the reinventions and their "attendant violence." "An insecure work force focuses more on security than on business," he says. "It will take years to restore morale." The work contract has been rewritten. It used to be, says West, that "essentially you come here, work hard, do what you're told, and you can work here the rest of your life." This may have been unwritten, but it was the reality. Now the contract is moving from dependence to counterdependence to interdependence.[15]

A more cautious approach to hiring might have avoided some of SEI's problems. Another rapidly changing high-technology company, VeriFone, has had to lay off some people but has avoided any large cutbacks by hiring conservatively. "It is not our intent to be a hire-and-fire company like one of the airlines," says the CEO, Hatim Tyabji. "We are constantly mindful that there is a down escalator, and therefore we have never been in a situation where we've had to take a hit." Will Pape, former senior vice president, explains, "We have a very thoughtful process for adding people. We monitor daily the hiring numbers—people in the pipeline, new hires, terminations, and so forth. We try to do a lot of arm twisting in the planning process ('Why do you need 14 people for your new plan?') We try to anticipate process improvements so as to obviate hiring too many people."[16]

The massive layoffs that marked Jack Welch's early tenure at General Electric ended long ago and GE has entered into a tough-minded relationship with its employees that may be more typical of the enterprise of the future. Robert Muir, the vice president for human resources at the Plastics Division, doesn't see corporate ruthlessness in GE's policy, but rather a drive to be competitive. "Perhaps we don't employ 400,000 [as GE once did], but we do have wonderful jobs for a quarter of a million people," says Muir. "It's exciting, fun. The contract is that you are compensated for what you do, we provide you with an exciting job, and with developmental and growth opportunities. And when you are not needed here, you will be able to grow somewhere else. Almost anyone here could leave for jobs elsewhere tomorrow, but they stay for the challenge and excitement."[17] GE people get 15 days training a year now and the incentive compensation is spread wider. While only 400 of the top people received stock options in the 1980s, 22,000 now qualify.[18]

RETAINING OLD STRENGTHS

Unless they are fighting for survival, in which case a quick amputation may be the only choice, companies should be able to deal with people decently in a way that does not shatter their lives or company morale. They may even be able to preserve the lifetime contract with modifications. Enough examples of a more human approach exist today to show that it is possible. Pioneer Hi-Bred International did get 180 key people, out of a total work force of 3,000, to take early retirement during a reengineering phase. The reengineering continued, but without big layoffs. Pioneer remains committed to long-term employment. "We assume when we hire we're hiring an employee forever," says Tom Urban, the chairman. "Most of the turnover takes place in the first 36 months, which is as it should be. But after you have been with Pioneer for three years, in most cases you're there for a long time."

Pioneer's continuing growth helps obviate layoffs, but it also helps that "we are somewhat leery about hiring." Urban explains that "every three years or so we stop hiring and say, let's understand where we are going. Let's refocus. We don't hire for three to six months and see if we really need these people."

Pioneer, which was built on the idea of lifetime employment for the hardworking Iowans it hired, has gone through what Urban calls a "significant redefinition of employment." Beginning in the 1980s, he began to talk about company responsibilities and employee responsibilities, and then he began to say "employment is not guaranteed here." The new policy evolved gradually, and Pioneer still wants people to work there for a long time, and to encourage their relatives to work there too. "We want to retain the old strengths," says Urban, "but we are telling people that you have to perform to work here. If you stop learning or you do not welcome change, then you'll probably limit your opportunities here. This company changes every day and if you want the same job you have now for the next ten years, then you probably shouldn't be here."[19]

In a company that is changing less, that is not forced to move fast by new technology, it's easier to keep the old social contract. Labconco, a privately owned, $32-million-a-year manufacturer of laboratory equipment in Kansas City, has laid off a handful of its 230 people in recent years but basically has not changed its employment policy. "There's nothing fancy here," says the CEO, John McConnell. "Just a big manufacturing job shop." Michael Wyckoff, the vice president for human relations, says that some turnover is healthy but basically Labconco wants to keep its people. "We spend too much to train them to see them leave. We give people an opportunity to learn new technology. We send them to school, but we don't let them go because they can't deal with new technology. That is not grounds for letting them go. You can find something. In eight years I haven't seen a failure."[20]

GETTING RID OF WORK, NOT PEOPLE

Corning Incorporated, having revived its fortunes in the 1980s with a fierce effort to improve quality, decided after a slump in 1993 to reengineer massively. The company tried to call it "Corning Competes," but the "R" word prevailed. Jamie Houghton, one of those four Rushmorean leaders, regrets that the company had to reengineer, but feels it was wise and that "we did it the right way." He turned the job over to President Roger Ackerman, who later succeeded him as CEO in 1996, but he kept an eye on some key matters. Since Corning has always been a family concern and is the biggest employer in Corning, New York, Houghton was sensitive to layoffs. "I'm not going to see Corning, New York, decimated and I'm not going to see 8,000 empty houses just because some consultants from Chicago thought it was a good idea." He and Ackerman agreed that anything that might have a devastating effect on a community if done overnight would be stretched over several years. In the past, when the company wanted to cut costs, Houghton recalled, "We'd say, 'Okay, on Friday we're going to shoot a bunch of people in the head and then, on Monday, those who are still alive go back to work.'" One problem with that approach is that the work doesn't go away. The whole point of reengineering is not to get rid of people but to get rid of work that doesn't add value. This time Corning took a year and put some very good people on teams to analyze the work. "We did it the right way," says

Houghton. Nevertheless, it was a time of tension at Corning and the stress seminars run by the medical department were "wildly popular." The one mistake he regrets is that Corning didn't bring the unions in on the process—even though in the end it was mostly the jobs of managers that were affected.[21]

Ackerman and his teams decided to focus on redesigning four areas in the company: manufacturing, innovation, purchasing, and senior management. Ackerman made what he describes as "a fateful decision" to deploy the best people in the four areas, as many as 200 at one point, and have them work for months full-time on redesign teams in open, bull-pen type offices. The results really did improve the company's operations. The manufacturing team, for example, cut the levels of management from six to two. The purchasing team took all the polymer buying out of different parts of the company and bundled it together so Corning could have one national contract. The management group cut the budget process from months and reams of paper to a few days and a few sheets.[22]

Since the people who would have to live with the redesign created it, it had their support. And it was accomplished with substantial but not massive loss of jobs. The rank and file believed it was their jobs that were in jeopardy but in fact management was hit harder. Blue-collar workers were hardly affected but the corporate staff of 3,000 in the Corning area came down by 700, mostly through early retirement. Half a dozen senior vice presidents' jobs were eliminated, as were the jobs of 60 people at the level of directors and managers (out of a total of 158). Corning used its imagination to reassure worried workers. At the Blacksburg, Virginia, plant, Corning created what it describes as six circles of protection against unemployment. Corning would take these steps progressively before laying off employees:

1. Use slack time to train workers so they would have skills to make them employable.
2. Let temporary workers go.
3. Go to partial shifts.
4. Go to job sharing by working half-days.
5. Consider pay cuts.
6. Help employees get other jobs, paying them to relocate if they go to another Corning facility.[23]

As of late 1996, only steps 1 and 2 had been invoked at any time.

Corning did not reengineer without pain or fear, but it did treat its people with humanity. Moreover, the reengineering appears to have worked. Between 1994 and 1996 Corning's net income from continuing operations grew 52% to $343 million.

When the pace of corporate downsizing abates, as it presumably will, we will still be left with a different way of looking at careers, security, and loyalty. It would be an exaggeration to say the career as we've known it is dead, or that a job in the old sense no longer exists, but certainly there will be more unease and insecurity. The degree of each that exists from one company to another will vary greatly. A loosening of the ties fits the direction of our culture. If people are more independent-minded, better educated, more willing to take responsibilities, then they should be more comfortable managing their own careers.

But people still need a sense of belonging, and corporations still need the brains and the enthusiasms of their employees. So while they continue to shake up their work forces and and reorganize themselves, they need to keep in mind a whole lot they can do to limit the damage. Best of all, of course, is to plan well so as to avoid any big layoffs. But if it comes to layoffs, then are they clearly justified? Have people had enough advance warning? Has management planned how to do it, attended to all the details, trained people in executing the changes? Is management sharing the pain? Is there a clear appraisal system and are there rules for deciding who goes? Are the employees involved in deciding? Will management make an effort to explain what is happening and to be accessible? Is there an opportunity for people to express their feelings? Are the people leaving really being helped? Are those left behind just saddled with more work, or has the work been reduced along with the jobs.[24] How well a company answers these questions affects not only those who leave, but also the performance and morale of the survivors.

Pointers

- In restructuring have you focused on getting rid of unnecessary work rather than getting rid of people?
- Have you planned the restructuring carefully and thoughtfully, with the participation of the people whose work is to be restructured?

- Have you resolved or made efforts to resolve the conflict between becoming more efficient and competitive, on the one hand, and treating people decently, on the other?
- Have you attempted to create a sense of fairness by sharing the pain, by treating people generously and with dignity, by the openness and accessibility of managers?
- Even in a major and rapid restructuring, can you avoid harsh or sudden departures?
- If the old social contract between employee and employer is frayed or broken, have you attempted to write a new one?
- Are you assuming too glibly that people can manage their own careers and flit easily from job to job?

Links

- Is your restructuring limited to a particular function (in which case it is unlikely to improve your overall performance) or is both broad and deep?
- Do you have a believable appraisal system which can help identify candidates for dismissal without creating a sense of unfairness?
- Have you planned training for the survivors to help them improve their performance and cope with new responsibilities?

Cautions

- Is there an obvious gap between the generous treatment of the executives who caused the restructuring and the treatment of those who lost their jobs?
- In spite of the enormous changes in business, are you working to create some sense of belonging, of security, and of loyalty?
- Are you simply assuming that normal jobs and careers have disappeared forever, or that lifetime employment is no longer possible in your company?
- Before choosing restructuring, which will often be disappointing, have you thoroughly considered growth strategies as an alternative?

9

THE INDISPENSABLE
EMPLOYEE

Our people are our most important asset.
—Old saw frequently found in annual reports and vision statements,
etc., etc.

Of all the management ideas that fit the 21st century enterprise, the one with most profound importance and power, the one with the longest and most checkered history, and the one that has proved the most difficult to execute is the idea that employees should have the power to make significant decisions. This is no fad. Consider this: During World War II, General Motors was so pressed to switch to weapons production without enough skilled managers and engineers that production workers had to make many decisions. Peter Drucker, in his visits to GM at the time, was so impressed by the contribution of the workers that he pleaded for what he called the "self-governing plant community." After the war, when Charles E. Wilson became CEO of GM, he liked the idea so much he prepared to implement what he renamed "work improvement programs" at the company. But the head of the United Auto Workers, the powerful and otherwise astute Walter Reuther, objected vehemently and said he would call a general strike if they were implemented. Wilson backed off.[1]

But that was just the beginning of the story at GM, which has experienced employee involvement in all its forms, good and bad, successful and unsuccessful, decade after decade. It was the UAW, surprisingly

SEI Survey	
It is critical to have responsible, trained employees working in teams	77%
We are doing that	26%

enough, who revived the idea. Irving Bluestone, then the UAW's vice president for GM affairs, drafted a resolution for the 1968 UAW convention promoting "quality of worklife." Bluestone did not have better quality or greater productivity in mind. He wanted dignity and respect for the worker. The UAW approved the resolution, but it wasn't until 1971 that GM, now bloody-mindedly adversarial, agreed to implement what has come to be known as QWL.[2]

Long before GM tasted the quality of work life, a theoretical basis for managing workers differently had begun to emerge. In the 1950s, the decade in which William H. Whyte's *The Organization Man* seemed to define the American corporation, Abraham Maslow laid out his theory of the hierarchy of needs in *Motivation and Personality,* pointing to a different kind of organization. Having satisfied workers' physical needs very well, he maintained, the classic corporation could not gratify their higher needs for self- fulfillment. Other books dwelt on workers' dissatisfaction with the mass-production system and their desire to contribute with their brains as well as their muscles. In 1960, Douglas McGregor published *The Human Side of Enterprise,* describing what came to be seen as the difference between the old and the new corporation: the rigid, autocratic "Theory X" company that whipped rebellious workers into line, and the enlightened "Theory Y" corporation that nurtured people's natural instincts to contribute their best.

If this really is the age of the knowledge worker, if we are to innovate better and improve quality more, if we are to work faster and use information technology skillfully, then the employee can't be viewed as a Theory X disposable cost. The employee becomes an indispensable Theory Y asset. Business now has to live up to the old saw that "our employees are our most important asset." Many companies already treat their people extremely well, but, as we hope we showed in the previous chapter, business has a long way to go. Even if they can't guarantee jobs, companies have to create a greater sense of caring. They need to provide more training, more flexible working conditions, new incentives, more rewards for team play, more opportunities for minorities, and, most of all, the right support and structure to encourage workers to use their talents. Companies need to think of developing their human assets rather than cutting human costs. Over the last two decades business has developed a whole box of tools for making employees more effective through teams, through training, through better management.

Authoritarian Japan became the first to enlist the brains of its workers on a large scale with the establishment of quality circles. The Japanese Union of Scientists and Engineers, the sponsor and focus of the movement, registered the first quality circle in 1962 and the idea caught and stuck so that the quality circle became the accepted way of solving lower-level problems in large Japanese companies. Nearly two decades later, when chastened American businessmen began visiting Japan to learn the secrets of its success, they discovered the quality circle and fixed on it as the answer. Aha! That must be why the Japanese had made so much progress! So they came back to the United States determined to do what the Japanese had done.

But these new enthusiasts failed to see that quality circles had a limited role; that they were only one aspect of the successful Japanese production system. Before starting to create the teams, Japanese companies had spent more than a decade immersing themselves in the techniques of improving quality. The Japanese managers understood what the circles were supposed to do: to work painstakingly to make many small improvements. The Japanese did not regard the circles as *the* way to improve quality, but as one of a number of tools to be used. The circles were not simply attached to an existing production and management system, but were part of a whole new system for improving the company. The Japanese also understood that workers had to be trained to make the circles work. In fact, the first circles were seen principally as devices to train foremen.

FALSE STARTS

Some experiments in teams started tentatively in the United States in the 1960s at General Foods and Procter & Gamble, among others. P&G established its first self-managed teams, which have now become standard at P&G plants. Lockheed's Missile and Space Center appears to have been the first to create quality circles in 1974. By the end of the 1970s a fully-blown fad for quality circles gripped American business. It didn't last. For example, when a new boss who didn't like quality circles took over the Lockheed division in 1978 they faded at that plant. Westinghouse started quality circles in 1980, rapidly created 3,500 of them, but had started backing off by 1982.[3]

But this was not the end of employee involvement, only a false start, one of many. After the early QWL efforts, General Motors had a whole universe of experiences, beginning with the use of teams at the Tarrytown, New York, assembly plant to raise the wretched quality of the cars made there and save the plant from being closed in 1973 (quality and productivity improved greatly but GM finally did close it anyhow in 1996). It took some GM plants three starts to get it right. An initial attempt at quality of worklife improvements at the Buick plant in Flint, Michigan, in 1977 foundered on the mutual hostility and misunderstanding of labor and management. When GM decided in 1983 to create Buick City as a model of efficient car production, a labor management team designed the plant. At first it was a disaster, as a factory and as a management experiment. The first Buick LeSabres shipped were terrible, but in 1987 they began to improve and by 1989 the cars were first-rate. Finally, the teams worked there.

During the 1980s employee involvement experiments went astray in multiple ways. Donald Burr launched People Express Airlines with high idealism in 1981 and organized the company on the basis of self-management and teams. Everyone at People Express was a manager (pilots were "flight managers," flight attendants and passenger agents were "customer service managers") and everyone served on a team. Although Burr retained the right to make final decisions, most decisions were made by teams up and down and across the organization. As the airline grew, groups were broken down into new teams to keep alive the idea of small, self-contained, self-managed teams. People people were supposed to help each other and rotate jobs, so that pilots might spend some time doing office work and selling tickets. (Ticket agents were not expected to fly the planes, however.) It was fun while it lasted. But eventually the pilots rebelled at having to do clerical work, the team structure became too cumbersome, and the strain of building an airline under difficult circumstances while conducting an idealistic experiment at the same time began to hurt performance. Although People's collapse in 1986 had more important causes (mainly the introduction of American Airlines' computerized, multiple-priced reservations system—see Chapter 2), Burr's approach to self-management had added to the burdens. Still, the experiment had shown how teams can break down barriers and drive out fear.[4]

When John Sculley left Pepsico in 1983 to take over Apple Computer he found a company where teams were out of control. Apple "was built around the idea of empowerment," he says, "but almost to an extreme where it was very difficult to manage the company." Apple was like a university where the tenured faculty members can do pretty much what they want and barely tolerate their deans (their bosses). The engineering teams had almost total autonomy to make important decisions and considered that management was there to serve them.[5]

WHY TEAMS FADED

Early employee-involvement efforts foundered for many reasons. For example, when Westinghouse created teams in 1980 each was made up of people from a single unit. Like quality circles on the factory floor, they were supposed to improve their own operations. But they soon discovered that the obstacles to improvement mostly lay not within the unit but in the links with other units. The need for cross-functional teams became apparent everywhere. The hostility that had built up between labor and management during decades of Taylor-type management was another reason for failures. But these early efforts at Westinghouse and elsewhere were also damaged by elementary mistakes. They included (and unfortunately often still include):

- *Failure to prepare workers.* Corporations assumed at first that if you just sat people down in teams they would figure out what to do and how to do it. But they need to be trained how to work in teams, how to focus on the important issues, how to deal with teammates, how to get results.

- *Failure to prepare management.* Corporate leaders neglected to train middle managers in the new approach (Southern Pacific Railroad) or deliberately kept middle managers out of the loop for fear they would be spoilsports (Florida Power & Light). Workers came back from training charged with enthusiasm to do things differently, only to be confronted by supervisors who had no idea what they were talking about except that it seemed to threaten their jobs.

• *Failure to provide direction.* Teams need to inhabit an ambiguous zone where they have both the autonomy to make decisions and enough direction from above to make decisions that matter to the company. Without leadership, or a corporate vision, or a set of goals or priorities, teams have floundered around, dealing with irrelevant or trivial matters.

• *Failure to follow up.* Nothing can douse the enthusiasm of a team faster than a lack of response or results. Teams that see that their work has no effect will fade away.

• *Failure to provide consistent support.* Unless a corporation commits itself long-term to the team approach, and sticks to that commitment, teams aren't likely to take root. But as CEOs and plant managers come and go, so may the support for teams, as happened at AT&T.

• *Failure to reward team efforts.* If performance appraisals and compensation plans are not amended to recognize and encourage team efforts, and if teams don't get applause, then contributions are likely to be halfhearted.

In spite of the disappointments, teams in many places and in many guises achieved such outstanding successes that they couldn't be ignored. Team Taurus, which designed Ford's best-selling car between 1980 and 1985, broke the auto industry pattern of letting designers control the creation of new models by including from the beginning representatives of manufacturing, marketing, and finances. Ford broke down the barriers between these groups so that they could all contribute their ideas from the beginning, and not have to come in late to undo the work already done by others. At the Big Three, the team idea spread from the factory floor to the design of new cars. Although it was slow to get the message, General Motors had its outstanding successes too, from the NUMMI plant in California, a joint effort with Toyota based on teams and the Toyota production system, to the Saturn plant in Tennessee. The so-called Group of 99, made up of labor and management representatives, the majority of them blue-collar workers, designed the Saturn plant and its production system. Everyone at Saturn sits on teams, from the Strategic Action Council at the top to the work teams on the floor.

NO KISSY-FACED STUFF AT BOEING

Boeing's very successful new 777 passenger jet came out of a new development process based on teams and information technology. Considering how well Boeing's authoritarian managers had designed the 707, 737, 747, 757, and 767 over nearly half a century, the switch to a new system was remarkable. The 777 was created by 235 "design/build" teams which included not only design engineers, but the customers (the airlines) who would buy it, the mechanics who would maintain it, the pilots who would fly it, and the suppliers, including many Japanese, who would help build it. The blueprints came to life not on paper but on a three-dimensional computer graphics system which allowed teammates to work together on drawings even if they were physically separated and showed them instantly not only their own changes but others' changes too. Gordon McKinzie spent five years in Renton and Everett, Washington, as the United Airlines representative on the 777 project, and when he visited his own home office in Chicago he was greeted as "the man from Boeing." He feels that customers contributed important points in the design. In fact, Boeing originally just wanted to stretch the 767 but the customers insisted on an entirely new model. When it went into service in 1995, the plane proved to be reliable and popular.

While Boeing acted like a "Theory Y" company to develop the 777, other parts of Boeing remained firmly "Theory X." That, combined with cyclical layoffs and hirings and the export of jobs and technology, soured Boeing's labor relations and made workers suspicious of the real reasons for having teams and quality improvement. The International Association of Machinists struck Boeing twice, in 1989 and 1995, over the issue of job security. James Pierre, president of the Seattle Professional Engineering Employees Association, the engineers' union, believes that Philip Condit, who headed the 777 program and then moved on to head the whole company, and his successor, Alan Mullaly, are "Theory Y" people. But the corporate managers in human relations, labor relations, legal affairs, and compensation have not come around. "There are a lot of old-timers around," says Pierre, "who don't want any of this kissy-faced stuff." With Condit now running the whole corporation, Boeing should become fixed more clearly in the "Theory Y" mode.[6]

Both the Ford Taurus and the Boeing 777 examples show the extraordinary value of teams that embrace people from different parts of the company, or from outside the company. It was a Japanese mechanic who suggested how to make the electronics bay under the cockpit of the 777 easier to serve—and since he made the suggestion in the design stage, no costly changes were involved. Until you start putting the facts together from different parts of an organization you don't realize that some serious problems may have simple solutions.

Over the last decade the concept of working in teams, rather than through hierarchies, has become a widely accepted practice. It's not the kind of "teamwork" American businessmen have always boasted about. The old teamwork meant coming aboard, not rocking the boat, playing along. The team player today is *expected* to rock the boat, in a constructive and civil way, of course, and to speak up for change.

TEAM TASKS

Professor Edward Lawler, director of the Center for Effective Organizations at the University of Southern California, established clearly the breadth and the trends of employee involvement in the United States in a series of surveys conducted in 1987, 1990, and 1993 of the combined *Fortune* 1,000 industrial and service companies. Although the results reflect disappointment with quality circles, their use remains widespread. About 65% of the 1,000 have QCs, but the percentage barely changed between 1990 and 1993, nor did the percentage of workers involved. A majority of companies did not plan in 1993 to add more circles. However, an increasing number of the companies said they would use more employee involvement in other ways. For example, the proportion of companies that planned to use more self-managed work teams grew from 60% in 1990 to 68% in 1993.

Lawler and his researchers were surprised to find that while most companies were thoroughly committed to more power sharing, they were not good at creating the conditions for sharing power. Lawler said that to participate effectively, employees need information about the company, they need training, they need to be encouraged with compensation for performance, and they need to know their jobs are secure. The sense of job security evaporated in the 1990s, of course. The Lawler surveys found that employers did little to give their employees more information (they got less than the stockholders), training increased only moderately, and performance pay, either for individuals or for teams, increased little.[7]

In a broader annual survey of management practices, *Training* magazine covered a sample of companies with 100 employees or more and found that the use of teams of one type or another is widespread in companies of all sizes. However, big companies make more extensive use of them (see Figure 9.1, top). The tasks most frequently assigned to self-managed teams are setting their own work schedules and dealing directly with customers (see Figure 9.1, bottom).[8]

As we said in the introduction to this book, every corporation has to custom-build its own responses to the 21st century. Nowhere are the responses more diverse than in the manner of giving more power to the employees, through various types and levels of teams, and through new incentives and policies on hiring and evaluating employees. Here are sketches of how some companies are responding:

MOTOROLA

Motorola did not have to make a clean break with its old culture when it decided in 1990 to take up teams on a big scale. People at Motorola already had a sense of self-mastery because most of them had never seen a time clock and they were encouraged to go around the bureaucracy to solve problems. They can choose the computer hardware they want on their desks because, as Chuck Blazevich, an executive responsible for teams, puts it, "If you want empowerment, you can't have many exceptions." Certain personnel policies are excepted, however, and one of the exceptions is that if a manager wants to lay off an employee with ten years' seniority or more he needs the approval of the CEO. That rule helps create another condition for getting employees to participate in making decisions: job security.

It's not surprising, then, that when Motorola began to encourage

FIGURE 9.1

In its 1996 annual survey of industry, *Training* magazine found that nearly three-quarters of American organizations (including schools, hospitals, and government units) have teams and more than half the workers in those organizations serve on teams. But organizations with self-managing teams are still a minority. Here are the findings, based on answers from 1,456 organizations with more than 100 employees:

HOW MANY TEAMS

	All organizations	More than 10,000 employees
Percentage with one or more teams	73%	81%
In companies with teams, average percentage of employees who are members	55%	57%
Percentage of organizations with at least one self-managed team	31%	45%
In organizations with self-managed teams, average percentage of employees involved	36%	32%

WHAT SELF-MANAGING TEAMS MANAGE

Among organizations with self-directed teams, percent indicating that teams perform these functions on their own:

Set work schedules	67%
Deal directly with external customers	67%
Training	59%
Set production quotas / performance targets	56%
Deal with vendors / suppliers	44%
Purchase equipment or services	43%
Budgeting	39%
Performance appraisals	36%
Hiring	33%
Firing	14%

Source: Training, "1996 Industry Report" (October 1996), p. 69.

teams it adopted a *laissez-faire* attitude. Teams are almost all self-forming, they pick their own members, they choose (or decide not to choose) leaders, they may or may not register with the company, and they may or may not report the results of their work. The teams generally don't handle performance reviews or decide on merit increases. They do focus on process improvement. Motorola's vision is clear—it has stressed quality improvement since 1980—and the team members know what matters. Generally the teams work on the key initiatives chosen by management. "It boils down to communications," says Blazevich. "Teams form themselves around management's hot buttons. Mostly they pick meaningful projects. They want to win." When the finance department decided to shorten the period it took to close the company's books from ten days to two, some 100 teams formed to work on the problem. Sometimes now the books get closed in one day.

Motorola has promoted enthusiasm for the teams by running an annual worldwide competition to choose the best. Top teams get to travel to regional and national runoffs and then 24 teams end up at the world championships, which were held in Orlando in 1996. When the company announced the first championships in 1990, 2,000 teams registered. By 1995, 5,053 teams registered and 1,000 to 2,000 more teams chose not to register. "Travel is a tremendous incentive," says Blazevich.[9]

CORNING

When Corning first started using teams, according to the recently retired chairman, Jamie Houghton, "the union people thought empowerment meant taking coffee breaks any time they wanted." Workers and managers alike resisted the idea of accepting more responsibility. When you tell people "'you're going to operate in a team setting and you're going to make decisions on your own,'" says Houghton, "it scares the hell out of them, absolutely scares them to death, especially at the lower levels, where they've never had any experience with this." At the higher levels of plant managers there were some who couldn't accept the idea of subordinates making decisions they were used to making. Houghton found that it took some discipline, some toughness, and some persuasion to get the teams focused, to encourage the frightened, and to see that plant managers were reborn or removed. But all that happened, and teams are what make Corning work today.[10]

Beginning in 1987 in Blacksburg, Virginia, at a plant that makes ceramic substrates for catalytic converters, Corning turned its plants over to what it calls "high-performance work teams." The teams design the processes that operate the factories—with enormous improvements in productivity in some plants—and they govern much of their own affairs, under the guidance of a person who is now supposed to be a coach, not a supervisor. At Corning's specialty cellular ceramic (SCC) plant at Erwin, near Corning, New York, the hierarchy, such as it was when we visited it, consisted of the plant manager, Chris Nagel, a woman, the operations teams leader, Calvin Johnson, a black, and three "high-performance work teams." The plant, which makes catalytic converters for foundries, also has a staff of specialists, such as the chief engineer and the maintenance engineers. And it has a steering committee, which includes representatives from the American Flint Glass Workers Union, to review business conditions, goals, and layoff proposals.

The teams at SCC cannot change production schedules or quality standards, but otherwise have large responsibilities without direct supervision. In addition to working to improve the processes, they plan their own training, schedule vacations, and take part in deciding who works on the teams and in evaluating fellow team members. The plant's shifts, 6 A.M. to 2 P.M. and 2 P.M. to 10 P.M. are the hours the workers prefer. SCC workers perform four types of jobs (firing, cutting, extruding, and finishing) and can take training to qualify for all of them. They can rotate assignments, performing any job for which they are qualified, and they add 10¢ to 15¢ an hour to their pay for each level of training achieved. In addition workers at SCC and all 40 of Corning's plants can qualify for extra gain-sharing pay depending on the performance of the plant. In the four years ending in 1996, SCC workers added 10% to their pay in gain-sharing awards.[11] The plant doubled its productivity in 1996.

AT&T

AT&T has discovered just how much the team approach may be undermined by downsizing and restructuring. Chairman Bob Allen's unsure hand has left it to the business units and even local managers to decide what level of employee involvement to have, or whether to have any at all. Both management and the union at AT&T agree that the company's experience has been erratic. The team concept took hold early at Western

Electric (recently reborn as Lucent Technologies), which manufactures communications equipment, but manufacturing has always been the easy place to start. Elsewhere at AT&T, the story is mixed. The network system offices have followed the team approach consistently, but operators' offices have been pushed and pulled in and out of employee involvement as the bosses changed. The Transtech operation, set up in Jacksonville to deal with stockholders after the the government split up the Bell System in 1984, started off with a manager who believed in an empowered work force and set up an advanced system of teams. He was followed by a marketing man who paid lip service to teams, but didn't understand them. The next boss was an old "Bell head" with a utilities mentality who set about restoring a firm hierarchical system. Finally, in the 1990s, Transtech got a female boss, Monica Menan, who set to work sensitively and successfully to restore the team system. "Morale was terrible," says Harold W. Burlingame, AT&T's executive vice president. "People were disempowered. Once you had this kind of life and it's taken away from you, that's the worst of all things." But Menan is rebuilding Transtech.

GENERAL ELECTRIC

Jack Welch has special terms for the ways General Electric tries to get the most out of its people. One is the famous "work-out," which Welch describes as a "natural act" when "people of disparate ranks and functions search for a better way, every day, gathering in a room for an hour, or eight, or three days, grappling with a problem or an opportunity, and dealing with it, usually on the spot."[12] The work-out is meant to bring together the people closest to the work and apply their hitherto untapped knowledge to solving the problem. The work-out combines with "boundaryless behavior," which Welch describes as "the soul of today's GE." Boundaryless behavior is meant to break down the barriers that have separated the fiefdoms of finance, engineering, manufacturing, and marketing, to remove the walls that separate the different GE businesses, and that keep customer and suppliers at arm's length, and to replace the NIH (not invented here) complex with a willingness to consider ideas from anywhere.[13]

The day-to-day achievement of boundaryless behavior is the work of the teams that you find throughout GE today. The Salisbury, North Carolina, plant that turns out lighting panelboards for customers in as little

When Worlds Collide

Although efforts to improve the "quality of worklife" characterized some of the earliest and less successful efforts to create teams, the idea remains alive. CEO Lewis Platt of Hewlett-Packard put QWL improvements at the top of the corporate priorities in 1996 by including it in the company's "hoshin" plan, which signals a corporate-wide, systematic effort to make a major change in the company. In a speech he titled "When Worlds Collide," Platt said he saw "two irreconcilable trends on a collision course: first, the ever-growing demands of the workplace, and se-cond, the people's desire to have more control over their personal lives."

He cited these changes in the work force at HP to show why the clash was coming:

	1960	1995
Women in Hewlett-Packard work force	33%	46%
Employees with working spouses	34%	60%
Employees with child care responsibilities	14%	21%
Employees responsible for parents		25%
Employees with parents living with them		25%

Platt also noted that professional men and women both worked about 50 hours a week, but women spent 33 hours a week on household and child care chores, while the men spent 19 hours on these chores. He said people are more interested in the effect of a job on their personal lives than they are in salary and benefits. Therefore companies like HP must do more to avoid a collision between the two worlds. HP is taking steps to improve the "QWL" by encouraging more telecommuting and other flexible ways of working, by making leaves of absence rules more generous, by providing more help for employees with elderly dependents, and by reducing overtime. It's time HP employees quit wearing the "badge of honor" of working 80-hour weeks. But he said not everyone is getting the message: one senior executive started a meeting to discuss worklife balance at 5 P.M. and wound it up at 9 P.M.

Source: Lewis L. Platt, CEO, Hewlett-Packard Company, speech, October 18, 1995.

as one day is run essentially by the plant manager and teams of workers. Work-outs, followed by the creation of what GE calls "high-involvement teams," lie behind the rescue of the company's huge appliance business in Louisville in the 1990s. The business had been headed for oblivion after a $500-million disaster in 1988 when refrigerators made in Louisville were shipped with faulty compressors.

When customers had a problem or question for GE's $6.6-billion plastics division, they would call an account manager or customer service representative, who might have the answer but more likely would have to root around the company to find it. Today when customers call the plastics division headquarters in Pittsfield, Massachusetts, they deal with a team of people with different specialties drawn from different parts of the company. The customer center covers the United States with nine regional teams of four to seven members each, usually including specialists in credit, customer services, logistics, pricing, and quality. (Separate international teams cover European and Pacific clients.) The teams sit together in an open space in their regional groups and have no formal leaders, although someone usually emerges as a natural leader. Each team creates its own goals, structure, and measures, establishes budgets, hours, and vacation schedules. Turnover runs as high as 50% as people rotate in and out from their home units. They have two bosses, their home unit boss and John McGovern, who is responsible for the customer center but does not manage it on a daily basis.

The teams try to go beyond answering the usual customer requests on the spot. They will send people out to customers to show them how to raise productivity, or help them deal with payment schedules or shipping questions. The actual sales are handled by account managers, but the teams are beginning to help with sales too. Once in a while, the whole customer service office goes into a work-out to deal with a particular problem. For example, the entire process of hiring new team members seemed to need improvement. A work-out focused on the lack of an organized way of comparing the many applicants they interviewed for jobs and devised a simple matrix for rating them.[14]

GE reinforces the work-out and boundaryless approach with appraisal, compensation, and promotion systems that make it unwise to act as if the fences are still up. The 360-degree appraisal system applies to managers worldwide and allows company people to comment electronically from anywhere in the world. People above, below, and alongside can comment on the person being appraised. The effect, says Welch, is to identify and get rid of those who "smile up and kick down." The two fastest ways to get tossed out of GE, says Welch, are to commit an "integrity violation" and to be "a controlling, turf-defending, oppressive manager who can't change and who saps and squeezes people rather than excites and draws out their energy and creativity." GE has turned toward a new way of dealing with people. With all these great goads and lures, GE, says the ebullient Welch, has "an absolutely infinite capacity to improve everything."[15]

SUPER FRESH FOOD MARKETS

The furthest you could go in distributing power in business would be the democratic corporation advocated by Russell Ackoff, the consultant and former Wharton professor introduced in Chapter 1. Ackoff accepts that an organization needs a hierarchy. But does it have to be autocratic? Why can't it be a democratic hierarchy, like our government? He argues for a hierarchy in which everyone participates, directly or through a representative, in decisions that affect him or her directly. This democracy would be created by a series of boards linked down through the organization. Every manager, except those at the very top and bottom of the organization, would sit on a board consisting at a minimum of that manager and his or her immediate superior and immediate subordinates. The boards would work by consensus rather than majority rule, and could make any decision affecting their part of the company alone as well as make recommendations to other levels.[16]

American business has not exactly embraced this level of employee involvement. However, some have tested it. The Great Atlantic & Pacific Tea Company announced in 1981 that it planned to close its Philadelphia stores because they were money losers. With other supermarkets also closing, that would have left 12,000 members of the United Food & Commercial Workers union in the Philadelphia area out on the street. The union approached the A&P to see what could be done to save the stores. What the company and the union agreed to amounted to something like Ackoff's democratic corporation. The union agreed to greater flexibility in work and seniority rules, and to a 25% cut in basic pay. The company agreed to some participative management and to incentive pay based on the stores' performance.

The stores began reopening in 1982 under the name Super Fresh Food Markets, with green and white striped awnings and displays stressing fresh produce. Within a year Super Fresh had 57 stores. Gerald Good, the A&P executive who became president of the new subsidiary, set a management style early on when the meat manager in a store about to open asked him for a plan for the layout of the meat department. Good said, "You figure it out" and walked away. The meat manager followed him out to the sidewalk and asked, "Do you really mean that?" Supermarket people weren't, and still aren't for the most part, familiar with the ideas of employee involvement.

Each store set up its planning board consisting of the manager, the department heads, and another representative of each department. As the chain grew it added zone planning boards for groups of six to eight stores each consisting of store managers and union representatives. Finally Super Fresh set up a corporate planning board of top management and representatives of the stores and the unions.

While the corporation kept certain powers to itself, such as setting prices and determining what promotions to run, the boards were free to decide other matters at their levels. The store boards focused on fairly substantive matters, such as displays, signs, and customer service, and they were particularly interested in how to earn the incentives that could raise their pay above the base. Within a year sales at the average store were double what they had been under the A&P logo and three-quarters of the stores were qualifying for incentive pay. But when new managers with other priorities moved into Super Fresh the experiment lost steam and the boards stopped meeting. In 1996, A&P started to revive boards and the incentives at the 70 existing Super Fresh markets in Philadelphia, and negotiated a new agreement with the United Food Workers.[17]

WHO THE HECK ARE WE TO SAY?

The shape of employee involvement can vary from the rather formal structure of Super Fresh or GE to the totally loose approach at VeriFone. Apart from three permanent councils dealing with marketing, shipping, and scheduling, says Will Pape, at VeriFone, "we form and abolish ad hoc

teams all the time." The team members don't have to be collocated physically. They operate from anywhere by conference calls. CEO Hatim Tyabji
says that at any given moment there could be 30 or 40 teams at work in the
company. He doesn't know exactly because he doesn't track them. They
are self-starting and are expected to do something about whatever problem they tackle. "We absolutely do not monitor them because who the
heck are we to say that we know more than they or better than they do,"
says Tyabji. Supervision would defeat the whole point of empowerment,
he argues, which is that you trust your people. If a team takes an action
that does not fit the company strategy, that would be management's fault
for not communicating that strategy. He believes the company has to convey its messages over and over again.[18] In his office he has a panel of nine
pictures showing him with his Irish setter, both standing. In the first eight
pictures he orders the dog to "sit" but the dog doesn't move. Finally, in the
ninth picture, the dog sits and Tyabji pats his head.

Although Tyabji does not monitor the teams, he does give them a
chance from time to time to make presentations at meetings, as a form of
recognition. A curious thing about teams is that when given a choice
about rewards and celebrations, they tend to choose small, symbolic,
even corny things, recognition rather than money. At the GE customer
service center they have parties, monthly awards, dressing down days,
or days when they come to work dressed up in national costumes. A big
celebration took the whole crew, with partners, to Boston for a weekend.

Pay practices lag far behind what corporations need to do and what
they say they want to do. Rewards are still based on short-term, individual achievements. They send the wrong message. They undermine the
whole idea of teams. Edward Lawler writes that his surveys of compensation practices in 1987, 1990, and 1993 show no increase in incentive
compensation and show that "gainsharing," which is most closely associated with the team approach, remains unpopular and little used.[19] In
gainsharing, employees benefit directly from increased profits with increased pay.

SEI Investments is one company that does base its incentive pay
largely on the performance of teams. The company emerged from its
turbulent reorganizations in the early 1990s flatter and split into 150
teams. Base pay for people making more than $75,000 a year has not
changed in recent years, but the incentive compensation has grown and

covers the whole company. It averages 25% to 35% of base pay but can reach 100% and even 200% in a few cases. CEO Al West wants each team to be a little entrepreneurial unit, and the bonus money is distributed among the teams according to their performance, which may be rated by customers as well as management. The team members themselves then decide how to divvy up the pot—with a "facilitator" on hand to try to prevent bloodshed and to stop the team from taking the easy way out by sharing the money equally. The difference in the amount of annual bonus awarded to members of the same team can amount to $7,000 or $8,000.[20] Management also has discretion to sprinkle some bonus money on people who fall outside the team award system. The SEI approach to compensation is still exceptional.

In a flattened, team-based company like SEI, defining a career becomes a problem. There's no ladder to climb, so the career path becomes a series of lateral shifts to different teams, with each shift supposedly adding skills and therefore enhancing a person's value and employability. But what happens at SEI is that some team leaders, facing deadlines and goals, resist letting their best people roam around to improve their résumés. "So you can end up with a flat organization with no mobility," says Scott Budge, senior vice president at SEI. "It's very difficult to deal with."

To the extent that a person's performance appraisal and pay depend on contributions to team efforts, boundaryless behavior has its reward. At Microsoft, every salaried employee qualifies for cash bonuses and stock options. The bonus can amount to anything from nothing to 15% of base pay and the annual options awarded could be 150 shares for an administrative assistant (what used to be called a secretary) to several thousand shares for a senior executive. These incentive awards are based on the appraisals run twice a year in February and August. Since the appraisals take into account adherence to the company's values, one of which is teamwork, the system to some extent encourages teamwork. As mentioned in Chapter 7, GE has added adherence to values to the criteria used in appraisals and those values include the ability to work with teams. GE has certainly achieved nominal adherence to these new ways of judging and dealing with people. How deep they have taken hold is another matter. One GE executive who looks at these matters points out that the old performance appraisals are based on the numbers, but the

---

Dress Down, Open Up

When you call on an IBM vice president and find him in an open-neck, short-sleeve sports shirt, with no jacket in sight, you know you are witness to a truly fundamental change in business. IBM used to be the company of "suits." But it is becoming almost an embarrassment today to be seen in the uniform of formal, dark suit, with crisp white shirt and silk tie. Corporate America began with dress-down days, usually Fridays. Now, to the delight of Levi Strauss and other makers of up-scale dress-down clothes, the days are stretching to the whole week (see Figure 9.2).

The suit might be considered the emblem of the old up-tight corporation, controlling and hierarchical. How could you expect liberated, empowered, team-working "associates" to wear the emblem of the old order? These people aren't likely to work happily in a private office furnished and sized exactly to the measure of the occupant's status, with the appropriate credenza under the regulation number of windows. The office of the future has been coming for a long time, but there are more of them now. Walls have come down, replaced by partitions, or nothing at all, so that people working in teams can see and talk to each other all the time. At Alcoa, they can gather around information centers, or in lounges or kitchenettes for an informal luncheon meeting. At "hotel" offices, employees can check into temporary office space, hook up the phone and lap-top, and then head out again on another trip or sales call. The CEO may have no private office, and in the case of Milliken & Company, not even a desk. For some time now, Roger Milliken has just wandered around his headquarters, seeing the people he needs to see. SEI Corporation has built itself new offices designed around the idea of flexibility. When Astra Merck laid out its new offices in Wayne, Pennsylvania, there was some debate about whether the CEO should have a large office, but in the end the company decided there should be only two sizes of offices. Yetter got an office which wouldn't be enough for even a junior secretary in the vast reaches of the executive floor at AT&T's headquarters in Basking Ridge, New Jersey.

---

new values appraisals are subjective and open to cronyism. Friends can exchange favors in mutual 360-degree appraisals. But even if the new systems are observed more nominally than in reality, they are pointing in the right direction.

A few companies base at least part of their incentive pay on team performance, as SEI has done, or on long-term goals, or both. Astra Merck divides its incentive compensation, which amounts to 25% of total com-

FIGURE 9.2

Going Casual

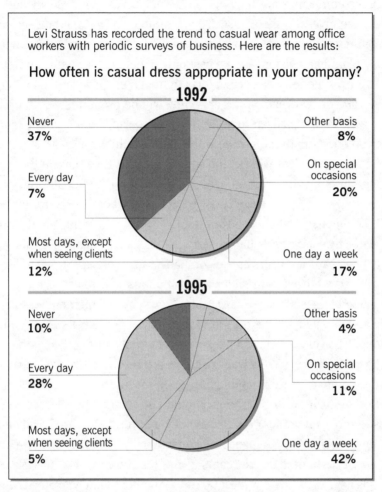

Levi Strauss has recorded the trend to casual wear among office workers with periodic surveys of business. Here are the results:

How often is casual dress appropriate in your company?

1992

Never
37%

Other basis
8%

Every day
7%

On special occasions
20%

Most days, except when seeing clients
12%

One day a week
17%

1995

Never
10%

Other basis
4%

Every day
28%

On special occasions
11%

Most days, except when seeing clients
5%

One day a week
42%

Source: Surveys for Levi Strauss & Company by Evans Research Associates.

pensation, into thirds, one based on corporate performance, one on individual performance, and the other on the unit's performance. Levi Strauss, which plans to have all employees covered by incentive compensation when it works out agreements with some of its unions, also divides its incentive pay into two segments, one for this year's performance and one for performance over a three-year period. The idea is to encourage Levi Strauss people to fit their actions to the company's long-term strategic goals.[21]

LOOKING FOR RESULTS IN JAPAN

Japanese companies are moving to use incentives too, if slowly and in a rather negative way. As of 1996, Toyota adopted a "more results-oriented personnel evaluation system," says Tokuichi Uranishi, general manager for the planning division. "In the past only people of the same age were eligible for promotion to a certain level of manager. Now we are looking at people one or two years younger." They will be promoted ahead of their class with commensurate pay. "As to poor performers," says Uranishi, "we won't demote them, but we won't increase their salaries." Not everyone in the same class will get the same salary, as they have in the past.[22] Honda announced a more aggressive approach in 1992, allowing three years of grace for its "associates" to get ready before the system took hold. Honda CEO Nobuhiko Kawamoto explains the company no longer promotes by seniority, as Japanese companies have long done, but by performance. After ten years at the company, managers are evaluated annually. Those who perform well get promotions and raises. "If you have performed less well," says Kawamoto, "your pay will be reduced substantially and you will also be moved to the rank of specialist so that you will no longer be very active."[23] The pay cuts amount to 10% off what the manager would otherwise receive. These are aggressive moves for Japan, but neither company is thinking of going so far as to fire anyone.

How high in an organization should the team concept reach? That question has not yet found a satisfactory answer. CEOs are hardly likely to submit themselves to managing consensually with a group of their colleagues. In a limited sense teams at the top might work. For example, SEI has a Growth Advisory Group (known unfortunately by its acronym, GAG) consisting of CEO West, the president, the heads of the 12 business units, and several other top people in the company. GAG, which meets for a day once a month, has proved successful at spreading information around the top of the company and focusing on growth, but not so successful at getting people to take off their unit hats and think in terms of the company as a whole. West does, however, see people taking a less parochial view. But another major issue of governance—whether GAG should make decisions or only make recommendations—remains to be solved. At the end of 1996 it had not gone beyond making recommendations.[24]

Few companies are ready to embrace the idea of teams at the top. David Nadler, a consultant who has worked with the top levels of management at AT&T and Xerox, points out some of the difficulties. At the operating level, say in a plant, people spend 100% of their time working together in the same place on the same product, they can rotate jobs, and they probably have no big career ambitions. But at the senior management level they all have different jobs, work in different places, spend maybe 5% of their time on a team, and they all want bigger jobs. Teams at the top can work quite well on matters like resource allocation, deciding how to divvy up capital expenditures, but not at running the company. You need a tiebreaker rather than a consensus-maker at the top. But it depends a bit on the kinds of people you have at the top. The more power seekers there are, the less successful teams are likely to be.[25]

Microsoft believes in the team concept, but when turf battles broke out between the Windows 95 and the NT groups, the differences couldn't be resolved by a team. That kind of problem has to be resolved at the top by management decision, says Microsoft Vice President Mike Murray. "Teams can't work them out, management has to settle them. If you push all decisions down, you get chaos."[26]

ATTRIBUTES OF SUCCESS

It may seem like a contradiction, but employee power isn't likely to work without committed leadership of one sort or another, whether that be the chief executive, the team leaders, or simply an explicit and consistent company policy. A major transition to something as fundamental as employee involvement doesn't stick unless the company commits itself to it. Otherwise there may be sporadic and scattered efforts in a company to adopt teams, but they come and go depending on the preferences of the boss of the moment. That's why AT&T's record on teams is spotty. The corporation favors them, but does not make them a way of life because, for example, contributions to teams do not figure explicitly in performance appraisals.

Mike Murray says he has found that teams (the best size being five or six people) that work well at Microsoft always have leaders with three attributes: they are good at setting goals, good at planning, and good at follow-up. If one of the three is missing, the team members will want out.

Tappas Sen, director of the workplace of the future project at AT&T, thinks teams need to have these attributes to be successful: clarity of goals; good communications, and training in business objectives so that the team understands where it fits in the general plan of the business.[27] Nadler would add another attribute: that the team follow an explicit process. If teams get too wrapped up in discussing process, they will founder on their own weight. But unless there is a specific process— such as Deming's "plan, do, check, act" cycle—it becomes difficult to learn why one team succeeds and another fails.

With some important exceptions, the idea of asking managers and employees to take more responsibility and make more decisions is central to the new enterprise. It is right for the times and right for employers and employees. People today are too well educated and too liberated to let others make all their decisions. The pace of change and competition require better and faster decisions than a bureaucratic organization can make. Giving people more say in their work is simply the enlightened, productive thing to do.

Pointers

- Do you agree that if this is the age of the knowledge worker the employee has to be treated as an asset, not a cost?
- Does your company accept that the best way to get the most out of a worker is to give him or her as much responsibility as possible?
- Do you allow that responsibility to be exercised through self-managing teams?
- Do your teams bring together people from different parts of the company, even from outside the company, so that they can see problems and solutions that might never have occurred to you otherwise?
- Do your teams have goals, accountability, timetables?
- Do your teams get coaching and training so that they learn how to act as team members, know how to solve problems, and are able to encourage others?
- Do your corporate leaders show consistently and by their actions that the teams matter and do they pay attention to the teams' ideas?
- Do your leaders convey a strong sense of the corporation's purpose so that teams can focus on what matters and not drift into irrelevant work?

- Have you allayed the fears of managers that employee involvement will threaten their authority?
- Are you keeping your teams small (as few as five or six people)?

Links

- Has training become pervasive in your company?
- Do you share significant business information with employees so that they know what is relevant and what needs to be done?
- Have you realigned appraisals and rewards so as to recognize team performance rather than only individual performance?

Cautions

- Do you recognize that for some purposes hierarchies and top-down decisions will still be necessary?
- Are you aware that the higher up in the company you try to install teams, the more difficult it becomes?
- What are you doing to preserve valuable functional expertise that may be lost as employees become immersed in cross-functional teams?
- What are you doing to assure rank-and-file employees that creating teams does not, as they often assume, have the hidden purpose of cutting jobs?
- Are you keeping in mind that the team approach may not be the right one for everybody or for every occasion? Turning a McDonald's eatery over to a team of teen-agers, for instance, might be a recipe for chaos.

III

THE RESPONSE—
THE WEAPONS

10

MASTERING INFORMATION

This thing is like a tidal wave.

—Hugh McColl, CEO, NationsBank Corporation

The trouble with computers, says Paul Allaire, the Xerox CEO, is that the technology "outstrips our ability to use it effectively." Thus the focus of discussion has shifted from gee-whizz at the wonder of it all to a rather sober and sometimes anxious discussion of what information technology means and how to handle it. Some of that anxiety comes from CEOs who have yet to meet a computer personally and have a hard time deciding just what they should do with it. But initiates have anxieties too—about the difficulty of forecasting the future of information technology, about security, about organization, about training and education, about the effects on managers' personal lives, and about the effects of an almost unimaginable mass of information.[1]

As everybody knows by now, the impact of computers on business is enormous and inescapable (Chapter 2). James Unruh, the CEO of Unisys Corporation, says that the typical *Fortune* 500 company stored eight billion characters of electronic data in 1970, 33 billion by 1990, and

---

SEI Survey	
The use of information technology and other high-tech tools is critical to being competitive	72%
We are there	17%

---

will probably have 400 trillion by 2010. The number of computers in the world grew from less than half a million two decades ago to 200 million in 1996. The number of Internet web sites is doubling every 53 days and the number of Internet users will grow from an estimated 40 million today to 500 million in 2000.[2] These numbers—if anyone can actually keep track of them—are almost meaningless except as an indicator of the breathtaking scope of change that business has to deal with.

To anchor these celestial figures to real business numbers, consider the case of SAP, a company founded in Germany by five refugees from IBM in 1972. Since introducing its R/3 client-server application software in 1992, SAP has leaped ahead to become the number-one provider of enterprise networks that connect all—well, almost all—of a business's activities. One seamless flow of information goes from the supplier and from the shop floor up to the boardroom and out to the customer. For example, R/3 automatically updates accounts receivable when a company makes a sale. Figure 10.1 shows how SAP's numbers have changed since the introduction of R/3.

The adoption of SAP systems on a massive scale by large companies such as Hewlett-Packard and Compaq and SAP's endorsement by all of the Big Six accounting firms hardly means their clients have settled into

FIGURE 10.1

SAP's Growth

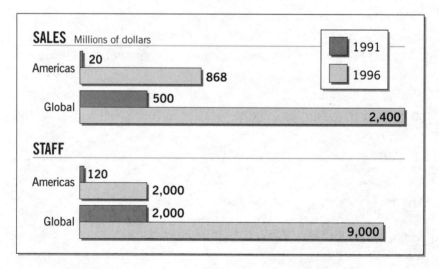

Source: Company data.

a new state of effortless use of powerful new information systems. It can take several years of painful work and buckets of expensive consulting to become a comfortable SAP user. However, it is a powerful system, which has obviously impressed a lot of customers.

"EXPERTS MYSTIFIED"

Beyond the sheer difficulty of adopting information technology on a large scale, huge strategic and management problems come with it. When computers start to transform an industry so much that totally new kinds of players may appear, when the shape of that transformation is unpredictable, when betting on the wrong system or technology can be devastating, then business leaders have reason to agonize about information technology.

The banking industry adopted computers early on and used them successfully, first to make their backroom operations more efficient and then to give customers better service, notably with automatic tellers, but today banks face risks and challenges of a new order. Will banking at home catch on? Will stored-value cards? Or financial services? Will Intuit be the bank's big competitor? Or Microsoft? Where will the Internet fit in? Will banks, with their customers' trust and their experience in handling a mass of transactions, come out on top? Or will it be the software companies with their flexibility and speed of innovation? Or will it be a partnership of the two? No wonder Hugh L. McColl, the martial CEO of NationsBank Corporation, sounds uncharacteristically unsure when he says, "This thing is like a tidal wave. If you fail in the game, you're going to be dead."[3] McColl planned to spend $1.4 billion on operations and technology in 1996 and wants to develop a technology-based strategy to replace the successful aggressive growth-by-acquisition strategy that made NationsBank the third largest in the United States.

Ironically, while computers give us the means to make more data-based decisions than we were ever able to make before, computers can't help us know the future of computers themselves. The span of predictability of information technology has so shrunk that experts don't even like to say what will happen a year ahead. At a gathering of business and academic experts at the Wharton School on the future of information technology, one participant imagined how a newspaper might interpret the uncertainties voiced at the meeting and suggested this headline:

"Experts Mystified by Future of Computing." While computers are giving managers more and better information to use for fact-based decisions, the computer systems themselves call for a measure of good intuitive decisions.

The annoyances, uncertainties, and risks of information technology need to be noted and considered, but they are hardly going to stand in the way of the most powerful strategic tool and technology of our times. In earlier chapters we have seen examples of how computers can fundamentally affect a business: how they enabled Boeing to create an aircraft in a completely different way, how they underlie the reorganization and marketing strategy of American Express, how they add to the value of Federal Express's already efficient and automated services by allowing the customer inside FedEx's computers to track his package. The examples could be taken from almost any company in any line of business.

As the shape of the 21st century enterprise emerges, we can see five fundamental ways in which information technology leads the way: (1) by enhancing the efficiencies and economies of existing operations, (2) by creating new products and services, (3) by creating new businesses, (4) by tying the customer more tightly to the company, and (5) by completely changing the nature of new and even traditional kinds of companies.

PIONEER: A SIMPLE CONCEPT

To begin with the companies that have changed, let's go back to Pioneer Hi-Bred International Incorporated, the Iowa corn seed company we met in Chapter 2. We quoted its former chairman, Tom Urban, saying "the information system is the firm."

When Henry Wallace founded Pioneer in 1926 he could not have made or imagined such a statement. Since then, the average yield of corn grown on North American farms has quadrupled from around 25 bushels per acre to more than 100 bushels—and much more than that in good years. Corn seed is no longer a commodity; nor can farmers simply save seed from last year's crop and plant it. To be competitive, they have to buy new hybrid seed every year. Pioneer's data-based research and development puts it ahead of competing seed companies by five to seven bushels per acre in yield, depending on the year. That yield, in turn, allows Pioneer to charge premium prices 10% to 15% higher than competitors' prices, which keeps Pioneer's return on equity above 20% a year.

Information technology allows Pioneer to speed and expand the development of new hybrids at a phenomenal rate. Between 1990 and 1995 Pioneer increased the samples of corn it tested every year for oil and protein from 5,000 to one million. Pioneer develops 70,000 new hybrids a year and picks about 15 winners from among them to send to market. A network of labs and growers all over the world, including winter nurseries in Central America and Chile, tied into its information system, have cut the time it takes Pioneer to develop a new hybrid from 13 years to seven. "Each year we reduce the time to release we dramatically enhance the return on the $130 million we spend annually on research and increase our lead over the competition," says Tom Urban.

Pioneer began using computers in the 1960s and developed an information system typical in business until quite recently. It had a central group of about 250 people running information management and another 100 people serving as "interfaces" in the operating units to interpret the system to some 6,000 users. Urban and his managers took a traditional view of the firm as a series of discrete functions requiring discrete information systems. They did not see the connection, for example, between research information and sales information. Information management was an adjunct to the company's operations. As far as they went, Pioneer's computers delivered what was expected. The e-mail system worked well all over the world. But even though they had the latest technology, Urban's team knew they weren't getting what they should out of their computers. They tried various tacks to get more without success until, in 1993, a senior management team headed by Tom Hanigan, vice president for information management, sat down and spent six months reinventing the system. This time it was the customers, that is, the business units, rather than the information management office, who decided what was needed.

The team realized, says Urban, that Pioneer "had missed a very simple concept . . . that all the pieces of information across the company could now be related to each other." Two other principles already governed information policy at Pioneer: (1) the data had to be accurate and trusted all over the company, and not regarded suspiciously as the product and property of one division or another, and (2) the data should be available instantly anywhere in the world. Limiting access to data does not enhance authority or define responsibility, says Urban, "but only reduces the benefits to be gained from the free flow of information."

The new system, based on a mainframe, a large server using Novell networking software, and PCs using Microsoft software, began to function in 1994. The flow of linked information throughout the company began to do things for Pioneer that couldn't be done before and to reveal things that Pioneer didn't know.

For example, Pioneer used to base its production and shipping of seed in the spring on what farmers had ordered in the fall. There was no connection between sales and R&D. But when executives began to understand the business as a flow of information and not a series of discrete steps, as Urban tells it, they saw that what farmers ordered in the fall was not what they bought in the spring. Instead, as winter wore on and farmers heard about the performance of new hybrids and discussed them with neighbors, they moved away from their fall orders and bought more of the new hybrids. In other words, R&D results were a better indicator of what farmers would buy than the farmers' own initial orders. Now Pioneer plans production and sales on the basis of the performance of new seed, not what the customers say they want, and can push plans ahead two or three years by predicting future performance.

To tighten its relations with customers through its new information technology, Pioneer has also entered joint information ventures in which its data can be merged into a flow of information from other sources that goes out to farmers and agricultural companies. Pioneer is part of a consortium called the AG Marketing Group which meshes the customer data bases of several noncompeting agricultural companies.

Pioneer's information systems will be even more critical in the future. Urban expects that genetic engineering will become a significant factor in the seed market around the turn of the century. Coordination of the continuing flow of data on the field performance of plants with new lab data on gene experiments will create data demands that are orders of magnitude greater than what Pioneer has been dealing with. The company is also looking to the time when satellites will scan a farmer's fields in small sections, take in the moisture content, weed cover, and whatever other information may be relevant, check that against soil type and past crop performance, and tell the farmer how much seed, fertilizer and herbicides to use. The information might be fed into a tractor's computer to adjust the flow of seed, fertilizer, or herbicides as the farmer rolls across his fields.[4]

ANDERSEN: GETTING ALL THE KNOWLEDGE OUT

Consulting firms have seen their traditional business fundamentally changed by computers. "Information technology is the driver in our business," says Charles Paulk, chief information officer at Andersen Consulting. Andersen specializes in showing its clients the nuts and bolts of how to use information technology. To demonstrate to clients what it can do for them, Andersen set up a "center for strategic technology" in Palo Alto with the facilities to create for executives an image of what advanced information technology could do for them. The center runs workshops, conducts research, and works on actual problems with clients. (Andersen also has demonstration-research-consulting facilities in Chicago for the retail business, in New York for financial services, in Dallas for health care, and others elsewhere.)

For itself, Andersen has created a global net linking its 35,000 consultants. "Before, when I went out, the client got all the knowledge that I had," says Paulk, and that included what he had learned in Andersen's extensive training efforts (to be considered for a partnership Andersen consultants need to take 1,000 hours of training at the firm's campus near Chicago). Company files and fax messages from colleagues might help a bit. "But what about the knowledge in the rest of the firm?" asks Paulk. "Our vision is to operate as one global firm, leveraging our best people."

The old system worked well enough when the firm's business was mostly in the United States. Since it split from Arthur Andersen & Company in 1989, Andersen Consulting has grown its international business from 20% to 50% of its fast-growing revenues, which totaled $5.3 billion in 1996. Today's clients need a broader base of knowledge because they want comprehensive solutions—and they want them quickly and they may well want them to be global. With the Lotus Notes–based network the firm has established, Andersen consultants anywhere can dive into data bases on 3,000 different subjects, swap presentations and slides, browse through libraries, and set up customized news summaries. Consultants are expected to contribute to the data. "We don't nurture Lone Ranger partners," says Paulk. A team of 100 Andersenites working on a major logistic and distribution project in the United States got stuck on a bug in the software and made no progress for several weeks. Then the team posted a question on the firm's worldwide net to see if anyone else had had the same problem, and overnight they got the software code to solve the problem. Teams have searched the personnel data bases to find someone with a particularly arcane specialty among the 32,000 consultants. (Anyone in the company can search the skills bank, but confidential matters such as pay are closed off.)[5] Andersen might say, with Pioneer, that information is the firm.

ASTRA MERCK: SOLUTIONS INSTEAD OF PENS, PADS, AND PIZZA

In the category of businesses created by information technology, take Astra Merck, where Andersen is deeply involved. When two giant drug companies, Merck & Company of the United States and Astra AB of Sweden, formed Astra Merck as a marketing company in the United States they had a chance to create from scratch a company fit for the 21st century. Beginning in 1992, Andersen provided up to 120 live-in consultants at a time, and some of them spent three or four years with Astra Merck. John D. Rollins, until 1996 the senior Andersen partner on the job at the firm's headquarters in Wayne, Pennsylvania, says "this exemplifies the relationship we'd like to have with some clients. I have never seen such depth and breadth of engagement." Rollins explains how the Andersen system works for him. "The critical success factor for a company like Andersen is global interconnectedness, so that we have a worldwide communications structure to share experiences, résumés, credentials, techniques, and so forth. We all have mail boxes. That's the biggest use. We also have discussion groups. I seek information every day on the net as I used to by phone or fax. You can start discussion groups on specific subjects. But if only two or three people are going to be involved, it's just as effective to use the phone. It's a new competence. Client data has to be confidential and a lot of our people will only put information on the net that they are comfortable sharing. Confidential stuff they share 'ear to ear.'"[6]

Andersen was brought in originally to help design Astra Merck's information network, but became deeply involved in the whole design of the company. As the company took shape in 1992 and 1993, Merck pushed Astra Merck to stretch the limits of organizational concepts—and the Merck team assigned to the new company ended up going perhaps further than parent Merck expected. When Astra Merck was born in 1994, says its founding CEO, Wayne Yetter, it wanted to "revolutionize the pharmaceutical industry." Yetter describes the experience as a "once in a lifetime opportunity to create an important company (with sales approaching a billion dollars) from a blank sheet of paper."

The result, says Yetter, who moved on in 1996 to become CEO of Novartis Pharmaceuticals in the United States, is that "we sometimes refer to ourselves as an information company that happens also to sell pharmaceutical products." Drug company "detailers" have always handed out promotional brochures and instructions, as well as trifling gifts, along with the drugs they sold. Astra Merck eschews the "pens, pads, and pizza" approach. The company provides not only instructions, but information about matters unrelated to its own drugs that a hospital, doctor, or patient might need. Astra Merck calls it providing "customer solutions"; that is, meeting customers' needs by giving them information showing them how they can deal with a problem. It might provide an economic analysis of alternative treatment programs, or run a seminar to show doctors how to negotiate with HMOs, or, in one case, stage a dummy OSHA inspection to prepare a clinic for the real thing, with an Astra Merck employee playing the part of the inspector. (Don't store sandwiches in the refrigerator along with specimens.)

Astra Merck is so focused on furnishing information that its organization grid shows three of its six key businesses or "process areas" relate to information (see Figure 10.2). At its Wayne headquarters is the "process area" called Information Services and Education. From six Unix business servers there Astra Merck can distribute information electronically to the field offices and to the laptops carried by sales reps. About half the information relates to products; the other half provides more general training and services. It includes patient information sheets, such as diet guidelines or how to get ready for endoscopy, and monographs, drug fact sheets, clinical studies, literature searches, and other materials for doctors. The whole system ties into the National Library of Medicine.

Astra Merck's 38 field offices are equipped with four-color desktop printing equipment to create their own materials or print information

FIGURE 10.2

Information Is Half the Game

This matrix of the Astra Merck organization shows how important information technology has become. Astra Merck is a pharmaceutical company, but of the six major processes shown serving the customer, three of them (the bottom three) are based on information technology.

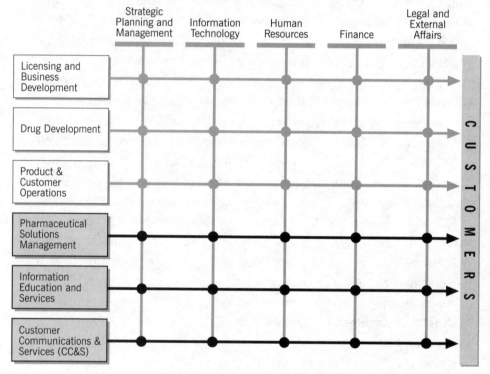

Source: Astra Merck: Capabilities + Solutions. A Year-End Meeting 1994 (a company publication).

downloaded from Wayne. The staffs include graphics specialists who can adapt the materials for individual doctors and hospitals, adding names, logos, and particular information. The field offices include on their staffs MDs or PhDs who can talk as equals to professional customers. These offices are encouraged to go out of their way to think up "solutions" for their customers. For example, the New York metropolitan area office, based in Norwalk, Connecticut, has helped one hospital evaluate physicians coming out of residency and is working with the New York chapter of the American College of Physicians to create a data base for a closed-circuit televised system to help rural doctors. Cathryn Gunther, who manages this office (but uses no title), asks rhetorically, "Does this sell our drugs? No. But when they come up for formulary, they will remember." In other words, when it comes time for a hospital or clinic to list the drugs its doctors should prescribe, Astra Merck hopes its good works will nail the sale.[7] In 1996, Astra Merck grossed $2.1 billion, more than double the starting level in 1994, and the company doubled its sales force, adding nine more customer centers.

MEDQUIST: A COTTAGE INDUSTRY GOES ELECTRONIC

In medical record keeping, information technology is creating a new business. Doctors' notes and medical records have always been transcribed, of course, but usually by typists working in the bowels of a hospital under conditions that were less than inspiring or productive. Transcriptions Limited, established in 1970, had improved on that system somewhat by distributing transcripts in the Philadelphia area to typists working in their homes. But the material was moved around by car and was processed by Dictaphone and typewriter. MedQuist Incorporated, a provider of medical information and business services, acquired Transcriptions in 1994 and is using information technology to create a rapidly growing national business in what was a fragmented cottage industry.

Doctors deliver their reports by phone to MedQuist's digital dictation system, which then passes it on to one of the 2,200 qualified medical transcribers who check in looking for work. They operate at home with PCs and modems, and where they are or what hours they work doesn't matter much to MedQuist. The system can shift work around the country to spread the load and a transcriber in Texas can be working for a Boston hospital one hour and a San Francisco hospital the next. The system can also pick transcribers with particular specialties if they are needed. They are paid by the number of keystrokes, which are easy to track on a computer, less a deduction for errors. Transcripts can be delivered back to the doctors by modem in a few hours and can be entered into a patient's electronic record.

By shifting the whole operation over to electronic systems, by letting people work at home, and by using transcribers all over the country, MedQuist creates an effective, low-cost system that easily competes with a hospital's own system. MedQuist saves costs because the transcribers don't have to commute to an office and because it can shift work from high-cost to lower-cost areas. James Emshoff, Medquist's CEO until 1996, sees the company as the kind of flexible, networked business that information technology makes possible. Emshoff thinks companies and executives will come in many shapes and sizes and offers himself as an example. He moves around between teaching (at Wharton), consulting, and running companies. He took the CEO job at MedQuist on a temporary and part-time basis. By growing its business and acquiring other transcription companies MedQuist pushed its revenues up from $24.8 million in 1994 to $45.1 million in 1995 and $61.5 million in 1996 after dropping other business to focus on transcription.[8] As well as it is doing now, MedQuist faces a risk particular to information technology. The business could be transformed by voice recognition technology. In this case, when doctors can start talking their notes into a computerized voice transcription system, MedQuist will need to lead the change or risk losing its business.

GE: TRADING ON THE INTERNET

It would be hard to find a major corporation today that is not making big investments in its information technology and systems and, as a result, changing the way it works. GE Plastics, a global business which would rank around 200 on *Fortune's* list of 500 American companies if it stood alone, spent a strenuous two years beginning in 1994 rolling out an entirely new information system. Like Pioneer, GE Plastics discarded the typical old "management information systems" approach in which a staff of designers and programmers created a separate system for each functional group in the company, which then became the owner of that system. In the first step, GE Plastics integrated the whole company, installing open, compatible hardware and software that made the system available to everyone. Then GE Plastics began building a "data warehouse" for the whole company to use to make quick, accurate analyses and dig deeper for information. The warehouse feeds information to the people who make decisions.

The warehouse came just in time to help GE deal with a burst of double-digit inflation in commodities at the end of 1994 that created chaos in the market for raw materials used to make plastics. "Now when we buy a commodity we can immediately calculate the effects on the market price," says Jack Sprano, manager of information systems at GE Plastics.

Major analyses that used to take a week or two can be completed in an hour or less. The allocation of production among GE's 31 resin plants around the world used to take two or three weeks of wrangling about the numbers and the final decisions were largely intuitive. With the warehouse, decisions can be made in hours and they are based on data, not intuition, Sprano asserts.

The installation of new "groupware," the third part of GE Plastics' information plan, was aimed at giving everyone in the company uniform but easy to use and powerful desktop applications. Everyone now has Word, Excel, and PowerPoint, operating on open, Intel-based PCs. Previously Plastics people could install whatever software or hardware they wanted. Hoping to acquire a common, improved e-mail system, the Plastics division offered itself as a test site for Microsoft's Exchange, which it has now installed in 16 countries. GE Plastics became in 1994 the first noncomputer company to get on the Internet and uses it to buy and sell commodities, market recyclable materials, and put out bids.

Like other companies, GE Plastics finds that the new approach to information requires different people. Programmers and systems architects are out. Subcontractors in India write the code. Well-trained programmers in India cost a fraction of what they cost in the United States and since the number of people needed during the development of an application follows a sharp bell curve, by using subcontractors GE avoids maintaining a large permanent staff. GE does not hire systems architects because today companies are more likely to buy integrated packages from SAP, Oracle, and others. Even IBM, Hewlett-Packard, and Sun Microsystems buy these systems.[9]

Here are a few more examples of the kinds of changes and innovations, even new businesses, that wouldn't exist without the new information technology:

- *Levi Strauss & Company* makes a highly visible use of information technology by "mass customizing" jeans for women. Customers can go to one of the company-owned Original Levi's Stores where a sales "associate" takes four measurements, and enters them in a computer, which recommends a prototype jean. The customers tries on the prototype and the associate adjusts the measurements to improve the fit and then gets another prototype. Once the measurements are right they are flashed by modem to the company factory in Mountain City, Tennessee, where lasers automatically cut the right pattern and operators stitch the jeans together. Delivery is guaranteed in three weeks. They cost $70, $10 more than the same 512 Jeans for Women ready made. As often happens, the software for Levi's Personal Pair jeans, as they are called, came from a small company, Custom Clothing Technology Corporation of Newton, Massachusetts, which Levi's bought in 1995.

• *Wells Fargo & Company* has closed 1,000 conventional branch banks since 1980 and has been replacing them with one- or two-person branches in supermarkets and with remote electronic banking in partnership with Microsoft and Intuit. In effect, Wells Fargo tells its clients, "Don't come to the bank—use the phone, use your computer or use the ATM." It has developed algorithms so loan officers can approve small business loans over the phone in minutes—and it makes these loans from Maine to Florida, even though it has no branches outside California. By the end of 1996, Wells Fargo had 200,000 "cyberaccounts," up from 20,000 early in 1995, so that clients could bank by computer."[10]

• On-line shopping services have their troubles, especially with the delivery of the goods once the order has been placed by computer. However, *Peapod LP,* founded in 1989, seems to be establishing itself with a business based entirely on information technology. Peapod customers can go on-line in Boston, Chicago, Columbus, San Francisco, and San Jose to order their weekly groceries from supermarkets signed up with Peapod. They can browse through a data base of 20,000 items by category, aisle, brands, prices, or by "specials," or just order from a personal list in the system's memory. The service isn't cheap. Customers pay a monthly fee and a delivery fee for each order plus a percentage of the order. A customer who buys $100-worth of groceries three times a month could spend $35 extra for Peapod. But Peapod hopes to have overcome the order fulfillment problem by putting its own people in the stores to pack the orders.

VERIFONE AND SEI: WELL WIRED

For top executives, the use of information technology presents some problems, not the least being that those over 50 learned how to work before computers became ubiquitous. It has been suggested that every

CEO needs a teenage computer nerd at his elbow. There are CEOs who know their companies depend on information technology, but have never touched the stuff themselves. Hugh McColl of NationsBank was one of those. When he saw his company's fate was tied to information technology, he started taking lessons in the use of a PC.

The age problem will be solved by time, of course, and many companies, especially new ones and those in electronics, have fully wired executives. The top people at VeriFone, for example, are tied in wherever they are. One of the founders, Will Pape, 47, travels with a few "road warrior" tools so he can link his laptop computer to a phone line if the hotel phone doesn't have a port. Typically he will get up at 4:30 or 5 A.M. to scan his e-mail and "clear his desk." He may check his e-mail two or three times a day. In between times, he can always be reached by cellular phone on an urgent matter. E-mail ranks fairly low in psychological effectiveness, he says, while the video conference ranks at the top, but that capital-intensive tool is confined to the company's offices in the United States. The phone and e-mail are only two of 32 modes of communicating available in the company. VeriFone's 3,000 employees send each other about one million messages a month, and when one person broadcasts a message to 200 fellow workers, that counts as one message. This kind of message muddles accountability, though, warns Pape, because no one knows who is supposed to do what.[11]

Another well-wired company, SEI Investments, in Oaks, Pennsylvania, went to open offices, gave everyone a PC, and abolished the job of secretary to switch to a new mode of working. (Secretaries were offered a chance to apply for other jobs in SEI and about 30 of some 90 qualified. SEI doesn't want to employ people who aspire only to be secretaries, or people who aspire only to be programmers.) The executives now have no buffers, no support. If CEO Al West needs an airline ticket, he calls the travel office (an in-house but outsourced operation). "Everyone here thought Al was nuts," says Mark Wilson, a vice president who deals with organization. "But a local area network, a good copy center, and e-mail make up for a lot of losing a secretary. We've never been paper intensive here. The culture is you just pick up the phone." To assuage the frustration of callers who can't get beyond West's answering machine, SEI created team lines so that if West doesn't answer, the caller punches "0" and gets a member of West's team. Callers learn that SEI's culture requires that their voice-mail messages have to be substantive—if they just say "call me back" nothing happens.[12]

Life for executives who are completely wired isn't all that much fun. One way or another they can be reached 24 hours a day by more people than they want to hear from with more information than they need. John Sculley, the former chief of Apple Computer, decided to carry a beeper and cellular phone when he started running his own businesses out of an office in New York. "That was the worst decision I could have made," he says. Instead of keeping in touch with the world, he found the world was keeping in touch with him, leaving him no privacy. So now he leaves both devices behind, perhaps setting a good example for other harassed executives. But he still telephones every hour or two to one of his two assistants—his "human interface"—who filter messages and handle scheduling.[13]

Older companies in more traditional businesses may with good reason take a more cautious approach to information technology, at least the communications part of it. Labconco Incorporated, a 73-year-old, $34-million-a-year manufacturer of laboratory equipment in Kansas City, faxes message all over the world and uses some e-mail internally, but does not let customers into the e-mail or voice-mail systems. CEO John McConnell, who says he is not a "power user" of computers, wants to keep the relationship between company and customers personal. "People buy from people," he says, and so when customers or outsiders call in, they don't get voice-mail, they get "voice fe-mail," in the person of a gracious, competent English receptionist.[14]

SAINT-GOBAIN: TOLERATING E-MAIL

Michel Besson, the urbane head of Saint-Gobain's operations in North America until 1996 (he became executive vice president of the parent), tolerates some of the new communications technology. He doesn't use e-mail himself but thinks it is a useful tool for communicating with places in distant time zones. He finds teleconferences useful for discussing specifics, such as plans for a new plant or budgets. But while in the United States he was obviously more comfortable with his monthly visits to headquarters in Paris and other face-to-face meetings to discuss operations, manufacturing, or sales or to talk to customers. At that time he wore four hats in Saint-Gobain's complex global management matrix, and believes the ambiguities and tensions of the job could only be worked out face to face. The speed of e-mail doesn't impress him because he rarely has to make quick decisions, and the lack of discipline among e-mail users distresses him. They transmit too much trivia, he said. When someone in Asia sends the same message to ten other people in Asia, nobody takes action because each one thinks the other nine will.[15]

In the end the real constraint on the use of information technology becomes time, the time of executives and managers to absorb and make use of the information. The amount of data available and all its renderings have become almost limitless, but the time available to use it remains finite. In fact, time has been curtailed by other new demands placed on executives, to get by with smaller staffs, to work faster, to get more training, to sit on teams, to pay more attention to customers and suppliers, to travel around the world. But that constraint can hardly stop or even slow the information revolution. It's here and it's growing. It's creating new products and new businesses. It's creating new markets and revealing markets that we didn't know existed. It allows us to mass customize products, to design them faster and better, to produce them more efficiently. It spreads useful knowledge through an organization and allows customers and suppliers to share in it. It connects all of a company's activities, wherever they may be. The successful deployment of information technology has become the central business strategy of the times and it changes everything we do.

Pointers

- Does the information system unify the whole organization, connecting activities from the supplier through to the customer?
- Is the information system centrally managed and compatible throughout? (Hewlett-Packard's new SAP package is replacing 24 existing, uncoordinated systems.)
- Has the information system been designed by the people who are going to use it?
- Is the information network widely accessible and as easy to use as possible?

- Does it capture the information you need to segment the market precisely?
- Does your information system allow you to know your customers well, track their behavior, and build a long-term relationship with them?
- Does it provide the support you need to make rapid, fact-based, accurate decisions?

Links

- Are your information systems and your structure, power relationship, careers, pay, training, and skills in alignment with each other?
- Since the number of people and the skills needed in information technology change rapidly, have you considered outsourcing your computer operations?

Cautions

- Future technology is becoming increasingly unpredictable so even the brightest experts find it hard to know what to do next.
- The scope and cost of new information systems are so huge that the choices may involve bet-the-company risks.
- As networks grow, the risk that intruders can invade an organization's information system becomes a major management worry.
- The biggest obstacle to installing information systems in a company is the way people work and the way companies are organized.
- If an information system simply produces a mass of data rather than usable information, it is part of the problem and not the solution.

11

SPURRING INNOVATION

The creative process . . . works well when it is not too structured. But, in the long run, it must be tamed, harnessed, and hitched to the wagon of mankind's needs.
—William Hewlett[1]

A merican business would seem to be in the grip of a frenzy of innovation. CEO Harvey Golub announces that American Express introduced more new products in 1995 than in the previous decade and then in 1996 the company kept on churning out new cards.[2] The Hewlett-Packard chief executive, Lewis Platt, says that the life cycles of new products last only nine to 18 months and he remembers a decade ago when they lasted for years.[3] Hewlett-Packard and Intel, among others, cannibalize their own products by bringing out new versions of them in as little as six months. And at Corning, 75% of the flat panels for TV and computer screens sold in 1995 were not made in 1994. Products in the flat panel market change almost quarterly.[4]

Are we—do we really want to be—that innovative? Rice Krispies still

SEI Survey	
It is critical for large organizations to become more innovative and entrepreneurial	79%
We are doing that	19%

snap, crackle, and pop as they did when we were kids, don't they? Aren't toilet paper and Kleenex pretty much what they always were, except maybe the wrapping is prettier? Brillo pads haven't changed, have they? Even the label on a can of evaporated milk looks like the one our parents and grandparents knew. Much of what we use all the time—shoe polish, Jello, umbrellas, toilet seats, hammers, nails, screws, screwdrivers, sticky fly-paper (if anyone still buys it)—has hardly changed for decades.

What's going on here? Let's keep a sense of proportion. Everything isn't changing all the time. Well, it is and it isn't. Even in industries that make the same things they have been making for years, the ability to innovate is important. Maybe the product doesn't change, but the competition may. New markets or new channels to the markets open up. Maybe the old products can be made more efficiently, with new tools or manufacturing methods. Or distributed in a different way. Innovation is not confined to products and to services, but to the company itself, its management, its organization, and its processes.

In certain industries the pace of innovation has indeed become frantic. The need to invent new electronic products constantly is obvious. The technology is new, the market is growing enormously, it has so many applications, its possibilities yield readily to the imagination. Presumably electronics will settle down one day into a more stable state where the products and the players don't change too much—just as the automobile industry, for example, settled down in the 1920s in the United States. The major players then are still major players today and an automobile is still an automobile. The electronics industry is still in the tumultuous state. A few months of inattention by top management can cause a company to miss a whole generation of products.

The need to innovate is overwhelming in other industries too—in banking and financial services, pharmaceuticals, chemicals, and retailing, for example. Foreign competition forced the auto industry to innovate on a massive scale, to improve the quality of cars, to raise the productivity of factories, to speed the design of new models, to clean out the blocked arteries of management. You can readily recognize the resemblance between a 1997 car and a 1980 model, but look at the corporations and you find little resemblance between the Chrysler or the GM of then and now.

A UNIVERSAL SPIRIT

To innovate successfully, you need four things: First, the entrepreneurial or inventive spirit; second, the willingness to commit resources to innovation; third, the methods to do it, and, fourth, the right type of organization to do it. The real problem in an advanced industrial society lies in the fourth point. How do you get large organizations to keep innovating, especially if they are successful at what they are already doing? This chapter will focus on organizing to innovate, but first let's look briefly at the other three points.

The Spirit. The spirit of innovation certainly exists, to a great extent in the United States and to a greater extent in many other countries than the laws, the culture, or the economy seem to allow. The number of garages, basements, spare rooms, and workshops that have been the birthplace of great American companies and even whole industries is legendary, from the Wright brothers' bicycle shop in Dayton and Leroy Grumman's workshop on Long Island to Hewlett and Packard's garage in Palo Alto and Steve Jobs's family garage in Cupertino. A list of immigrants whose entrepreneurial spirit was released in the United States would begin with Andrew Grove of Intel. The spirit is universal, even in conformist, bureaucratic Japan. A visitor to Japan just after World War II could have seen the founders of Sony working around benches in a leaky shed and Soichiro Honda, a bicycle and motorcycle mechanic, fitting tiny war-surplus motors to bicycles.

The Resources. Well, maybe the spirit exists, but what about the willingness to support innovation? Periodically we hear that American business people are too short-term oriented, too cost conscious, too scared of product litigation to take the risks to innovate. It is true that industrial spending on research and development in the United States stagnated from 1987 through to the mid-1990s. Reengineering and cost cutting certainly hurt R&D. Labs were closed or shrunk and researchers laid off. Just as important, the turmoil of downsizing tended to break the network of informal relationships that are so critical to getting research done in an organization. When researchers undertake a project that is both risky and iffy they need friends and sponsors, trusting relationships that take time to build.[5] However, industrial R&D spending started to pick up in

1995 and seems likely to continue showing real growth. In fact, U.S. industry is by far the world's biggest contributor to research and development.

Who's Falling Behind?

Although U.S. industry is often criticized for a shortsighted disregard for research, it is in fact the prime performer of research, not just in the United States, but globally, and not just in applied and developmental research, but in basic research too. U.S. industry paid for $113 billion of the $184 billion spent on R&D in the United States in 1996, or 62% of the total. While spending did stagnate from 1985 to 1995, the National Science Foundation estimated American businesses increased their R&D budgets by a real 3.5% in 1996 and the Industrial Research Institute said its members projected an increase of 5.6% for 1997. Since university spending on research is flat and the government has been cutting R&D spending since 1990, all the increase in research funds comes from business.

Total spending on R&D in the United States exceeds the combined totals for Japan, Germany, France, and Great Britain. However, in terms of spending as a percentage of gross domestic product, they are comparable. Spending on R&D in all five countries falls in a range between 2.19% (Britain) and 2.69% (Japan).

Business funds most of the pure or basic research in the United States—an estimated $6 billion in 1996, compared with $900 million funded by the government. Basic research accounted for 6% of business spending. Admittedly, though, the purity of that spending may be tainted by a trend to "directed basic research."

The Japanese are famous for the quality and volume of their developmental research—as well as their ability to copy. Toyota is probably the best and fastest developer of new cars and Japanese companies are indefatigable patent seekers. Among companies obtaining the most patents from the U.S. Patent Office in 1996, eight of the top 10 (see Figure 11.2) were Japanese. However, Japan performs pitifully in basic research—the source of future products. Japanese business focuses on applied and developmental research and the universities are underfunded and insular. Since 1970, just three Japanese have won Nobel prizes in physics, chemistry, and medicine, while 89 Americans have won or shared them, and Germany produced 16 winners and Britain 15. However, the Japanese government has endorsed a plan to invest $155 billion in science and technology by the year 2000.

Sources: Institute of Industrial Research, National Science Foundation, U.S. Patent and Trademark Office, *Business Week* (September 2, 1996).

FIGURE 11.1

Patent Champs

Although Japanese businesses and universities may be weak on basic research, they are geniuses at getting patents for new products. IBM has usually come in first in the number of patents granted by the United States Patent Office in recent years, but an increasing number of the runners-up are Japanese. No. 2 Canon spends 10% of its revenue on R&D, more than double the average of the top 100 American companies in R&D spending. Had the U.S. government been included, it would have ranked 7th in the 1996 list. Here are the rankings at six-year intervals since 1978, with the number of patents granted:

Rank	1978	1984	1990	1996
1	GE 820	GE 785	Hitachi 908	IBM 1,867
2	Westinghouse 488	IBM 608	Toshiba 891	Canon 1,538
3	IBM 449	Hitachi 596	Canon 868	Motorola 1,064
4	Bayer 434	Toshiba 539	Mitsubishi Electric 862	NEC 1,042
5	RCA 423	Philips 438	GE 785	Hitachi 961
6	Xerox 418	Canon 430	Fuji Photo Film 767	Mitsubishi Electric 932
7	Siemens 412	RCA 430	Eastman Kodak 720	Toshiba 912
8	Hitachi 387	Siemens 404	Philips 637	Fujitsu 868
9	DuPont 386	Mobil 370	IBM 608	Sony 854
10	Philips 364	Nissan Motor 372	Siemens 506	Matsushita Electric 852

Source: U.S. Patent & Trademark Office.

The Methods. Since the early 1980s in the United States, and earlier than that in Japan, new approaches have improved the process of innovation markedly. Since creativity is involved, there will always be differences between people, companies, and nations in their approach to innovation. Pharmaceutical companies will presumably continue to rely on the genius of outstanding individual scientists. Big industrial companies will presumably continue to deploy large teams of engineers.

Corporate research in the United States tends to be structured and staged. The Japanese are less formal and have also made an art of disseminating knowledge so as to spur more applications of new ideas, which is one reason Japanese companies win more U.S. patents than American companies (see Figure 11.2). "Organizational knowledge creation is the key to the distinctive way that Japanese companies innovate," write two leading Japanese business professors, Ikujiro Nonaka and Hirotaka Takeuchi, of Hitotsubashi University. "They are especially good at bringing about innovation continuously, incrementally, and spirally." What the authors are talking about is "the capability of a company as a whole to create new knowledge, disseminate it throughout the organization, and embody it in products, services, and systems."[6] (For more on the learning organizations, see Chapter 16).

New approaches to innovation are much like the new "lean" methods of manufacturing. The team approach to R&D is perhaps the most important of these tools. Now, instead of having engineers work in isolation on a new product and then, in the endlessly repeated phrase, "throwing it over the wall" to manufacturing, the team includes manufacturing people from the start, as well as people from marketing, suppliers, and so forth, who can contribute when it counts most, near the beginning. Some 80% of a product's cost is determined in the design stage.

From the team idea flows the associated idea of parallel or concurrent development. For example, the manufacturing process for a new product can be developed while the product itself is developed. That leads to another important emphasis in R&D—greater speed. The faster you can get a new product to market, the more likely you are to win a greater share. Computer-aided design makes it possible to turn concepts into drawings faster and more accurately, to test more of them, and to exchange them more readily with other designers. With good communications, companies can globalize their research teams, so while their American colleagues sleep, engineers in Indonesia and India can carry on their projects—and at salaries about one-third or less of what they are in the United States. "Value engineering" pushes designers to come up with products that are simpler and easier to make. The idea of handing over parts or all of a development project to partners or subcontractors is becoming popular as a way of getting help and spreading the risk of innovation. (For more on outsourcing, see Chapter 15.)

The focus on the customer has also spread to the R&D process. Bell Labs, General Motors, and other corporations have consumer centers attached to their central research labs. The big commercial customers are often included in the design teams for new projects so that they help design a product that suits them. Suppliers can also be drawn into the design work—or may design a piece of the product themselves. By marketing open systems, companies may get more out of a product than they could by keeping a proprietary system to themselves. They get a lot of help from the outside creating new uses and applications that will work with their products, which in turn makes their products more popular.

The Organization. By definition, small, new enterprises are at least entrepreneurial if not really innovative. But what about the large, successful, established enterprises? The most difficult and controversial part of innovation is how to keep the spirit alive in large organizations. Some of the best minds in business management disagree on how that can be done, or even whether it can be done. James Brian Quinn of the Amos Tuck school of business at Dartmouth College, who has made a study of innovation, believes that "the innovative environment is always dynamic, opportunistic, and unpredictable." The most innovative organizations, he writes, use some form of ad hoc "skunkworks," or small teams with extensive networks.[7] Henry Mintzberg of McGill University would agree. "The innovative organization cannot rely on any form of standardization for coordination," Mintzberg writes. "It must avoid all the trappings of bureaucratic structure."[8] By contrast, Peter Drucker argues that in the last 40 years *"purposeful* innovation—both technical and social—has itself become an organized discipline, which is both teachable and learnable." Therefore, he says, "every organization of today has to build into its very structure *the management of change.*"[9]

The argument between the organized and the fortuitous schools of thought about innovation might be partly semantic. The big breakthroughs, the ground-breaking innovation, probably cannot be planned and organized, but developmental innovations, the improvements or the new versions of existing products, which use most of our R&D resources, can to a large degree be organized, scheduled, and even budgeted. Still, a distinction remains between the two approaches and we can find examples of both today. But before examining these examples, let's look at another factor which is probably more important than any formal policy, and that is the ability to create an innovative culture.

3M: THE MOST INNOVATIVE

The 3M Company's culture nurtures both kinds of innovation, incremental and breakthrough. Among a number of novel management practices, 3M has a 15% research allowance: engineers are encouraged to spend 15% of their time working on a favorite idea, regardless of what their assignment may be. There's no management discipline attached to this free research time. In fact, there is no formal rule about the 15%. It's a tradition and the 15% is loosely applied. The idea came from William McKnight, who created the modern 3M during the 52 years he spent at the company, finishing up as chairman before retiring in 1966. The story they tell around 3M is that one day in the 1930s McKnight discovered a young technician, Richard Drew, trying to develop something called masking tape when he was supposed to be working on sandpaper. McKnight told Drew masking tape would never work and to get back to his sandpaper. Drew kept on with the masking tape until he had created a product that turned out to be one of 3M's most successful. McKnight, who fortunately did not have a big ego, then vowed not to get between 3M's engineers and their ideas. (Drew later invented Scotch tape.)

The culture created by this kind of legend is what makes 3M one of the world's most innovative companies. Engineers are given plenty of freedom and encouragement and they know they work in a company whose management is committed to innovation. The culture has had a long time to take hold and since 3M has always picked its leaders from inside the company the culture doesn't get disrupted. Unlike other companies which send their big brains off to pastoral settings where they can think undistracted, 3M concentrates its researchers around the corporate headquarters in St. Paul, Minnesota, where they can keep in touch with what the company is doing, attend forums, and exchange ideas with colleagues who become friends over the years. They are encouraged to get to know the customers, not just by asking them what they want, but by watching them enough to decipher the customer's "unarticulated needs," as 3M's senior vice president for R&D, William Coyne, puts it. The way 3M thinks and behaves is far more important than its formal structure. In *Fortune's* description, "Beneath its orderly, AAA-rated, Midwestern exterior, the place is dotty."

The most successful part of that dottiness is the 15% time allowance for researchers to spend doing their own things. Post-it Notes were invented in 1980 by an engineer on his time. Where would the world be today without Post-it Notes? They have proliferated into 56 shapes, 18 colors, 27 sizes, and 20 fragrances. A dozen competitors have tried unsuccessfully to copy the idea.

Having created a new product, 3M doesn't stop there. If it can, it uses the product to create a platform for a whole family of new products. Since 3M has an open, collegial atmosphere, ideas can migrate into different parts of the company. On his 15% time in 1964, a company scientist, Roger Appledorn, developed a way of focusing and brightening the image cast by overhead projectors. He created a plastic coating for the lens with a surface of tiny three-dimensional patterns. For years microreplication, as the new technology is called, remained a limited, one-purpose line. But around 1970, 3M saw that it could also be used to focus traffic lights so that only drivers coming from a particular direction could see them. In the 1970s and 1980s 3M found other optical uses for microreplication, the technology migrated into other areas, and in the 1990s its uses exploded.

Today microscopic prisms brighten the flat screens of most laptops by 50% and newer versions will extend the battery life of the laptops by using less power. Glass tubes coated on the inside with sheets of the stuff can be used as illuminated railings extending as far as 300 feet with just one bulb lighting the tube. The technology is used to make fasteners for diapers, to make ID cards that are hard to alter, and for mouse pads for computers. With some difficulty, 3M applied microreplication to abrasives and came up with all-purpose Apex. One grade can do rough or fine work on a variety of materials. That means a worker using sanding belts doesn't need to change the belt each time he needs a different "grit." After Dennis O'Connor's *Stars & Stripes* turned in disappointing performances in the trials for the 1987 America's Cup races in Australia, the hull was sheathed with a 3M plastic that replicated the rough surface of a shark's skin. Presumably it helped, since *Stars & Stripes* defeated *Kookaburra III*. The American sailors in the 1996 Olympics wanted to coat the hulls of their boats with the same material, but the Olympic

Committee turned them down. The company expects annual sales of microreplication products to exceed $1 billion by 2000.

In spite of 3M's success as an innovator, the company decided in the 1990s that it had to improve. To reach its goal of a 27% return on capital, it would have to focus R&D more clearly on big projects. One of the important measures of the success of a company's R&D is the "new sales ratio"—the proportion of sales attributable to new products. The sales goal ratio had been 25% of sales in products brought to market in the previous five years, but in 1993 3M raised that to 30% and four years—and achieved that level the next year. The goal tightened even more when 3M decided 10% should come from products introduced within the last year. Another important ratio is R&D spending as a percentage of sales—3M keeps that ratio at a relatively high 7% and didn't cut the dollar spending when business fell off in the mid-1900s.

But 3M also realized that to achieve the vision of being "the most innovative enterprise," as Vice Chairman Ronald Mitsch says, it would have to be "much more market channel and customer focused." R&D choices had been somewhat informal. "You picked a champion and he pushed you," says Thomas Wollner, head of the central research laboratories. "He had a lot of emotion involved. The top people used to go by their gut sense." A project with a $3-million sales potential would get as much attention as one with a $100-million potential. Moreover, as the company matured, R&D people had a tendency to do more incremental things, short-term improvements suggested by customers and salespeople.

In 1990 3M started a "pacing program" with the aim of selecting and pushing the most promising projects, ones that had a minimum sales potential of $20 million. By 1995 3M had 100 of these, and the ones that had reached the market were averaging $60 million in sales. But, says Mitsch, some divisions did not really push their pacing programs or reallocate resources. So in 1995, when 3M reorganized (see Chapter 6), it tightened the focus further with a "Pacing Plus" program that would identify projects with a potential of $100 to $1 billion in sales—things that could really change the basis of competition or redefine the markets— and put them at the top of the priority list. By the end of 1996, 3M had designated 30 Pacing Plus projects and two had reached the market (a breath-activated inhaler for asthmatics and a seven-day estrogen patch).

At the same time, 3M has somewhat formalized its approach to R&D, using larger teams with more team training and various techniques that came out of the quality movement. The teams are global, embracing labs that 3M has established overseas. The company is also relying more on outsiders, working jointly with companies such as Hewlett-Packard and licensing the output of nonprofit research institutions such as the Battelle Institute.

The pacing program "does not knock out grassroots stuff or skunkworks stuff," Mitsch maintains. "But it does state which projects are really going to make a difference. We are not going to be 100% correct, but I can almost guarantee you that we'll do better this way than just by trying to kick everything along at the same pace." At least half of 3M R&D spending still goes to projects that haven't been selected for pacing. As a signal that creativity matters as much as ever, however, 3M left the 15% elective time intact, without attaching performance or measurement standards. By doing this, 3M hopes to perform the difficult feat of making its R&D more market-directed while keeping that innovative culture alive.[10]

HEWLETT-PACKARD:
FIGHTING CREEPING ELEGANCE

Like 3M, Hewlett-Packard is enormously inventive. It too has a carefully nurtured culture that encourages innovations. Each of its 60-some divisions exists as a separate entrepreneurial business and when a business gets too big, it's broken down to keep the units small. Like his predecessors, CEO Lew Platt keeps that entrepreneurial spirit alive. "Most decisions are made by people who really are close to customers, not some corporate council that can slow innovation through bureaucracy," Platt says. "I work very hard every day to make sure centralization doesn't creep into our organization and slow people down." He encourages risk takers and is careful not to punish those who fail.

It's understandable that Platt preaches the gospel of innovation since HP depends even more than 3M on sales of new products. As Platt points out, a decade ago HP products had a life cycle that lasted years, whereas today nine to 18 months is more common. Where 3M says 30% of its sales should come from products introduced in the last four years (or 10% for one year), HP exists in such a fast-moving high-tech world that two-thirds of its revenues come from products introduced in the previous two years. HP introduces new PCs and printers to replace its older models as often as twice a year.

FIGURE 11.2

Big R&D Spenders

One good indicator of the scale of a company's R& D efforts is the ratio of total spending to total sales, or the R&D "intensity," as people in the field call it. Here are the ratios for the top ten biggest R&D spenders among American corporations in 1995 (dollar amounts are in billions):

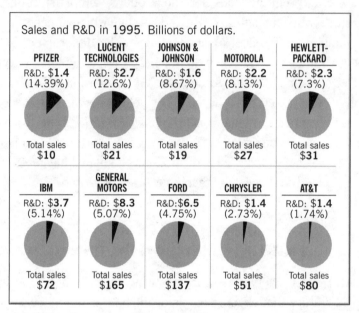

Source: Standard & Poor's Compustat, August, 1996.

HP has evolved policies that clearly get the most out of the 7.3% of company revenue that it spends on R&D. (For spending by other companies, see Figure 11.2.) Through its participation in a Sloan Foundation study, HP learned that the critical part of a successful development project comes right at the beginning, when the product is defined. The description begins with ensuring that the product fits the organization's strategy, then looks at the customers' needs, confirms that the company has the necessary skills, and so on through ten steps. If any step is skipped or performed poorly, the resulting domino effect increases the level of damage as the project grows. The most common mistake comes right at the beginning, in failing to understand the users' needs. To avoid that risk, HP spends plenty of time with the customers, watching what they do—"almost like cultural anthropology," says Platt. In fact HP did hire cultural anthropologists in England to watch "mobile professionals" in action to see how they would use HP equipment.

To assess the quality of the definition, HP hands a questionnaire to everyone associated with the project asking them, for example, how important the project is to achieving the division's strategic objectives. The answers, says Platt, have given HP insights into what is likely to work. Better definitions have helped fight the sin of what Platt calls "creeping elegance"—the urge that makes engineers want to keep adding features while a product is being developed. In the last ten years HP has reduced the average number of "design turns"—that is, the number of times a design has to be returned for a new version—from six or seven to two.

The results of HP's approach to innovation show up in many new products—PCs, workstations, servers, printers, and scientific and medical equipment and software. Behind it lies an almost paranoid fear of being left behind. Platt would rather cannibalize his own products than let the competition kill them.[11]

XEROX: END RUN AROUND BUREAUCRACY

Large successful companies are famously incapable of exploiting their best ideas. Their bureaucracies stifle innovation. Sometimes the companies try to outsmart their own bureaucrats by going around them and sponsoring "intrapreneurships" that in theory will be free to innovate. In practice these dependent start-ups rarely escape the corporate fetters and the approach hasn't won much of a following. However, Xerox has had some success. In the late 1980s Xerox finally saw that too many of the great ideas coming out of its Palo Alto Research Center were being used by others because Xerox hadn't seen their potential. "We invented the laser printer, the local area network, the PC, the mouse," says Bill Buehler, executive vice president. "It's phenomenal what's come out of our research facility." But it was the likes of Steve Jobs and Bill Gates who actually saw their potential and sold them successfully in Macintosh computers and Microsoft software. When a whole book called *Fumbling the Future* was devoted to Xerox's missed opportunities, David Kearns, then CEO, thumped the book down on the desk of Robert Adams, one of the company's senior executives, and said, "I don't ever want this to happen again."

Adams became CEO of Xerox Technology Ventures (XTV), the company's end run around its own bureaucracy. XTV, established in 1989, takes promising ideas out of Xerox and puts them in startup companies with the help of regular venture capital. The Xerox executive or researcher who goes with a spin-off has no assurance of getting back into Xerox if the venture fails, but gets his or her share of a 20% piece of the enterprise if it succeeds. Xerox could hold on to the company or take it public. XTV launched a dozen startups, two of which went public. XTV is being absorbed into a new business development arm of the company called Xerox New Enterprises. Xerox now intends to retain a majority interest in any new startup, but without losing the venturesome, nonbureaucratic spirit of XTV.

To alert its leaders to good ideas, Xerox also created a technology decision-making board which brings together operational engineers and research scientists once a month to talk about emerging technology and what they have that might work. "The stuff that's commercially viable goes into a holding area to nurture it and if it looks like it's going to have some customer appeal, they put it into a division," Buehler explains. Another forum Xerox created looks at the architecture of new products to make sure that products from different divisions of Xerox are compatible and can talk to each other. Large customers want total systems and they don't want a printer with one architecture, a scanner with another, and a copier with yet another.[12]

AMERICAN EXPRESS: AN AVALANCHE OF CARDS

At the end of 1993, American Express had 11 cards (the regular old green card, plus various gold, platinum, senior, corporate, and student charge cards, and its first credit card, the Optima). By the end of 1996, Amex had 36 cards, including the first co-branded card, with Delta. Amex kept pouring out cards: additional co-branded cards with ITT-Sheraton and Qantas, platinum cards in Italy and France, credit cards in Hong Kong and Canada. It launched a special card for gold enthusiasts and tested a "smart" corporate card with a chip embedded. In addition, American Express put its name on co-branded cards issued by other companies, including the credit arms of the French auto companies, Peugeot and Citroën. Having for years spurned issuing cards through banks, it campaigned to break through the VISA by-laws that prohibit Visa banks from selling other cards. It got its first bank card in the United States through Natwest Bank (not a VISA member).

As the company's CEO, Harvey Golub, explained it, "we are deliberately cannibalizing the consumer charge card business to grow other businesses—when it better serves our customers and shareholders—by offering small business cards, credit cards, corporate cards, and co-branded cards." Golub wants to introduce more cards faster. Although the Optima True Grace card, Amex's first revolving credit card, was introduced successfully in 1994, it took the company 18 months to launch it. By Golub's reckoning that was far too slow. "Our competitors had a True Grace clone in the market within seven weeks of our launch," he says. He wants to get Amex's launch time down to six to eight weeks, or the time it takes to order plastic, and to raise the pace of introductions to 15 to 20 new cards a year. American Express put out 14 in 1996. This blizzard of innovation is intended to stem the loss of Amex's market share to VISA and MasterCard. Golub argues that the banks should join the American Express network as a way of "differentiating their card products from the avalanche of new bank cards saturating the market." Presumably, the American Express brand name makes its avalanche better than those other avalanches.

American Express's information technology is the key to its ability to introduce new products rapidly. Since Amex operates a "closed loop"— that is, unlike other companies, it issues the card, deals with the merchants, and handles the billing—it has information about its customers that other card companies don't have. As Amex builds its data warehouse, it acquires data that helps it segment the market, find new niches, decide what cards to issue, and find the people who will be interested in them. To get the cards out faster Amex uses multidiscipline teams so that all the players who make the important decisions get together from the beginning. Amex has studied the process of decision making to help the teams make the right tradeoffs, to get the most benefit from the least investment. Executives who follow the process successfully get more funding and bigger projects, while the less successful ones get managed more tightly.

In its zeal to get out more cards, Amex has gone beyond its "closed loop" and signed on partners who are allowed to issue American Express cards themselves and who handle the customer and merchant relationships. By the end of 1995, Amex's deals with eight foreign banks had produced 500,000 new members and $1 billion in charges. But the open loop also loosens the relationship that allows Amex to build its warehouse of data about customers—the thing that differentiates its cards from the bank cards.[13]

A BIG MENU

The tension between the contradictory needs of nurturing creativity and following a structured process is something that no innovative company will probably ever fully resolved. The sources of creativity cannot be pinned down to a formula. Logically, creativity would flourish most where it has the most freedom and encouragement, but it certainly can flourish among the oppressed, the impoverished, and the paranoid, as the lives of any number of inventors, artists, and writers prove. Of course, much of the innovation in business falls short of being really creative. Making marginal improvements on existing products and services doesn't take genius—and that kind of innovation can certainly be organized.

But what about the big breakthroughs? The important inventions? Most of them will always come from the entrepreneur, the start-up, the scientist or inventor. But large organizations can do much better than they have done. Part of the answer lies in the kind of culture found in a place like 3M, an openness and receptivity that becomes part of the corporate mind-set. It lies also in giving individuals the opportunity to create their own skunkworks, as 3M does with the 15% rule and Xerox with Xerox New Enterprises.

Corporate creativity requires a certain dexterity, the ability to do one thing well while preparing to do something different. When transistors came along, RCA wasted time worrying about whether shifting to transistors would spoil its profitable market for vacuum tubes and ended up with neither. The Swiss watch industry invented and ignored quartz technology, then shrank to less than half its size when Seiko walked off with the quartz business. RCA and the Swiss watchmakers couldn't juggle two ideas at once.[14] To innovate successfully, a company will need to juggle a lot of things.

Managing innovation is a complex, tricky process. A corporation needs to keep its eye on as many as seven different innovation activities: (1) R&D on forthcoming products, (2) support and extension of current products, (3) fundamental research related to strategic goals, (4) development related to strategic goals, (5) the internal infrastructure of research labs, (6) the external R&D relationships through joint ventures and partnerships, and (7) the blue-sky inventions that may come of inspiration or genius.

Stephen Rudolph, vice president for technology at Arthur D. Little Incorporated, believes that a corporation needs to develop "a big menu, a rich flow of products that exceeds its ability to invest in." Since predicting is hard and any organization will make some bad choices, it needs to develop more opportunities than it can exploit—and it's easier to kill projects that aren't showing enough promise when you have a big pool to choose from. One of the strengths of corporate R&D in Japan is that the Japanese fire broadsides of new products while Americans tend to target more narrowly. The Japanese practice may result in more failures, but it also reveals new product niches, and covers more ground. Rudolph describes what he sees as four stages of technology (emerging, pacing, key, and base) and argues that you should always feed the pipeline to make sure you don't find yourself suddenly with no competitive advantage. "The short-term guys" will always fight the long-term investment needed to push emerging technologies ahead, but some of those technologies will be what give a company its edge in the future.[15]

Pointers

- Do you have a culture that nurtures innovation, gives people the freedom to follow good ideas (and make mistakes), and encourages a healthy flow of information around the company?
- Do you assign your development projects to teams that include people from marketing, manufacturing, finance, and other parts of the company?
- Do you make sure that your customers and your suppliers contribute to the development process?
- Do you have a systematic way of identifying the most promising R&D projects and giving them priority treatment?

- Do you have a balanced portfolio of projects ranging from blue-sky R&D to product extensions?
- Do you have a balanced portfolio of low-risk and high-risk projects?
- Is the pipeline of new products properly filled from beginning to end so that you can produce a cadenced flow of introductions?
- Are you willing to let your new products cannibalize your existing products, and are you able to do one thing well while preparing to launch another?
- Are you speeding the introduction of new products?
- Even if the products or services you sell are not subject to much innovation, are you looking for ways to innovate distribution, marketing, processes, and management?
- Are you developing platforms of new products which can be the basis for a family of extensions?
- Even though genius cannot perform on schedule, do you have a methodical process for developing products?

Links

- Innovation is not just the concern of development engineers, but also of manufacturing, marketing, sales, legal, and other departments.
- The costs, scope, and risks of innovation today will often require partners, joint ventures, or consortia.

Cautions

- Innovation needs to be on the leading edge of technology, but not ahead of it.
- Innovators will always have to resist the calls of short-termers to switch spending to things that will pay off immediately.
- R&D needs to be organized, but not bureaucratized.

12

STEPPING UP THE PACE

It's not the big companies that eat the small;
it's the fast that eat the slow
—*Wall Street Journal*

Ultimately, speed is the only weapon we have.
—Andrew Grove[1]

The idea that everything must be done faster has surfaced repeatedly in the earlier chapters of this book. New products and services must be first to market or they'll fail to win their potential market share. Flexible factories switch the models coming off their assembly lines in a moment, responding to reports of that day's sales flashed from cash registers across the country. With the help of information technology, managers assemble data from all over the world to make an informed decision on a strategic issue in hours instead of weeks. Research projects keep going 24 hours a day as labs on one continent hand their day's work electronically to labs on the next continent in the sun's path. What's the rush? Speed alone will not make a company successful in the 21st century. Doing everything in a rush will probably do more harm

SEI Survey	
Speeding up all of a company's processes has become critical	79%
We are doing that	21%

than good. The effective approach to speed is not to hurry up or to skip important steps, but to get there sooner by eliminating waste and improving processes. In fact, the most important thing about speed is not necessarily to work faster but to learn faster.

In high-tech industries, tougher competition, faster technological change, and shorter product life cycles are all working to pressure business to work faster. "Shorter life cycles mean that whoever gets there first garners the bulk of market share while the remainder are left to compete on price," writes Christopher Meyer, a management consultant who specializes in speed. "Those who are late find that the product life cycle ends too soon after introduction, thus making the cost of each development quite expensive."[2]

Business leaders are clearly fascinated by the power of speed. Some executives, like Andy Grove of Intel, would make speed the governing driver for a company's activities. Jack Welch keeps referring to speed in his well-crafted letters in the GE annual reports as one of the "behaviors" that define GE. "*Faster,* in almost every case, is *better,*" he wrote in the 1994 report. "From decision-making to deal-making, to communications to product introduction, speed, more often than not, ends up being the competitive differentiator." In the 1993 report he said:

> While speed has had its most striking impact on our new product introduction process—the driver of tomorrow's top-line growth—it's most immediate quantitative impact has been on our asset management. Focusing on the speed of our order-to-remittance cycle—from time of order to when we get paid—has increased our inventory turns 27% in two years, throwing off almost $2 billion in cash in the process.
>
> Speed "redefines capacity," reducing plant and equipment investment. In the past three years, our faster pace has freed up nearly five million square feet of manufacturing space across the company. To a business like plastics, that has meant a savings of nearly one-half billion dollars that would have been required for new capacity—like getting a new plant, free.
>
> Speed is allowing us to shift the center of gravity of the company rapidly toward the high-growth areas of the world, particularly Asia. . . . And finally, speed, in the form of a technique called quick market intelligence, originally learned from Wal-Mart and evolved and adapted in our business, has GE leadership at all levels of the company, in every business, living in the field with customers.[3]

In spite of his enthusiasm for speed, Welch is careful to situate it as one of several keys to GE's actions. The list of his keys changes from year to year, but speed is always there. He doesn't make the mistake of seizing on speed as the panacea that will ensure a company's success, which is what happened in some companies in the 1980s when the power of speed was first widely recognized. Speed is a powerful management weapon, but it has its unintended consequences. When will computer owners get fed up with too many software updates and too frequent model changes? And what happens when a company that has hyped its profits with a torrent of new products runs out of steam, as seems inevitable sooner or later? Those impressive sales and profits may turn out to be a temporary blip.

KINGSTON: A HIGH-VELOCITY MARKET

Kingston Technology Corporation of Fountain Valley, California, built its enormous success on the idea that it can fill an order for computer memory upgrades in 24 hours. When John Tu, a quiet, studious emigrant from Shanghai by way of Germany, and the younger David Sun, a boisterous native of Taiwan, founded the company in 1987 they had some creative ideas about the company. It would be like a Chinese family. Employees would come first, suppliers second, and customers third (the assumption being that happy employees and well-treated suppliers will do the best for the customer). Tu and Sun prefer to do business on the basis of trust rather than complicated legal documents. And they made speed critical to their business.

When Tu and Sun entered the business of providing memory upgrades for computers it was the norm to take two weeks or more to fill an order. They saw a chance to change the market by cutting that time down to one day. "We've created a computer industry that believes that everything is more or less the same as anything else," says Gary MacDonald, vice president for marketing at Kingston. "It's all a commodity market. They are essentially virtual products, things that can be acquired anywhere, anytime, and in any quantity. If I can't get it from you, I'll get it from someone who is equivalent to you. It's only when things are perceived as unique that the customers are tolerant of delay. Speed is intrinsic to the industry. It is a high velocity market."

The market for Kingston's memory add-ons and other upgrades is built on the familiar experience of computer owners who find that their brand-new hardware almost immediately becomes inadequate because some more powerful, demanding application has come along. Businesses often want the upgrade delivered along with the new computers. Kingston can fill the orders out of a tight five-day inventory of components that it tries to keep on hand, updating it constantly and anticipating what customers are going to order. Kingston can replenish its finished product inventory rapidly by sending the circuit boards and other ingredients with the specifications out to two closely allied manufacturers five minutes away by truck from its offices in Fountain Valley. The finished items come back the same day. Every afternoon the FedEx trucks begin to back up against the loading dock and that day's orders, typically thousands of items worth about $200 each, start moving out for delivery the next day.

"It's like an orbiting warehouse in the sky," says MacDonald. Kingston has no inventory of finished products on hand, although it does keep a lean inventory of boards and other materials necessary to make the add-ons. The trick is to anticipate what the market is going to want. When Compaq introduces a new computer, Kingston tries to have the memory upgrades designed and ready to go at the moment the computer hits the market. Microsoft's introduction of Windows 95 produced a predictable surge in the demand for upgrades. If a customer requests an entirely new upgrade that Kingston has not yet designed, then delivery may take two days. MacDonald compares the operation to a Burger King because you have a basic stock, in this case boards rather than buns and ground beef, and a collection of ingredients, electronic instead of edible. You assemble them according to the customers' demands and your success depends on learning to anticipate the demands and then applying operational excellence to filling the orders correctly and quickly.

"You have to have a general sense of what product mix is likely, and then just have your active inventory," says MacDonald. "That's one of the things we do here incredibly well." Well enough so that Kingston now has 40% of the market for PC upgrades. Sales climbed rapidly from $120,000 in the first year, 1987, often doubling each year. They crossed the $1 billion threshhold in 1995 and grew rapidly in 1996, but Kingston won't reveal the amount because the company was acquired for $1.5 billion by Softbank, a Japanese company with a similar culture that puts workers first.[4] The ingredients that go into Kingston's hardware are standard. What makes the product competitive is speed. So long as quality and service don't suffer, the speedy win.

SNAIL MAIL

When we work with computers we seem to become so infected with their speed—with time stated in terms of millions or even billions of instructions per second—that we want everything to move at warp speed and delay becomes intolerable. Our lives do, in fact, move faster. Banks have finally awakened to the obvious fact that people detest standing in line for more than a few minutes to get access to their own money, so we now have shorter lines and ATMs. We have virtually instant access to our records, whether they are at the brokerage house or the Social Security Administration. The airlines can make a reservation and assign a seat in a couple of minutes. L.L. Bean and Lands' End will deliver an order in a day or two with the help of FedEx or UPS. Lenscrafters makes us a pair of glasses in 60 minutes. We are no longer willing to wait 45 to 60 days for a car ordered to our specifications, so Ford is trying to shrink that cycle to 15 days.

Customers come to expect that everything be done quickly. We want faster modems, faster printers, faster copiers. Businesses learn that it's important to respond quickly to customers' inquiries. Not only has that bank shortened its lines, but it may also be able to answer your queries by phone at 1 A.M. with an automated system or, if necessary, a live banker.

Some sluggards survive still, and may even be getting worse. It takes weeks to get a watch repaired. Ask a furniture store to order you a new sofa, and you probably won't get it for ten weeks or so. The airlines may make your reservations in a few minutes, but they still haven't figured out how to keep boarding an aircraft from being an ordeal of discomfort and delay. And the United States Postal Service, like the post offices of many other countries, has achieved the unusual feat of slowing down with automation. The Postal Service can deliver a letter in a day, so long as you are willing to pay $10.75 for overnight delivery, which is what you used to get for a first-class stamp when it cost 4 cents. But thanks to fax, FedEx, phone, and e-mail, the postal service has become almost irrelevant for important communications.

The systematic, organized acceleration of business has appeared over the years in a variety of guises and under a number of labels. Just-in-time manufacturing is the most venerable and perhaps the best known. The fact that some of these techniques have been around for years indicates that speed is not a fad, but nor does it mean that business has really yet learned how to be fast.

THE DISCIPLINE OF SPEED

The idea of just-in-time manufacturing can be traced to the late Taiichi Ohno, an up-from-the-shop-floor Toyota executive and the architect of the Toyota production system, which is probably the best ever devised. Those prone to think of management ideas as passing fads should consider that the JIT idea was planted in Ohno's head in the early 1950s when he began to think about how to eliminate the waste that made a Japanese worker so much less productive than an American worker. He made JIT one of the two pillars of the Toyota production system, the other being what he called "autonomation," or "automation with a human touch."

The tool for making JIT work was *kanban,* an idea that Ohno got from the American supermarket on a visit to the United States in 1956. In contrast to the archaic system of distributing food in Japan at the time, largely through street peddlars, the supermarket was a place where customers could get what they wanted, when they wanted it, and at the time they wanted it. Supermarket operators made sure the flow of goods responded to the demand. The *kanban* or order card applied the supermarket idea to the factory by creating a way for workers at one point to order just what they needed, just in time, from up the line.

It took decades for Toyota to get all its processes up to speed. Die changes, which took two to three hours in the 1940s, were cut to between 15 minutes and one hour in the 1950s, and to three minutes by the late 1960s. By Ohno's estimate it took ten years to establish *kanban* in Toyota, which adopted the process company-wide in 1962.[5]

As many American companies that adopted JIT in the 1980s discov-

ered, it can be a powerful weapon that can have benefits far beyond simply getting products out faster. A large company like General Motors can
reduce inventories by billions of dollars. The size of factories can be reduced too, because all that work in progress isn't hanging around, perhaps rusting, or getting damaged. Warehouses can be reduced or
eliminated. JIT is a tough disciplinarian that puts everyone on their toes.
Defects in parts or processes that could be concealed by a fat inventory
now surface immediately and have to be corrected immediately.

However, as Ohno had warned in oracular fashion, "a halfhearted introduction of *kanban* brings a hundreds harms and not a single gain."[6]
Unless a whole lot of other changes are made at the same time, JIT can
create chaos. Quality must be superb, transportation, warehousing, accounting, and accounts payable systems have to be redesigned, and the
whole network of suppliers must be brought into the system. In Japan,
the adoption of JIT was far from universal or wholehearted. While Toyota did refine its system to the point of getting deliveries to the factories
every few hours, Nissan didn't push the idea beyond daily deliveries
(which was a big improvement over the one-month inventories Nissan
used to carry). Japan's congested streets and terrible highways turned
out to be the biggest obstacle to pushing JIT further. Trucks with their
engines pouring out pollutants stacked up in the neighborhoods around
JIT plants, waiting to make their deliveries at the right moment. Even the
auto companies saw they would have to modify their schedules.

Good highways and easy access to plants made JIT deliveries in the
United States easier, but the idea proved disappointing in other ways.
The high quality of supplies and the trust necessary between supplier
and customer often doesn't exist. JIT makes a company more vulnerable
to disruptions such as strikes, bad weather, and parts shortages. Many
American companies saw just-in-time not as part of a whole effort to
achieve a lean production system but as a way to cut costs by squeezing
suppliers. In effect, the burden of carrying inventory shifted from the
prime contractor to the supplier. That, of course, defeated the whole purpose of JIT because the potential cost, quality, and flexibility benefits
were not realized. The supplier that ships just in time but doesn't update
its accounting procedures to collect money faster gets no financial benefit: it simply replaces the inventory asset with an accounts receivable
asset. JIT proved not to be the panacea that so many managers seek, but

it is widely used and—although barely mentioned now in the fad-chasing business press—certainly will be one of the tools of the 21st century enterprise. Applied selectively, with the proper analysis, it works very well. There is not much point, for example, in requiring frequent shipments of small, cheap electronic components from distant plants, but it makes sense to make frequent deliveries of bulky materials made nearby.

TEXTILES: THE POWER OF SPEED

Other techniques for speeding business processes have appeared since JIT, with names like Quick Response, Fast Cycle Time, Efficient Consumer Response, and Time-Based Competition. The textile and apparel industries sorely needed to move faster. What changes faster than fashion? Yet in the early 1980s, it took the industry 66 weeks to move a piece of fabric through the pipeline. Roger Milliken, chairman of the family-owned textile business based in Spartanburg, South Carolina, conservative to an extreme in politics but quite a daring innovator in business, discovered the power of speed. Factories made for long production runs had to be redesigned to handle short runs and quick changes. Distribution points had to be eliminated or streamlined. Information had to flow quickly throughout the chain. The Milliken company cut its lead time for deliveries from 42 days in the early 1980s to seven days in the 1990s, started filling orders for small batches of materials that it would not have bothered with before, and its on-time record got close to 100%.[7]

The quick response concept spread around the apparel and textile industries and into other industries. It involved major expenditures and reorganizations of some of the largest apparel companies. Levi Strauss & Company, unhappy with the service it was giving its customers, announced in 1993 a $500-million program to speed the delivery of its jeans and other clothing. In 1995, it increased the amount to $850 million, of which about one-third was for improving distribution.[8]

Information technology has made it all possible. Companies now have a clearer idea of what's happening all along the line and can integrate their supply chains. Detailed point-of-sale information, created automatically at the checkout counter, flashes right back to the plant and the supplier so that they know from day to day what is selling and what to replenish. New standardized bar codes, advance shipping notices, and, for overseas shipments, pre-clearance through customs have all helped speed response. Since the cost of distribution often exceeds the costs of manufacture, companies have radically changed their ideas about warehouses and transportation. A lot can happen in a warehouse to delay shipments—clothing has to be unpacked, verified, ticketed, given a security label, and put on a hanger. That may take four to six days. But if the merchandise comes in "floor ready" the stay at the warehouse can be cut to a few hours.[9]

TRANSPORTATION: ELIMINATING THE STOPS

Even if it weren't good for serving the customer better, speeding and synchronizing the whole supply chain makes economic sense because the costs of storage have grown faster than the costs of transportation. Speed changes the role of the warehouse and its design. Instead of being a place to store things it becomes a place for processing shipments. The retail and apparel industries are consolidating their warehouses and distribution centers. When Federated Department Stores merged with Macy's it cut the number of distribution centers in the Northeast from five to two. Shippers such as United Parcel are thinking of the day when goods will be transported from the factory or, in the case of imports, from the port of entry, directly to the point of sale, skipping the intervening warehouses and distribution centers.

When Levi Strauss started its $850-million restructuring of its distribution system, Bob Rockey, president for North America then, pointed out that it took seven to 14 days for Levi Strauss to fill an order and the store might take another four to 12 days to put the goods on the shelves. "That's from two to four weeks to replenish what's already sold out," he said, "—a month of consumers who are potentially unsatisfied." He said Levi Strauss intended to cut the time it took to replenish sold-out goods in the stores from 14 to three days and he wanted suppliers to deliver fabrics in three weeks instead of 16.[10]

The adoption of the quick response method can be extremely expensive and can require major changes in a corporation's process, so although the techniques are successful their adoption has been slow. Moreover, the information technology that makes speed possible is more powerful today than it was even a few years ago. The bar codes can carry more detailed information. The idea of using speed as a competitive tool has taken hold all over business—in banking (reducing the time required to approve loans, for example), in autos (the time to develop new models), office products (reducing inventory and increasing inventory turns), as well as textiles, retailing, and manufacturing in general. George Stalk, a Boston Consulting Group vice president who specializes in "time-based competition," states that companies that implement these techniques cut waiting time 60% and inventories 50% to 60% in two years, as well as achieving productivity and quality improvements.[11]

AUTOS: STRETCH GOALS

The auto companies use speed to compete on three levels: (1) how fast they can develop a new model, (2) how quickly they introduce new models, and (3) how quickly can they deliver the car when the customer orders it. In the early 1980s, Detroit discovered that Japanese manufacturers could do all these things much faster than the Big Three. They have made great progress since, but are still relatively slow.

When an American sees a new car he wants, he wants it right now, off the lot if possible. A Japanese consumer goes about car buying more deliberately, studying and thinking about the choices. But it is the Japanese who gets the specially ordered car first. Back before speed became a competitive as well as a cost and quality improvement strategy, it took up to 26 days to deliver a Toyota and 45 to 60 days to deliver a Ford. Slow distribution and slow information handling caused most of the delay. The actual assembly of the car did not offer much potential for improvement. However, Toyota did cut the time it takes to build a car from two days to one day, and Ford has now converted most of its plants to 24-hour assembly. Better information technology gets the customers' orders right back to the assembly plant and beyond to the supplier—so the car and its components are pulled through the system. Toyota can deliver a car in a week in Japan, and Ford has set a "stretch goal" of delivery in two weeks, which means redesigning the whole pipeline.[12]

The annual model changes, at least the superficial alterations of chrome and body metal, used to be a sacred rite in Detroit. Getting "Job #1" out the door on time was everything. Today at Ford, Job #1 doesn't mean the first car in a new production run but assuring quality. Annual model changes are no longer important. Getting significantly different new models out every four or five years is important. But that may be the limit. Honda's CEO, Nobuhiko Kawamoto, sees a danger in trying to shorten the life span of a model any further. He says Japanese customers are buying more European cars precisely because their manufacturers don't change models so often. Honda doesn't plan to shorten (or lengthen) its four-year model cycle.[13]

The most significant kind of time-based competition is the third kind, the length of time it takes to develop a new car. The development cycle is important not because we need to change models faster, but because speed creates enormous cost savings and quality improvement, and gives the automaker the flexibility to compete with the right product at the right time—while the fashion or fad remains hot. Fast development gives the manufacturer a weapon to hurl at the competition.

Development cycles are sometimes hard to pin down because of differences in stating starting and finishing times, but certainly American producers have been slower than the Japanese. In the mid-1980s, for example, it took the Japanese an average of 46 months to develop a new car and the Americans 60 months.[14] By then the Japanese were well along in developing a lean production system, but the Americans were only beginning to get the idea. The creation of three new competing family sedans illustrates the strength of speed. Ford decided in 1980 to create the Taurus, and GM decided in 1981 to make a competing car platform designated the GM-10. The Taurus, designed by a team with the real power to command the resources it needed, came on the market five years after the start. It had some initial quality problems but ultimately was very successful. Although the GM-10 was nominally a team effort, in fact it was designed the old way with a lot of pushing and pulling between different divisions and no strong team leader. The first model, a Buick Regal coupe, didn't come off the assembly lines in Flint until 1988, seven years after the start. It had serious quality problems at first and it took two more years for other GM models on the GM-10 platform to reach the showroom. Even Saturn, designed the new way in a new kind of factory, took six years to get to market (1984–1990). While all this was going on in Detroit during the 1980s, Honda had gone through two generations of Accords and in 1986 decided to build another larger Accord to compete with the two new American family cars from Ford and GM. This Accord reached the market in 1989 and was so successful that it competed with the Taurus for the title of the best-selling car in the United States.

Look at the U.S. manufacturers in the mid-1990s. They have all made great progress in developing cars faster, but the Japanese are still well ahead. Honda and Toyota have both got their development time below three years. Toyota is shooting at an 18-month goal and Honda at 24 months. Chrysler is close behind at 29 months, but also has a goal of 24 months. GM was still taking 48 months from concept to production in 1995, but with a new innovation process aims to cut that to 38 months, then 26, and eventually 20 or 22 months. Ford planned to go from 36 months to below 24 months.[15]

The other manufacturers have adopted essentially the same methods to speed development which were pioneered by Toyota. Each new project is turned over to a multifunctional team with a strong leader, what the Japanese call a *shusa*. He has the power to command the resources the team needs. Development and manufacturing engineers work together to make sure that the design is manufacturable and that the tools to make the car are ready when the design is finished. Traditionally in the United States the manufacturing engineers would take over only when the design engineers had finished, and the company would spend twice as much on the development as on the manufacturing. In Japan the proportions of spending are reversed and the factory people start to work on the manufacturing process at the beginning, so when the new car is ready so are the plants. Simplicity in design, reduction in the number of parts, and bringing suppliers, dealers, customers, and top managers into the process early on all play a role in speeding design. Building families of cars on standard platforms makes it quicker and cheaper to develop new models. With computer-aided design, parts are more likely to be compatible from the outset. Ford even claims to use its communications technology and labs around the world to keep development work going around the clock, with a lab in Detroit handing work over to a lab in Asia when it closes up for the day, and so on to Europe and back to Detroit the next morning.

In the auto industry, as in others, speed reduces inventories, the size of plants and warehouses, and the amount of capital tied up. If it takes a 500-person design team two years instead of four years to create a new car, the costs obviously drop dramatically. Speed exposes quality mistakes right away, rather than after a long production run of faulty products. Speed allows a company to be more responsive to the customer, to mass-customize the products, or rapidly change the models, colors, or whatever features the customers seem to prefer.

Does it matter if new automobiles can now be developed faster than the models themselves change, that is, in two years versus four or five years? It does, because speed creates options and flexibility as well as saving money. The company that develops new products more rapidly can respond to consumer taste as those tastes change, or it can delay the start of a new development project to see where the market is going.

Speed, properly applied, has profound effects up and down a company and has many applications. Speed can be applied to decision making, and can even involve the customers. If a company wants to be agile, decisions need to be made faster and that means distributing power to push decisions as close to the market as possible. When you have a new product, achieving peak sales and getting maximum market penetration quickly are both important too.

The development of the IBM's AS/400 family of midsized computers in the late 1980s opened that company's eyes to how much customers could help speed the process—and in general improve it and the product. An earlier project to replace a mess of incompatible midsized computers got into such trouble that IBM abandoned it in 1985 and started a whole new project code-named Silverlake at the IBM facility in Rochester, Minnesota. Because of the delay, Silverlake had to produce its AS/400 new computer in three years instead of the usual six. Silverlake got stuck by a disagreement over whether AS/400 should be able to use applications from earlier systems. The Silverlake executives decided to invite lead customers to help them decide, a move totally contrary to IBM's tradition of extreme secrecy. The panel was so helpful not only on that point but on others too, that the Silverlake team began convening regular customer panels, not only in Rochester, but in Japan and Europe too. With the help of customers, Silverlake met the three-year target— and even before it went on sale hundreds of customers had already developed thousands of applications for the new system. "We reaped a virtual bumper crop of benefits," members of the team said in describing the contribution of customers.[16]

THE LIMITS OF SPEED

In industries, such as electronics, in which new products appear constantly, a fast development cycle is even more important than in the auto industry. A 1983 study by Donald G. Reinertsen of McKinsey & Company is still frequently quoted to demonstrate how important speed is to the success of a new product. Based on modeling studies rather than actual experience, the study concluded that if a product is six months late to market its potential lifetime earnings will drop by 33%. But if the development costs run 50% over budget, the profits will only be reduced by 3.5%. So hang the expenses and work faster.

However, the McKinsey study also made some further points that don't seem to get quoted by the advocates of speed. The study attached the overriding importance of speed over cost of development specifically to a product with short life (five years) in a fast-growing market (20% a year) with rapid price erosion (12% a year). However, if a product has a long life (20 years) in a slow-growing market (7%) with no price erosion, then the cost of a six-month delay is only 7% of potential profits (and the penalty for an overrun in development costs is still trivial). But in the slow market the cost of the product itself is of overriding importance. If the product is priced 9% too high, that will cut the lifetime profits by 45%. Pricing too high in a fast-growing market also cuts the total profits, but only by 22%. Therefore, the relative importance of speed and production costs depends on the market. "The new-product race does not always go to the swift," Reinertsen wrote. "Speed is sometimes secondary and, if unduly emphasized, can lead to disaster."[17]

Reinertsen said recently that the misuse of his study has been a thorn in his side for years. "What everyone picked up is the cost of a six-month delay," he says. "It's easier to make that into a slogan and stick it on the wall than it is to make an analysis. My real message was that you have to make the analysis." He points out there are lots of products with ten- or even 30-year life cycles, screwdrivers and electrical connectors, for example. The cost of delaying the introduction of a new screwdriver will probably be very low. Most managers have no idea how to calculate the cost of delay and when asked to come up with estimates produce wildly different numbers. But if they analyze the facts surrounding the product and its market, they can make reasonably accurate estimates.[18]

Christoph-Friedrich von Braun, former head of technology strategy at R&D for the Siemens Corporation, has argued that shorter product life cycles (i.e., faster-paced innovation) can raise sales or profits so long as the cycles keep getting shorter, but inevitably a limit will be reached some time before the cycle reaches zero. When that limit is reached, the increase in sales and profits will prove at best to have been a temporary spike. Sales will settle back down to their former level. "Only during the switch from longer to shorter cycles will total revenues surge," von Braun wrote in a theoretical analysis in the *Sloan Management Review* in 1990. "Total revenues of the company will not increase on a sustained basis."[19]

As von Braun's research makes clear, a distinction should be made between two kinds of speed—the cycle of introducing products and the cycle for developing those products. Reducing the life cycle may be necessary for competitive reasons but of itself it is not necessarily desirable. But reducing the development cycle is always desirable, even if the development time gets shorter than the life of the product. Quicker development cuts costs, reduces the drain on the company, and increases flexibility because you can wait and make decisions closer to the time when the product will reach the market.

Speed must be treated with caution because it can have unintended results. For example, when Analog Devices decided in the late 1980s to set new corporate goals they included getting orders to the customers in three weeks instead of ten weeks and reducing the product development cycle from 36 months to six months. But it turned out the customers were more concerned with reliable delivery than rapid delivery. Some could wait a year, so long as they could count on getting the order on schedule. The pressure to speed up development had the unintended result of encouraging engineers to work on easier, short-term projects and avoid the bigger, riskier ones. So the development goals were scrapped and the delivery goal was amended to mean meeting the customers' requested dates.[20]

Management has clearly acquired an enormously powerful weapon in the idea of speeding all its processes. Like quality improvement, speed works in ways that are counterintuitive—at least to conventional thinking. Historically, business has said that if you want better quality or if you want it faster, it's going to cost you. What business has now learned is that quality, at least quality defined as lack of defects, and speed in fact cost less—and support each other. But being quick does have limitations and risks that may in the future limit its usefulness.

Pointers

- Are you trying to make all your operations move faster, rather than only the obvious ones such as manufacturing and product introductions?
- Are you using speed to create value for your customers and to differentiate your products or services?
- Are you able to anticipate market demand so as to be ready to serve that demand as it arises (whether it be hamburgers or computer add-ons)?
- Have you reduced your plant and equipment needs to the full extent made possible by accelerated processes?
- Have you changed your distribution, warehousing, and transportation to get the most economies from greater speed?
- Have you made your production processes as flexible as possible to adjust rapidly to changes in demand?
- Have you used just-in-time methods to speed all the processes in your business, improve quality, reduce inventory and capital requirements, or have you just shifted the burden of inventory to somewhere else?
- Are you using concurrent reengineering to speed development of new products?
- Do you spend enough time and money on preparing for the production and marketing of new products, so that introductions won't be delayed?
- Are you taking full advantage of speed as a discipline to make the whole company sharpen all its operations?
- Are you differentiating between speeding product development (which is always an advantage) and speeding product introductions (which may not always be desirable)?

Links

- A company needs to know how to learn quickly if it is to move faster.
- It also needs workers who are prepared to make decisions. A long chain of command is the enemy of speed.

- Good information technology, linking the company from customer to supplier, is essential to an agile corporation.

Cautions

- Speed as a management tool does not equate with haste. Rather, it means removing waste motions and simplifying products and processes to get there faster.
- Speed applied alone won't help.
- A just-in-time operation makes a company vulnerable to strikes, bad weather, and shortages.
- Speed achieved by short-cuts and lower quality will hurt more than it will help.
- Speed is not equally helpful to all products and all industries. In industries where products change slowly or where they sell in spikes, such as toys, it is of less advantage.
- Acceleration has its limits. It can't be infinite and at some point it may make more sense to look for other ways of expanding business.
- Customers may get fed up with too many updates, model changes, savings plans, and alternative choices.

13

REDEFINING QUALITY

Quality isn't complete until it makes an impression
on someone.
—Lew Platt, CEO, Hewlett-Packard[1]

Total Quality Management and its various offspring and cousins
have seniority over all the other current initiatives, fads, theories,
and metaphors that we talk about to describe how we are changing the
way we do business and manage corporations. We could go back further,
but let's start in Japan soon after World War II when the U.S. occupation
forces brought in three American engineers to help improve Japan's de-
plorable communications network by showing them how to use the statistical process controls developed two decades earlier at Bell Labs.
They produced a simple textbook for the use of companies like Nippon
Electric Company (NEC) and Tokyo Communications (later known as
Sony). The late W. Edwards Deming went to Japan in 1950 to preach his
quality message, and another American, Joseph Juran, soon went too.
Japanese executives followed the advice of the two Americans dutifully
and meticulously and added some ground-breaking concepts of their

SEI Survey	
It is critical that all of a company's activities add value for the customer	81%
We are doing that	36%

own. By the mid-1970s, after nearly three decades of patient painstaking work, some select Japanese companies achieved levels of quality and productivity unimaginable in the West at the time.

By the end of the decade, American business awoke to a nightmare. Canon threatened Xerox's existence with copiers far better and cheaper than the unreliable machines with which Xerox dominated the copying industry it had invented. Ford and Chrysler (and GM, much, much later) feared for their lives as well-made, reasonably priced Japanese cars captured a huge piece of the U.S. market. Hewlett-Packard bought thousands of Japanese-made random access memory chips when supplies fell short in the United States and, assuming that Japanese products would be second-rate, tested them rigorously. Not one failed. So it went. Corning, Motorola, and others saw their livelihoods threatened by competing products from Japan that were better and cheaper. The consumer electronics business in the United States was almost wiped out.

After a period of denial that ended only after many American executives visited Japan and returned to say that the Japanese really were working smarter, U.S. business set about improving the quality, first, of its products and later of its services. Quality improvement became the first and most significant of the new management ideas that are transforming business around the world. Companies that took the first small steps to improve their quality soon found that unless they changed the way they did most things they wouldn't improve. Total quality management became one comprehensive cover for all the things business had to do to become more competitive.

The 1980s became a period of experiment when businesses, in their attempts to achieve higher levels of quality, kept making basic mistakes. At first, quality was assigned to low-level quality circles, as if workmen could do it all themselves on the shop floor without management disturbing itself. Then it was assigned to directors or vice presidents of quality. Finally CEOs began to see that unless they took charge of quality measures themselves, nothing would happen. Through many failures and disappointments, business learned just how much needed to be done. People had to be trained, not only in the tools of quality but in the arts of dealing with people in a different way. The reward system had to change to encourage quality improvements and teamwork rather than short-term profits. Companies had to get to understand their customers better and work with their suppliers more closely. Managers had to be different, to encourage the independence of the people they once commanded. Organizations had to change, to break down the functional walls so as to focus on improving processes.

In short, to reduce the number of flaws in new cars or to get a better yield rate on computer chips, companies had to reinvent themselves. Quality became the testing lab for the other things business had to do. Whether they wanted to be more innovative, or speed their processes, or make better use of information technology, or compete in a tougher global market, or make better use of skilled employees, or reeingineer intelligently, companies would have to do much the same things as they had to do to improve quality. Often they made the same mistakes companies had made when they first approached quality improvement. For that matter, they continue to make them today.

THE FAD THAT WON'T GO AWAY

Being the trailblazer for new management, TQM came in for a lot of criticism and ridicule for its missteps and failures. Indeed by the 1990s, it was being dismissed as a fad that was fading. Consultants who specialized in quality improvement found that their business slipped away, unless they put a new label such as "reengineering" on what they were preaching. The truth is that TQM is tiresome. Perhaps the Japanese character is more suited to it than the American, for it takes years of patient, detailed labor to make quality improvement take hold and even then the work is never done. The quality professionals are not much help. They tend to practice an off-putting combination of righteousness—TQM, after all, is not a religion—with a maddening compulsion to put quality matters in excruciating, abstract detail. A conference or text on TQM tends to be a mammoth bore. Unleashed, quality professionals can wrap up their companies in a new bureaucracy of procedures, teams, measurements, and reports. No wonder managers often regard their quality professionals as irrelevant and find some joy when reengineering eliminates them or cuts them down. W. Edwards Deming did transcend the pettifogging cant of the quality profession, and fired the imaginations of managers and workers, but as he aged and continued his extraordinarily vigorous campaign into his 90s, his attacks on management became so vicious that he put off some of the people he meant to convert.

With all its handicaps then, has the quality movement spent itself? Quite the contrary, it is probably stronger than ever. If the reader has any doubts about that, consider how much quality practices have changed our basic ideas about management since around 1980. Management practice today says do it right the first time, rather than achieve quality by inspection and correction, as we used to do. Quality should be defined by the customer, rather than simply by technical specifications. Set stretch goals far beyond what used to be thought possible. Rather than work in secret isolation, benchmark your activities with other companies to see what you can learn. Examine how you work, see where you can improve, measure the results, and then look again. Most of the new management concepts in this book have been reinforced if not originated by the drive to improve quality: cross-discipline teams, pushing power downward, working faster, better training, a new role for leaders. Here is what can be said about the status of the quality movement today:

- Those early efforts almost certainly saved Xerox, Motorola, Ford, Chrysler, and many other companies from extinction, or at least from disappearing as major players.
- A high level of quality in products and services, higher than anything that could have been imagined in the 1970s, has become a given in the market place. Without it, many companies just could not compete.
- Some of the earliest and most successful converts to total quality management have in the mid-1990s set off in a new direction to make their quality better yet. These companies include Hewlett-Packard, General Electric, Motorola, and Xerox.

THINGS GONE WRONG

Before looking at these new directions, we might pause briefly to see what has been accomplished. Since quality managers like to measure everything, we can show here some measurable results (keeping in mind that some of the most important values of good quality cannot be measured). When American industry woke up in 1980, the poor quality of the cars made in Detroit was perhaps the most damning evidence of what was wrong with U.S. management.

One simple measure of the quality of cars is the number of "things gone wrong" per 100 cars. A TGW could be anything from a flaw in the paint or a misaligned door or panel to a functional breakdown. At the beginning of the 1980s, Detroit-made cars had 300 to 400 TGWs per 100 cars, about three times the level of Japanese-made cars. By 1985, Detroit was down into the 200s, while the better Japanese cars were in the low 100s. As Figure 13.1 shows, the ratings for American cars were mostly in the low 100s by 1996.

What these numbers mean is that most brands of new cars today are essentially defect-free. If you buy a Lexus, the chances are 50–50 you will find nothing whatever to complain about and if you buy a Saturn or a Lincoln you are likely to find one defect, and a pretty small one at that. The difference is not enough to influence your choice. It is taken for granted, a given for any company that wants to compete seriously, that new cars will have no defects.

THOSE INNER FEELINGS

The rough quality parity among the major automakers does not put an end to competition for the best quality. The basis for judging quality shifts, or rises to a new level that is more subjective and more emotional. One Japanese auto executive, Shinji Sakai, CEO of Toyota Motor Sales USA, reflects a widespread opinion when he says we need "a wider concept of quality." "Today quality is not just about statistics measuring defects, it reflects customers' inner feelings about the product," says Sakai. ". . . rediscovering quality means improving on the concept of total quality. We cannot talk about good quality in terms of the physical product or production process alone. It must encompass the total ownership experience and make customer satisfaction the target." In addition to providing transportation, he said, presumably with some help from his PR department, the automobile must be a private moving room or space, an "entertainment center providing fun and recreation while traveling," and it "must be responsive to public and environmental demands."[2]

The quality movement has reached a point where it needs to be refreshed. One of the first to experience this was Yotaro (Tony) Kobayashi, chairman of Fuji-Xerox. His company launched its effort in the 1970s, long before parent Xerox itself or for that matter any other American

FIGURE 13.1

Getting Better All the Time

The improvements in the quality of American, Japanese, and European autos over the last decade can readily be seen in these ratings from the J. D. Power surveys of 1985, 1995, and 1996 automobiles. The numbers refer to the problems per 100 cars reported by their owners 90 days after buying the cars. A rating of 100 would mean an average of one problem per car. This is just one of a number of ways of looking at auto quality. It does not, for instance, tell you about the long-term reliability of a car. All cars have improved markedly since 1985, but some show a slippage from 1995 to 1996. Both the manufacturers and the individual nameplates are rated. They are listed in order of their 1996 ranking. The list is not complete, but includes the best and some of the worst and the most changed.*

Car	1985	1995	1996
World Average	**247**	**103**	**100**
1. Lexus	—	60	54
2. Infiniti	—	55	67
3. Volvo	315	86	71
4. Honda	150	78	71
5. Toyota	135	74	80
6. Saturn	—	91	81
7. Mercedes-Benz	169	79	83
11. Lincoln	231	100	86
13. Jaguar	350	132	90
16. Cadillac	253	91	95
22. Ford	255	116	116
24. Chrysler	315	109	124
25. Volkswagen	241	183	125
26. Chevrolet	262	105	128
31. General Motors	255	155	145
33. Mitsubishi	242	164	150

*Data from J. D. Power & Associates initial quality surveys in the authors' files or published in *USA Today,* May 8, 1996.

company, and by 1980 it had won a Deming Prize in Japan. By the mid-1980s, says Kobayashi, TQM had made the company "a little too structured and people lost interest. It's not interesting enough. Not fun. It's dull. . . . People were saying individualism is being killed by the so-called quality approach." In 1988, Fuji-Xerox added what it called the New Work Way to TQM. People were encouraged to be more individualistic, to take risks, to ask "why not?" instead of just asking "why?", and to have fun.[3]

For one reason or another, in the mid-1990s some of the quality pioneers in the United States, some of the best performers, decided they would have to refresh their approach, to raise their standards or to take a new tack. Motorola realized that its much publicized Six Sigma standard—which means a phenomenal level of not more than 3.4 failures per million parts—would not be good enough for the new electronic equipment coming in the 21st century. Hewlett-Packard decided it just didn't understand the feelings of the customer well enough and launched a new quality drive to do that. Xerox, which had saved and then rebuilt the company in the 1980s on the basis of its quality strategy, found that it was too cluttered with tools and programs, most of which didn't work. It set about creating a more disciplined, focused effort. General Electric discovered, somewhat to its surprise, that its quality levels simply were lagging far behind the leaders and with characteristic energy Jack Welch launched a new attack on quality.

MOTOROLA: BIG GOALS

The best performers in quality have set themselves extraordinarily difficult goals, achieved them, and then set even more difficult goals. Motorola is probably the most famous example. To put a perspective on what Motorola and others have done and are trying to do, the typical American business in 1980 had an 8% defect rate. That didn't mean that 8% of the cars or copiers sold had a defect. It meant that 8% of the parts produced for those cars or copiers were defective. The cars and copiers themselves were riddled with defects. Quality has improved so much since then that defects are now normally measured at Motorola in parts per million rather than percentages. An 8% defect rate equates to 80,000 defects per million parts. In 1981, when Motorola started its quality drive it set a "reach" goal of reducing defects tenfold in five years. That was not good enough, so Motorola decided to improve another ten times again by 1989, and then ten more times by 1991. That would have brought Motorola's defect rate down to about eight in one million parts.

Motorola tweaked this goal a little more by announcing its Six Sigma standard in 1987. Statisticians use the Greek letter sigma (σ) as a symbol for standard deviation. Six sigma amounts to 3.4 mistakes per million parts and Motorola aimed to reach that by 1992, from a starting point of 6,000 mistakes. Motorola didn't make the Six Sigma target, although some of its products and processes did and even exceeded the goal. The company as a whole got to 150 parts per million (ppm) by 1992.[4] By early 1997, Motorola had squeezed errors down to 20 ppm, not Six Sigma but vastly better than what the rate had been. In the old percentage measure, Motorola achieved a .25% failure rate. Richard Buetow, Motorola's senior vice president for quality, explains that 20 ppm doesn't mean that if Motorola built one million space stations, only 20 would have a problem. Rather, in each step in the process of putting together a space station, problems would arise only 20 times in one million steps. "No other company in the world has reached this level and most don't even know where they are," he says.

While still a bit short of the Six Sigma goal, Motorola changed the whole scale again. "Our products keep shrinking and the processes become more difficult," says Buetow. "In the 21st century we'll have semiconductors with one to 20 billion parts. So we are scaling up to parts per billion. We have to keep improving. We haven't reached a point yet where quality costs money. It's still worth it. We have to do it for the future and because our costs still come down." Motorola is already measuring some processes in parts per billion.

Half of the failures at Motorola today come through its doors from its suppliers. They haven't quite kept pace with their customer, although Motorola has certainly worked on them. Motorola has cut the number of its suppliers from 10,000 to about 1,000 preferred suppliers, and they are required to show they have a serious quality improvement program. But much of the machinery Motorola purchases simply cannot turn out products at a virtually flawless level. So Motorola is investing in research to bring tools up to Six Sigma.

Like most companies, Motorola sees speed as part of the effort to improve quality and has set another of those big goals: to shorten the time it takes to develop a new product by ten times in five years. In other words, if it used to take 36 months to create a certain type of product, it should take three months or a little more. Motorola is also trying to understand the customer better, and is using new tools to do it. The company hires third-party interviewers to talk to customers about their experience with Motorola products. That's how Motorola learned to consolidate software updates because customers were irritated by the way they kept dribbling in.[5]

GENERAL ELECTRIC: ONE OBSESSION MISSING

GE has a long history of involvement in quality improvement. Its one-time director of quality, Armand Feigenbaum, became one of the most respected gurus in the field and his *Total Quality Control* has been a standard text for more than 40 years. In recent times, Jack Welch thought that with his constant focus on the three "S"s—speed, simplification, and stretch—GE would achieve world-class quality standards. GE was in fact doing many of the things that a company should do to improve—the teams, the idea of the boundaryless company, delayering, and training, for example. Welch thought these actions or ideas would embed quality into the company's activities. But GE did not have an explicit policy labeled TQM or something similar.

GE woke up in 1995 to find that its quality was nothing to boast about—as readers of *Consumer Reports* would know. GE appliances (and the Hotpoint machines made by GE) generally rated in the middle of the scale in surveys of *Consumer Reports* readers. The clothes washers and microwave ovens got very good ratings in most sizes, but new refrigerators free of CFCs (chlorofluorocarbons) and dishwashers got middling grades, or worse. The ratings for GE ranges varied from first place to the middle, depending on the price category. As for frequency of repair, GE appliances showed up mostly in the middle, usually behind Whirlpool, but the statistical differences were not great.[6] The *Wall Street Journal* reported that design mistakes created problems with GE's locomotives and gas turbines, and even delayed the delivery of its giant new jet engines for the Boeing 777.[7]

When GE compared itself to other companies, it found its overall performance was good but far below the best. GE benchmarked itself against the leaders, Motorola, Texas Instruments, Hewlett-Packard, and Xerox. All these companies, as Jack Welch put it, "were squarely in the eye of the Asian competitive hurricane" whereas GE "had the luxury of choosing its battle-grounds." They made quality "a defining management focus—an obsession." GE didn't. So while the others drew closer to Six Sigma, GE found itself with a rate of 35,000 defects per million, no more than average for a good company. At that rate and with $70 billion in revenues, GE could be throwing away $7 billion to $10 billion a year in scrap, rework, and rectifying mistakes. So at the end of 1995, GE set itself the goal of cutting that rate from 35,000 to 3.4 defects per million, or Six Sigma, in five years.

To get there, as Welch explained it, GE would turn from fixing products to fixing processes, so that they would "produce nothing but perfection, or close to it." The company adopted a four-step method to accomplish this: measure each process and transaction, analyze it, improve it, and then control the results. To lead the effort, GE designated what Welch flamboyantly described as "champions" in senior management, training 200 "master black belts" and 800 "black belts" as full-time quality executives to lead teams and focus on the processes. All of GE's 20,000 engineers were to receive training. With less flamboyance, but perhaps with more effect, GE changed the bonus system so that 40% of a manager's bonus would depend the contribution to getting to Six Sigma.[8]

XEROX: A NEW MODEL

Unlike GE, Xerox made quality the center of its struggle to revive beginning in 1982. What it called its "Leadership Through Quality" model worked well (although Xerox has not yet come close to returning to its pre-1980 levels for return on assets and market share). But like other companies, as the program matured and the 1990s passed, Xerox saw that it needed refocusing and refreshing. The company's "senior managers and quality experts saw shortcomings in the company's quality approach and were struggling with ways to overcome them," writes Richard J. Leo, vice president and general manager of Xerox Quality Services in Rochester. He said that Xerox "had a large number of quality tools and processes, but its people weren't using them consistently or effectively." The company was suffering from "concept clutter." The CEO, Paul Allaire, said Xerox would not be able to take advantage of market opportunities and its own technology "unless we can overcome cumbersome, functionally driven bureaucracy and use our quality process to become more productive."

The new "Xerox management model" which Allaire and his team began to roll out in 1994 was intended to apply more discipline to the use of all those tools and to increase Xerox's speed, not just at turning out products but at making decisions. Allaire meant to focus Xerox's quality efforts "on two critical objectives: profitable revenue growth and world-class productivity."

Xerox's shift to relating quality directly to profits coincides with a similar shift in the criteria of the Malcolm Baldrige National Quality Award. In the 1980s, when the award was established, quality was considered its own reward. No external justification was felt necessary. Improving quality was the right thing to do, and business would improve naturally. But by the mid-1990s this idealism had been replaced by an insistence on practical results. In the earlier Baldrige prize criteria the effectiveness of a company's quality efforts was judged by customer satisfaction. Out of a possible total of 1,000 points, 300 were in the category of customer focus and satisfaction. But the 1997 Baldrige criteria include a new category called "business results," with a possible score of 450 points. Customer satisfaction, worth 130 points, was folded into this new business results category—and there is a separate category called customer and market focus worth 80 points.

The rather formal, elaborate structure of the new "Xerox management model" assigns each of Xerox's quality tools, initiatives, and activities to six business practices: leadership, human resources, business process management, information utilization and quality tools, customer and market focus, and business results. The last category in effect measures the performance of the company in the first five. The idea is that everything that Xerox does will now be aligned with its quality goals, and that all its units and all its people will know what tools and what methods to use.[9]

HEWLETT-PACKARD: AN EMOTIONAL MATTER

Like the others, Hewlett-Packard found itself with a case of the quality blahs in the 1990s. HP had done extremely well since the beginning of the 1980s, both in improving quality and in its business results. However, it felt its quality effort was lacking something, that it had stalled. Hewlett-Packard benchmarked its efforts against those of the other major players and found that "these other companies felt utterly stuck in the way that we felt stuck," says Richard LeVitt, director of corporate quality. They were all using the same imported tools and the same ideas that had become embedded in the various quality prizes in Japan, Europe, and the United States. "The technology of quality wasn't moving fast enough," says LeVitt.

LeVitt drafted a plan for a new approach to quality which the chairman, Lew Platt, picked off his desk on a Saturday night in October, 1995. He read the plan on Sunday and began implementing it that Monday. They called it "Quality 1 on 1." As Platt explained it later in a speech, HP wasn't discarding the old concept of quality, with its emphasis on metrics and managing processes, but was going beyond it to learn more about the experiences of the customers. "Our usual habit is to think of quality as a producer does, focusing on the processes and controls in our daily production activities," said Platt. "Yet quality isn't complete until it makes an impression on someone."

The standard "producer" approach to quality, with its faith in "conformance to requirements" and "fitness for use," were natural to a high-tech company like HP: engineers building sophisticated items for use by other engineers. The specs were all-important. But as HP's market shifted towards selling more consumer items in the retail market to less sophisticated people, the idea of quality needed to change. As LeVitt puts it, instead of being so absorbed with the exciting evolution of technology HP had to think more along the lines of how the Disney organization creates an experience for visitors at its theme parks. LeVitt says HP found customers had strong emotional reactions to things that didn't seem important to the company. "We had to understand a day in the life of the customer," says LeVitt. "What happens when they first try to use the product? They take it out of the box and they try to set it up and use it. Does that experience lead to satisfaction? To delight? Dismay? Anxiety?" Analytic readings only give a surface impression of the customer's reaction.

HP's efforts to get into the customer's head include getting videos of customers opening and setting up their purchases. Its people spend time in the stores. Not only salespeople, but engineers, assembly line operators, staff people from finance and personnel, and general managers— people who may never before have dealt with a customer face to face—go out to the stores, set up displays, and then start talking to real customers.

Platt says he has meetings with customers, individually or in groups, five or six times a week. The whole idea is to take the producer's rational view of quality and blend it with the consumer's subjective, emotional view.[10]

As with any management practice, TQM can be carried too far, as many companies have discovered. Too many tools, too many measurements, too many meetings can tie up a company in a quality bureaucracy created by what *Quality Progress* magazine has dubbed "qualicrats." "There are hundreds of tools," says Martin R. Mariner, Corning's director of quality. "You can go tool crazy. I haven't introduced any for two years." Corning also found it had a whole staff of people just answering queries from and giving briefings to other companies, without helping Corning's quality at all. So Corning stopped all free help and instead started giving periodic briefings for which it charges $100 a head.[11]

Motorola, GE, Xerox, and Hewlett-Packard, all companies that took the lead early on in finding new ways to manage and improve their quality, all reached the same point in the early to mid-1990s where they needed to restart their engines. Each one has taken a different approach to the next generation of quality improvements—which shows again how every company is going to have to find its own way of approaching the 21st century. However, the same basic themes underlie each company's actions: the insistence on measuring results, setting goals high enough to make everyone gulp, the use of cross-functional teams, training people in the use of tools, spreading quality practices throughout a business and into all its activities, always looking for new ways to improve. Far from being a stale fad, quality improvement is becoming embedded in business. It is part of the price of admission to the market. But it is taking a lot longer to bring to maturity than anyone might have expected back in 1980—unless, of course, they had looked at and understood the Japanese experience.

Pointers

- Is the effort to improve quality focused on what really matters to the customer?
- Has your company's quality effort matured from requiring "conformance to requirements" or "fitness for use" to understanding the cus-

tomer's whole experience with your company as well as the product it-self?

- Is the company trying to improve the quality of everything it does?
- Is the company encouraging—or forcing—its suppliers to improve their quality?
- Do you periodically revise your targets upwards to meet the rising expectations of the customers?
- Are you using the statistical and other tools of quality improvement and giving people the training they need to use them?
- Do your pay and incentive plans encourage people to improve quality?
- Has top management demonstrated a long-term commitment to improving quality?
- Does your company use teams, benchmarking, and other management devices to improve quality?
- Beyond these and other specific measures, has your company basically changed the way it operates? If not, real improvements in quality are unlikely.

Links

- Unless your company is making many of the other improvements discussed in this book, such as speeding processes, improving product innovation, using teams, the quality effort on its own won't get far.

Cautions

- Achieving a high level of quality takes a long time—in fact, the quest never ends.
- Quality tends to lie in the details, and sweating those details can be tiresome, boring work.
- The search for excellence can run out of steam after a while and will likely need refreshing.
- The quality expert may try to smother a company in tools and try to create a bureaucracy that is an enemy of real quality.

IV
THE RESPONSE—
THE ORGANIZATION

14

THE GLOBAL REACH

Small, even tiny, niche markets can become amazingly large
when extended to the whole world.
—Hermann Simon[1]

Michel Besson, "Mike" to his friends in the United States, wore four
hats before returning to Paris in 1996. As executive vice president
of Compagnie de Saint-Gobain, a global French glass, packaging, and
construction materials company, he sat on its management committee,
which met once a month in Paris. As CEO of Saint-Gobain in North
America, he ran CertainTeed Corporation (building materials), Norton
Company (abrasives and specialty chemicals), and other subsidiaries
from his regular office in Valley Forge, Pennsylvania. He was also in
charge of Saint-Gobain's several worldwide businesses, such as construction materials, abrasives, and ceramics, which took him frequently
to Asia. He wore a fourth hat as overseer for Saint-Gobain's businesses
in Latin America, which of course meant frequent trips there.

This headful of hats seemed to sit lightly on Besson, a genial French-
man who lived in the United States for 16 years and speaks English with

SEI Survey	
It is critical to operate as a global, rather than national or multinational, organization	64%
We are doing that	30%

one of those French accents that conveys infinite worldliness. The complex "matrix" arrangement of organizations and lines of authority which so many executives find a maddening part of going global has worked now at Saint-Gobain for many years. Perhaps Saint-Gobain's secret is that it takes a relaxed view of formal organization. It has no organization chart and doesn't want one. The matrix keeps changing as people change. "We define the jobs according to the personality of the individuals, according to the situation," says Besson. Inevitably tensions arise across oceans and between businesses, but the Saint-Gobain culture has little tolerance for internal wars, so managers tend to work out their differences before too much damage is done.[2]

Going global presents management with layers of intricate problems and tradeoffs. The company with a real world strategy, which most large companies will need if they want to be around in the 21st century, has a scope that can yield enormous advantages and savings. But that doesn't mean the whole company goes on a global footing. In fact, each company has an array of choices to make in three separate areas:

1. *The Portfolio.* Rather than one set of global products or services, you may need a portfolio of them, some global, some regional, some local.
2. *The Domains.* You have to choose the domains in which to be global. The products may not be global, but the supply chain may be, or the R&D, or the business processes.
3. *The Mode.* You have to choose a mode of operations. You may operate on your own, or through a joint venture or alliance, or, if you are just getting your feet wet, through sales representatives or licensing deals.

What kind of organization do you create? How do you mesh different cultures and ethical views? How do you exercise control? The existence of the global market doesn't mean the world is just one big market. We may think so because we see MTV, McDonald's, Levi's, and Coca-Cola everywhere. But these ubiquitous products mean quite different things in different places. Eating at McDonald's in Los Angeles means a quick, cheap meal. In Beijing it's a special occasion. So the product is the same, but the market, and therefore the market segment, is different. Some markets are local. Many foods, drinks, clothes, and publications are local or regional. Many luxury items—expensive watches, jewelry, expensive cars, French champagne, for example—sell in a global market. Rich people everywhere want the same things. Top executives constitute a global market for travel and lodgings. Whatever their nationality, they stay in the same places, travel the same way. Although the product may be global, the marketing and the advertising may be local. The ads and the pricing are different. You will almost always need some local expertise to guide you through unfamiliar laws and customs.

Assessing the risks of operating in different regions and countries is critical for the global company. The banks purport to put out risk assessments by countries, but they refer mostly to the risks of lending money. The risks attached to operating a business are different. They depend on trade policies, exchange rates, central bank decisions, and on who your partner is. If your partner is the son of the local strongman, then your risks are minimized—unless, of course, there's a revolution.

Most corporations are struggling with these problems of global business, and if they are not now they probably soon will be. In the Conference Board survey of American manufacturers in the world markets mentioned in Chapter 3, all 64 companies in the survey with sales of $5 billion or more have overseas plants. In the entire sample of 1,250 companies, only 94 are purely domestic and the majority of these have sales below $500 million a year. Even among the smaller companies, nine companies out of ten have overseas activities.[3] (See Figure 14.1.)

It is not as if all these companies are just learning how to work outside their own borders. Alcoa, Coca-Cola, Du Pont, Eastman Kodak, Ford, General Electric, Gillette, H.J. Heinz, NCR, Quaker Oats, Sherwin-Williams, Standard Oil of New Jersey (now Exxon), and Westinghouse Electric were among 41 large American corporations described as multinational in 1914, and they are still there.[4] So are many of the other 41, under new names or ownership.

What makes it difficult for these veterans and the many newcomers to perform in the market today is that the terms of competition have changed radically. The old multinationals are referred to now disparagingly as "flag planters," colonial outposts of essentially domestic companies. They owned some plants, or mines, or sales organizations in foreign countries. Today's markets require globally integrated companies. The domestic and international units must merge so that the whole

FIGURE 14.1

Global Profits

Companies that operate internationally are likely to grow faster than purely domestic companies, and those with the deepest international commitment are likely to be the most profitable. These are the findings of a Conference Board survey of American manufacturing companies, classified according to how global they have become. The Conference Board categorized companies with majority-owned plants in all three major economic regions as "multinational"; those with one overseas plant or joint venture as "internationally committed," and those with foreign sales operations or licensing agreements as "internationally leaning." The return on equity (ROE) and return on asset (ROA) percentages are before interest and taxes.

Type of Company	Number of cos	5-yr sales growth	3-yr ROE	3-yr ROA
Total	1,250	15.9%	20.9%	8.4%
Multinational	155	10.9	29.6	12.3
Internationally committed	548	15.9	20	8.4
Internationally leaning	384	19.8	20.7	7.5
Domestic	94	8.2	21.4	7.3

Source: The Conference Board, *U.S. Manufacturers in the Global Marketplace, Report Number 1058-94-RR* (New York: The Conference Board, 1994), p. 35.

functions as a single organization, not a collection of fiefdoms or outposts. Depending on the business, it may need to globalize its products, or its purchasing, or R&D, or manufacturing, or marketing and sales, or information technology, or all of these activities.

For all the talk about globalization, most multinationals are still basically flag planters. The SEI survey for this book showed that about one-third of the companies surveyed felt they were achieving the proper global stance and structure—and some of them were probably exaggerating. When you are dealing with different cultures and languages, recognizing the need to do something is a long way from doing it. Take the case of Canon, an excellent company and a strong performer on the global market. CEO Ryuzaburo Kaku says he may have to take apart the product division structure he established in the 1970s. "This product division system now seems to be failing," he says. "Now we are facing an era of multinationalism, and vertical walls between divisions run contrary to the mainstream. Therefore, although I instituted the product division system, because it has become rigid, we are now thinking of restructuring it completely."

But what about globalizing Canon at the top? "So long as I am chairman of the company," says Kaku, "there will be no chance for foreigners to serve on the board of Canon, for a simple reason—I don't speak English. Other people, starting from the president down, do speak English. At the point where all the officers on the board can speak English, we may have lots of non-Japanese members. . . . So, when that time comes, Canon can be truly globalized. I don't know whether Canon should be completely decentralized or not. For now, I want to run Canon as a centrally controlled operation. My own feeling is that the company should be centralized with divided responsibilities and rights."[5]

ABB: RADICALLY GLOBAL

Like the idea of pushing decisions down as low as they can go, the idea of becoming truly global is so at odds with traditional practice that executives have trouble making it work. The result is confusion, many different approaches, and a lack of models to follow. If a global company does exist today, it would have to be ABB, an electrical engineering conglomerate based in Switzerland. Seven nationalities are represented on its 11-member board and four nationalities on its executive committee of eight. People from 19 countries make up the skeletal headquarters staff of 171 in Zürich. English is the official language of the company although it is the native tongue of only 20% of its employees. But English is the native tongue of global business. The man who put the company together, Percy Barnevik, says that even when two Swedes in the company talk to each other, they are likely to do so in English.

ABB was created in 1988 out of two sleepy old companies, ASEA of Sweden and Brown Boveri of Switzerland. How Barnevik, an animated Swede, brought the two companies together and transformed them into a global enterprise is already business legend. Barnevik has become a management hero, the Jack Welch of Europe, a man with a cult following. He moved first to cut fat radically. He unified the two headquarters staffs and cut them by 90%. He later took another 50% of the people out of headquarters. He made it a practice, as he reorganized the operating companies and acquired new ones, to reduce their headquarters by 90%. Many of the people displaced were moved out to the field. At this point in ABB's development, Barnevik was emphatically not a hero, at least not at home in Sweden. But globalism, he says, means that millions of people will lose their "present labor-intensive, low-tech jobs and must find employment in higher technology areas and in the service sector." Excess capacity and redundant plants, particularly in Europe, will become more obvious. While the United States has two locomotive plants and Japan three, Europe has 37. "The European shops will merge and maybe half the number of people will be required to make the same number of locomotives," says Barnevik.

He created what he describes as a "radically decentralized" network with 5,000 profit centers in 1,300 operating companies around the world. They were grouped into 51 divisions or business areas. What he achieved was—for a $36-billion-a-year company—a very flat organization with a lot of entrepreneurial authority out in the small profit centers at the extremities of the company. Only one person, in the division office, stands between the head of an operating company and the executive committee in Zurich. The operating companies control most of the R&D money, make their own decisions about capital spending and borrowing, and are responsible for the profits, part of which they keep.

The heads of the operating companies work within a matrix, one axis being the heads of the business units (which are global) and the other being the country managers. "We didn't choose a matrix," Barnevik has said. "We just have a matrix, whether we like it or not." The head of an operating company has two bosses—to the extent that he has any bosses at all. But what is important about ABB is not so much the form, but the way it works. The matrix is not used to drive a top-down organization, but to support the operating companies in a bottoms-up organization.

Those 1,300 companies, obviously, don't run free on the global range. Barnevik made everyone aware of what mattered. In spite of its spread, ABB has a tight focus. Barnevik has no use for the old, we-can-run-any-thing type of conglomerate like Litton Industries and ITT. ABB sticks to the electrical engineering industries. It has clear goals, in terms of growth and profitability, and it has a defined culture. Right after the merger in 1988, Barnevik brought the top managers together in Cannes to describe the new company, which was "decentralized under centralized conditions." He issued a mission and values booklet which said things such as: "Taking action and doing the right thing is obviously best. Taking action, doing the wrong thing, and quickly correcting it is second best. Creating delays or losing opportunities is the worst course of action." Another theme focuses the company on the customer, an idea that was hardly part of the old ASEA and Brown Boveri philosophies. The company is also held together by an automated global reporting system and by what has been described as a Praetorian Guard of 500 to 600 young global managers who move around the world being carefully cultivated and watched while they absorb new cultures and skills. ABB has grown, by acquisition and expansion, from $17 billion in sales in 1988 to $36 billion in 1996 and has pushed vigorously into Asia and Eastern Europe. But for all the global push more than half its business still remains in Europe. At this point, ABB is more of a fascinating experiment than a new business model.[6]

WHIRLPOOL: GOING ABROAD
TO STAY STRONG AT HOME

Until 1988, many of the top people at Whirlpool Corporation's headquarters in Benton Harbor, Michigan, didn't own passports. Today Whirlpool is the world's top appliance maker and is arguably the best example the United States can offer of a global company. Whirlpool's executives know their way around Milan, Stuttgart, Hong Kong, New Delhi, and São Paulo. A decade ago Whirlpool was comfortably situated as the leading manufacturer of appliances in the United States. It was competing successfully by changing from a top-down corporation to a leaner, more entrepreneurial organization driven by teams and gain-sharing plans that reward employees for improvements in quality and productivity. No low-cost, high-quality foreign firms had shown up to threaten Whirlpool's washers, driers, refrigerators, and other appliances.

However, Whirlpool had already seen that improving quality and productivity weren't going to be enough to keep on top. You had to have these attributes to stay in the game, but they wouldn't keep you ahead of competitors who were doing the same things. When David Whitwam became CEO in 1987 he launched an eight-month study of the company that reached an unexpected conclusion: the appliance business was inevitably going to become global, whether GE, Maytag, Whirlpool, and the others wanted or not, and becoming a global company would be the best way to sustain a competitive advantage. Appliance features varied from country to country, but the technology, the process, and the business were the same everywhere.

A risky chance to make a big bet in Europe came when Philips Electronics offered its sickly European appliance business for sale in 1989. Whirlpool took part ownership then and acquired the whole thing for a total of $1 billion in 1991, becoming immediately the world's biggest appliance maker. Philips had a collection of national businesses that offered the obvious opportunities that a global business could seize. As Whitwam pointed out in an interview with the *Harvard Business Review,* the washing machines made by Philips in Germany had more features and were more expensive than the ones made in Italy, but essentially they were the same machines. Yet they didn't have even a single screw in common. Philips had a collection of national companies offering different appliances in each market.

The classic American corporate way of dealing with a sick acquisition like Philips would have been to send a team of tough managers over to Europe to whip the company into shape, slash costs, and kick butt. Whitwam chose a slower, more careful approach. He felt the new partners had cultural problems to straighten out before they could start rearranging the businesses. Hardly any Americans were put in Europe, and none of them had senior jobs. (Whitwam later did put American executives in charge of the European operation.) Instead, Europeans and Americans visited back and forth, examining each other's operations. They hadn't signed on to be part of any global company and at first, Whitwam says, each party found fault with the way the others worked. In their quality processes, the Europeans followed the ISO-9000 system, which essentially sets quality standards, while the Americans followed the Baldrige Award criteria, which pay more attention to quality processes. Whirlpool appointed a transatlantic committee to take what it thought was the best of several quality systems and create a new global quality plan for Whirlpool. Other teams developed worldwide policies in a range of areas, from strategy to personnel.

As the two opposing sides drew closer, Whirlpool began to rationalize its operations. Today a plant in Varese in Northern Italy turns out squarish-looking ovens under the Bauknecht label for the top-of-the-line market, rounder models with the Whirlpool name for the middle market, and utilitarian ovens with the Ignis brand. They are all basically the same on the inside. Whirlpool is well on the way to cutting the number of former Philips warehouses in Europe from 36 to eight. The company has half the 1,600 suppliers it used to have. Instead of buying refrigerator power cords from 17 suppliers, it buys from two.

After the acquisition, appliances at first bore the joint Philips-Whirlpool brands names in Europe, but the Philips name has now disappeared. The technology, as well as the brand, is becoming global. When Whirlpool produced a new CFC-free refrigerator in the United States in 1994, the insulation was developed in Europe and the compressor in Brazil. These kinds of exchanges are showing the global company how products from one place may fit an unexpected niche in another. The American company acquired some improved styling from Europe and learned how to make stainless steel tubs for its KitchenAid clothes washers to replace the cast iron-and-porcelain tubs it had been selling.

Whirlpool had no ready-made opening in Asia like the one it found in Europe, so it chose to compete in the rapidly growing Pacific market through joint ventures rather than through acquisitions. For example, Whirlpool joined up with Shenzhen Petrochemical Holdings Company to boost the Chinese company's production of air conditioning units from 500 to 1,000 daily. Together with partners in India, Whirlpool is building a refrigerator plant there with a capacity for 1.5 million units a year. Whirlpool and its partners in China and India produce or soon will produce refrigerators, washers, microwave ovens, and air conditioners in Asia. Whirlpool, basically a domestic company a decade ago, has plants in 12 countries now and sales in 120. (For more on joint ventures and alliances, see the next chapter.)

Becoming a global company with a good grip on the number-one spot in its market gave Whirlpool a boost. Sales have increased nearly 50% to $8.8 billion since the acquisition of Philips. Profits increased 4.5% a year from 1990 to $397 million in 1994. But being global doesn't call off the market forces. Whirlpool hit a snag in 1995. Appliances sales were sluggish in the United States, and then the European economy went into a slump. Whirlpool's sales in Europe were hurt additionally when the lira's value rose, because Whirlpool manufactures more in Italy than in other European countries.[7]

DOES ANYONE WANT A WORLD CAR?

The approach to globalism at ABB and Whirlpool seems relatively straightforward compared with the complex plays, reversals, and replays attempted in the auto industry. If you make cars and want to be global, you make a global car, right? One that will sell in every market. That seemed feasible in the 1970s and even early in the 1980s. The competition among car makers was less intense then and the markets less demanding. Toyota had a world car and Ford began its efforts to create a world car in the Escort in the late 1970s. But it turned out to be a lot more complicated than that. The auto companies found they could get a lot better by going global in a number of directions, but not necessarily by making one car for the whole world.

As Toyota said in its 1995 annual report, "Our global strategy used to center on 'world cars,' which we would modify slightly to accommodate demand in different markets. Today, our focus is shifting to models that we develop and manufacture especially for selected regional markets." Toyota concentrates production near the markets where the models are the most popular—the Avalon and Camry in the United States, the Carina E in Europe, and the Toyota Utility Vehicle in Southeast Asia, for example. Toyota has globalized its logistics and purchasing, which allows it to exchange parts around the world, and its data base, which helps Toyota operations anywhere find the most competitive supplier.

For a company that has been a world leader in so many concepts that will be part of the 21st century corporation, Toyota is strangely conservative in its global corporate organization. Tokuichi Uranishi, general manager for corporate planning, acknowledges that Toyota has too many separate operating units in the United States that need to be consolidated and that headquarters in Japan is still too divided functionally to operate as an effective global headquarters. Purchasing needs to be more integrated, for example.[8]

Use of the phrase "world car" is forbidden around Honda headquarters in Tokyo. CEO Nobuhiko Kawamoto says, "if you look at the countries in which autos are used heavily, the environments are all quite different, which means that the ways that autos are used will be quite different. I don't believe it is quite correct to envision developing the same car worldwide." So Honda now bases its organization on regions. In 1992, Kawamoto created four regional operations: the Americas; Europe, the Middle East, and Africa; Asia and Oceania; and Japan. In 1994 he made these regions autonomous, with responsibility for developing, manufacturing, marketing, and selling vehicles in their regions. Specific steps to support that autonomy included doubling the R&D effort and expanding engine production in the United States. Honda is using the United States as a base to push deeper into Latin America.[9]

FORD: ANOTHER ESCORT, AGAIN

In contrast to Toyota and Honda, Ford has not let go of the idea of creating a world car, in spite of its frustrated efforts since the late 1970s to design an Escort that would sell all over the world. The Escort market segment for economy cars constitutes 33% of the world market for cars, so it would seem that if there is a market for a world car it would be at the low end. In the 1980s Ford presented the global Escort as the world's best-selling car, a somewhat disingenuous claim. Ford's European operation had indeed been given responsibility for developing a world car, but the actual design and manufacturing operations were not merged under a single management. So the engineers in Detroit had the right to tinker with the designs coming from England and Germany and, being engineers, tinker they did. The result: two Escorts that resembled each other visually but didn't share a single important part. There was no way either design could be manufactured on the other side of the Atlantic. The body panels, for example, were stamped out in different modules. If you add the two economy cars made for North America and Asia by Mazda, then 25% owned by Ford, you had four distinct economy cars. Looking back, Richard Parry-Jones, the 47-year-old Welshman who now heads Ford's global small and medium vehicle center in England, says, "We couldn't offer leading value if we followed wasteful parallel development. We multiplied the development costs by four, each working separately and not learning from the others, so we were not world class in quality, cost, or speed. We had a poor internal learning process."

With the development of the 1995 Ford Contour and Mercury Mystique compact line, Ford improved its coordination somewhat. By the late 1980s, when Ford began to create the European version of the car, the Mondeo, Ford had reorganized to create a worldwide Ford Automotive Group with a global planning staff. Ford Europe got lead responsibility for developing the car, then designated the CDW27. The Mondeo with its North American relatives can plausibly be described as a world car. The platform is the same as are most of the essential parts, although different engines were developed in Europe and North America. However, Ford was still only partway towards reorganizing and simplifying its design process, its parts, supplier base, and manufacturing. The European and American teams were still fighting each other, as they had been a decade earlier. In fact, development of the Mondeo cost $6 billion and took six years—both hugely bloated figures for the 1990s. Considering that the Japanese already have their development cycle down to below three years and are shooting for two years, which is where Ford would like to be too, Ford had far to go.

Ford's latest and most ambitious effort to be global was launched early in 1993 by Alexander Trotman, the Englishman who was to become CEO of Ford later that year. He had always liked the idea of making Ford truly global and he commissioned a study of running "power trains," that is, the design and production of engines and transmissions—as a unified worldwide operation. The advantages seemed obvious. Ford made five four-cylinder engines, but needed only two. The team that studied power trains, says Robert Transou, group vice president of manufacturing, concluded that it was a great idea—but did not recommend it. Instead, the team said Ford would really benefit only if all the vehicle development teams were unified.

Trotman bought the idea and at the beginning of 1994, 27 particularly promising or senior people, more of them from Europe than North America, detached themselves from their jobs and took over a section of the seventh floor of Ford's world headquarters in Dearborn to work on a "Ford 2000" plan.

They labored in virtual quarantine, seven days a week, for four months. Their style was Spartan. They had one secretary. They met at 7 A.M. as a group to discuss schedules and assignments, and then split up. They were supposed to have completed their assignments when they met again at the end of the day, unless an assignment was especially complex. They started by trying to write organization charts for the future Ford but then decided they had started from the wrong end. People who came in with an organization chart from then on were hooted down. Instead the team started looking at principles and processes. The chief principle was that one worldwide organization would run manufacturing. The company would share platforms, powertrains, technology, and best practices.

The Ford 2000 plan that emerged radically reorganized the 90-year-old company at the beginning of 1995. Ford Automotive Operations (FAO) took over the worldwide auto business and was assigned five "vehicle program centers," each with global responsibility for designing and engineering a particular family (small cars, big front-wheel-drive cars, big rear-wheel-drive cars, light trucks, commercial trucks). Trotman and the executives appointed to the new FAO, including the vice president of product development, Jacques Nasser (an Australian considered a likely successor to Trotman), deployed to spread the message. Trotman called for "passion, passion, passion," and prodded his managers: "In the past, I've said you're like a layer of clay soil. I could pour water on you and nothing gets through."[10]

Since Ford developed the Contour-Mondeo before the reorganization, the next Escort, yet another attempt to make one world car, will be the first to emerge from scratch from the new system. This time there are no competing efforts in Europe and North America. All the development work comes under the small car vehicle center in Europe, which is responsible for creating a car that will sell all over the world. Plants in Britain, Germany, Mexico, the United States, Argentina, Taiwan, India, and Indonesia will build the car. Richard Parry-Jones, the head of the center, says that had someone in the old Ford asked him to develop a car that would sell in China and Brazil as well as Europe, he would have told them to get lost. Now he knows the responsibility is his. He believes one economy car can sell all over the world with some adaptation for specific markets. For example, in India the Escort will be a family car and most families that can afford a car there will also be able to hire a driver. They will want more space in the rear. The answer: longer runners for the front seat so the driver can squeeze forward. The Indian version will have to be more tolerant of random variations in octane levels of the gasoline. In North America, the Escort is considered a starter car, but almost all buyers will want automatic transmissions. Only 5% of the European drivers will want automatic shifts, but they will want a stiffer ride and they are more likely to order a sunroof. These adaptations can all be made, says Parry-Jones, without any fundamental changes to the car.

Parry-Jones directs the project from what he calls an office in cyberspace. He travels a lot and has PicTel (televideo) conferences weekly with Nasser in Detroit and with his operating committee spread around the world. He goes back and forth between offices in Dunton and Cologne, as do many of the 2,000 people working on the project in England and Germany. To try to make travel between the two centers virtually spontaneous, Ford uses an MD-80 jet with seats for 118 to run a shuttle four times a day between Cologne and Stansted airport, near Dunton. Engineers in both places can also work together without traveling by throwing drawings on the PicTel screens, making changes as they talk. Once engineers have met face to face, says Parry-Jones, they work well together on the screen.

Even before the introduction of the new world Escort, Ford's global plans showed signs of strain. Ford's costs were still too high. Chrysler could produce a car for $1,000 less in North America and GM's costs per car were $800 lower in Europe.[11] Ford was losing money in Europe. To reduce costs, it cut the total number of platforms for its cars from 32 to 16 and reduced the number of power trains too. By selling off the commercial truck division and combining its two large-car vehicle centers, it cut the number of vehicle centers from five to three (small and medium vehicles, large and luxury vehicles, and light trucks, which includes vans and sports utility vehicles).[12]

GENERAL MOTORS: CENTRAL PURCHASING

General Motors executives think Ford is wrong to believe that being global means building global cars. "We wouldn't start by saying let's do a world car," says Arvin F. Mueller, group executive of the Vehicle Development & Technical Operations Group. "Rather, we ask what do customers around the world want and then, how do you satisfy the regional needs. The idea of a world car is not externally focused." Maybe there is a global market for an economy car and there is one for the most expensive luxury cars, the Rolls-Royces and Jaguars, but all those cars in between, the family cars, sporty cars, utility vehicles, are at best regional.

GM thinks it makes more sense to put its processes rather than its products on a worldwide basis, and take them one step at a time, rather than trying to make the whole company global at once. GM has centralized its purchasing worldwide. Company officials admit that José Ignacio López de Arriortua, the supercharged Basque accused of carrying off GM secrets when he defected to Volkswagen in 1993, did the corporation some good by shaking up the whole supply system during his brief, turbulent reign as GM's head of purchasing. He forced prices down and got rid of marginal performers. GM has globalized all its purchasing to give it leverage. "Even if the purchase is regional, it would be determined centrally," says Miller. "We can choose for a specific market."

Richard Wagoner, president of GM's North American operations, says that global purchasing is one of two ways GM has lowered its costs, the other being lean, flexible manufacturing. Central purchasing has the effect of allowing suppliers to grow with GM around the world and of pulling GM's engineers together as they try to use common components and systems. The results, says Wagoner, are "absolutely astounding." GM has also gone through the massive task of putting all its 100,000 Lotus Notes users on one global system. The hardest part was reducing 26 different CAD/CAM design packages to three by 1994. In 1996 GM chose Electronic Data Systems' Unigraphics to create one global system.[13]

SMALL COMPANIES, BIG MARKETS

Discussions of globalism focus mostly on the big multinationals who want to move up from being mere flag planters. The world in fact offers grand opportunities to many smaller companies which can sometimes slip into big global markets without the disruption that afflicts the big companies. The Conference Board study of American manufacturers in global markets says that "smaller corporate size poses no barrier to international roll-out early in the firm's development cycle. Foreign sales account for 22% of total annual turnover for firms with sales of $100 to $500 million."[14] Information technology gives even the smallest companies some of the attributes of large companies: they can reach and service clients anywhere quickly, they can readily pull in other resources, they can offer sophisticated benefits. Through the Internet they can reach huge markets cheaply.

Labconco Corporation, a privately owned maker of lab equipment in Kansas City, was founded in 1925 and established an international department in 1979. Sales outside the United States and Canada now amount to 30% of the total $34 million a year. Labconco's glove boxes, hoods, dryers, concentrators, and other pieces of lab equipment now go all over the world. The business is relatively simple to handle. Labconco has three foreign sales representatives, one each for Europe, Latin America, and Asia, who peel out of Kansas City to swing through their territories six to eight times a year. They work through exclusive dealers in each country. Since there are no more than a handful of dealers in lab equipment in each country, finding the right one is not a complex task.[15]

Having at hand a huge domestic market, small and middling American companies have never felt the same urgency that European companies felt to find markets around the world. In a fascinating book, *Hidden Champions,* Hermann Simon, a consultant in Bonn and a visiting professor at the London Business School, describes how many little-known German companies with annual sales under $1 billion have become dominant in their markets around the world. As Simon says, "even tiny, niche markets can become amazingly large when extended to the whole world." His hidden champions include Hauni, the world's leading manufacturer of cigarette-making machines, Tetra, which supplies half of the world's tropical fish food, and Brita, which makes 85% of the world's point-of-use water filters.

These are not newcomers to the world market. Most of them have been around for decades, under consistent, long-term leaders, steadily focused on their particular markets (as mentioned in Chapter 7). They have not rushed to adopt new management styles. They didn't need to, because they have always been close to their customers, they are already lean, and simple and fast, they already work to improve continuously, they are well-focused, and they are innovative. In other words, they aren't burdened with the handicaps that large companies are now trying to overcome by making all the changes discussed in this book. Beyond these sensible principles of good management, Simon did not find any patterns in how these companies achieved their global markets.

They didn't follow any well-organized plan to reach foreign markets. "Rather they started to internationalize very early, very rapidly, and often chaotically."[16]

Small companies typically venture abroad first with licensing agreements and sales operations. That strategy gives the company some relatively low-risk experience in working abroad and, according to the Conference Board report on American manufacturers, often achieves rapid sales growth. However, sales and licensing as a long-term policy yields relatively low returns on assets. In fact, the poorest performers in terms of returns on assets among multinationals are those that don't progress beyond this stage. Their returns aren't much better than those of companies that stay home. The most profitable international operators are the true multinationals that own manufacturing in the three major industrial regions of the world. Having a good geographic spread is more important than which particular countries you pick, the Conference Board said. Locating R&D facilities overseas also seems to engender higher returns.[17]

KNOWING THE LOCALS

What should be local and what should be global? That's a critical question for any multinational. As information technology and other support activities become more sophisticated and more international, a corporation can globalize more of its activities. That's why the auto companies and others can now put their purchasing on a worldwide basis. Other activities, particularly those affected by local laws relating to labor practices and the environment, for example, may have to remain local. Retail companies have to be especially careful about local tastes. Sports shoes seem to have a universal market, but other markets are national. When the Swedish furniture company IKEA, came to the United States in 1985 it thought it could operate just as it had done so successfully all over Europe, selling good furniture kits at moderate prices from big warehouses. By 1990 it became clear that IKEA was going nowhere in the United States. When the company's Swedish managers took a good look at their operations, they found that Americans didn't like IKEA's narrow beds (especially since the sizes were measured in centimeters), or their small kitchen cabinets, or the shallow drawers in their bureaus. IKEA's dimensions had worked all over Europe, but they didn't suit American tastes. So IKEA localized by giving its American products more generous dimensions (measured in inches), and incipient failure turned to success.[18]

When businesses start to be truly global they tend at first to make all their operations global, which is probably not a bad beginning. For example, when Rhône-Poulenc went on an acquisition binge in the United States and it bought 18 big businesses (such as Stauffer Chemical's basic chemicals business and Union Carbide's agricultural products) between 1986 and 1989, it needed to bring a lot of diversity under one umbrella. Peter Neff, the CEO of the North American operations until 1996, says "we overbalanced for a while and said, OK, everything is global." For the time being, managing its businesses centrally suited Rhône-Poulenc's style of making all the decisions in Paris. However, Jean-René Fourtou, the consultant who took over the moribund company in 1986, had plans to turn it into a decentralized, empowered organization.

Therefore, in the 1990s the company backed off its total globalism and began to look at each unit and activity. "One really has to understand what can be managed globally and what needs to be managed locally," says Neff. "That's a perception and an understanding that takes some time for a company to work through." Pharmaceutical research is clearly global but providing water treatment chemicals for oil refineries in Houston is clearly local, for example. Compensation practices are different around the world and marketing and sales are local processes, so a global sales or personnel organization is not likely to work, Neff maintains. But a global R&D operation makes sense in pharmaceuticals. Eventually, Rhône-Poulenc looked at each of its North American business units, by now 19, and decided which should be managed with considerable local autonomy and which should be managed more centrally.[19]

Neff observed with some insight the difficult adjustments Americans and Frenchmen had to make in the new Rhône-Poulenc. Americans are more individualistic while the French are hierarchical and communitarian. Americans want fast action; the French like to get everything synchronized before they act.[20]

East and West have a bigger divide to bridge. When America meets Japan, for example, the American blurts out his opinions, while the

Japanese waits until he has heard everybody, thinking that only a fool speaks first. The American admires youth and achievement; the Japanese respects age and seniority (although perhaps less so today); the American thinks he controls his destiny, the Japanese believes more in external forces. So it goes around the world. These are the kinds of contradictions and conflicts that global companies have to work out through training, travel, and some forceful persuasion, if they want to be the best in the world's markets.

There's nothing simple about being a global corporation and there are a few straightforward choices. You are faced with difficult tradeoffs and complex decisions at many levels. You have to decide what to do globally, what to do regionally, and what to do locally, how to organize to do it, what markets to enter, what partners to pick, what risks you can afford to take.

Pointers

- Assuming you want to be a global enterprise, have you selected the right mode, whether it be through licensing deals, or joint ventures, or direct investment in your own ventures?
- Have you selected the right domains in which to be global, if not in products or services, then in procurement, or R&D, for example?
- Have you chosen the right portfolios of products and services that should be global, regional, and local?
- Have you seen how markets for the same products may be segmented differently in different parts of the world?
- Have you taken the time to know the people, especially partners and customers, and the culture of the places where you operate?
- Have you assessed adequately the different types of risk in the different areas you plan to go?
- Have you taken steps to internationalize your staff? Your executives? Your board?
- Have you achieved the right geographic spread to cover your markets and minimize risk?
- Have you tested the opportunities for conducting R&D overseas and otherwise learning from global operations?
- Do you operate your business as an internationally integrated whole?

- Do you have the right architecture to deal with matters at their appropriate level, whether it be local, regional, or global, allowing local autonomy where necessary and exerting central direction when it is required?

Links

- Is the quality of your goods or services up to the world standards that a global operation requires?
- Is your information technology capable of knitting the company together into one global operation?

Cautions

- Resolving the cultural clashes between employees in different countries or regions may be the hardest part of going global.
- Using licensees and sales representatives may be a relatively risk-free way of starting off internationally, but it limits your possibilities in the long run.
- Global markets don't necessarily require global products.
- Don't globalize everything the company does. You will need a balance.

15

THE EXTENDED CORPORATION

There is the concern that we will outsource our way to the
hollow corporation.
—Joe Neubauer, CEO, Aramark Corporation[1]

The idea that companies must open up to networks, alliances, part-nerships, joint ventures, and outsourcing keeps getting more pow-erful in spite of some well-publicized failures. It gets harder and harder to be a Lone Ranger. Naturally there will be many failures in the begin-ning, when companies are experimenting with partnerships, especially if performance is judged against inflated expectations. But the reasons for working more closely with others are overwhelming: sharing costs and risks, getting your products into new markets, getting new products into your markets, acquiring skills and knowledge you need from others, shedding peripheral work to focus on the heart of the business, getting help to move faster, improving quality—the list could go on and on to

SEI Survey	
It is critical for companies to become more networked and less vertically integrated	49%
We are doing that	25%

cover most of the things that companies need to do today. New information technology makes networking easier and more effective.

Working with others can take many forms and the differences among them are large. However, they all involve a common element. If you really want others to work with you effectively, you have to open up to them. They have to know more about your business, your plans, your future products, even your proprietary secrets, and you probably have to know more about theirs. Therefore trust is the basic ingredient of any of these networking or cooperative arrangements. You need a good contract outlining the deal, but without trust the contract will mean nothing.

The idea of trusting outsiders is so foreign to business, at least to American business, that it takes courage and a huge change in attitude to become part of a network. Jordan Lewis, a consultant and writer on alliances, writes that when he was talking to a group of some 100 CEOs he asked those who supplied other companies if they had real alliances with their customers. Only a handful did. Beyond some rhetoric, nothing much had changed, said the CEOs, because their customers didn't trust them. Then Lewis turned the question around and asked if any one of them had alliances with their suppliers. Only two did. Why didn't the others? The answer: Because suppliers can't be trusted![2]

The matter of trust gets more complicated when international partnerships are involved. If you tie up with a Japanese company, won't they learn all your secrets and then set themselves up in competition with you? A McKinsey & Company survey of joint ventures with Japan that had been terminated in the 1980s found that in three quarters of the cases the Japanese partner had absorbed the joint venture. Gary Hamel, a professor at the London Business School, describes partnerships "as a race to learn."[3] The one who learns the most, gets the most. Partnerships are all about learning. It should be mutual. At the NUMMI partnership in California, for example, GM learned (slowly) about the Toyota production system, while Toyota learned (quickly) how to work in America and deal with the unions.

Trust obviously can't be achieved on a flying visit to Tokyo or Seattle. It takes time and socializing—placing yet another demand on the time and stamina of the top executives—and in Japan maybe a little *karaoke* singing to show you are among real friends and can let your hair down. It takes a personal chemistry, as well as the necessary business chem-

istry. But the need to be open with others in one way or another has become pervasive.

Almost any major company will provide an example of the change in
attitudes toward working with others. Until around 1980, IBM was totally
buttoned up. It built closed systems, it was self-contained, it didn't share
its technology with others, and meeting with a competitor was a firing of-
fense. Then, to create its PC, IBM took Intel as a partner and went to
open systems. Over the rest of the decade on into the 1990s, IBM built
an extraordinarily complex web of new relationships with customers and
suppliers, with other companies such as Motorola and Apple in the
United States, and Toshiba and Siemens overseas, and in consortia such
as Sematech.

Many new alliances and partnerships have failed, petered out, or just
not been very productive. Those that fail normally don't resound as
much as, for example, the failure of AT&T's alliances with Olivetti and
Philips. In the SEI Survey, only 25% of the participating companies
thought they were properly networked. But as Figures 15.1 and 15.2
show, the formation of alliances continues strong.

FIGURE 15.1

Trends in Alliance Formation

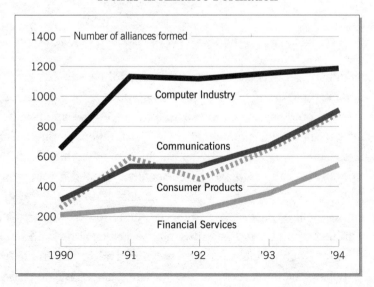

Source: Praschant Kale, Wharton School, from Alliance Analyst data.

FIGURE 15.2

Alliance Mania

U.S. corporations have become alliance intensive, as this listing of the top ten alliance-makers illustrates. The list, compiled by *The Alliance Analyst,* covers agreements announced publicly from 1990 to 1994. *The Alliance Analyst* said that the average shareholder return on equity for the top 25 most active companies averages 17.2% a year, compared to 7.7% for the *Fortune 500.* JV refers to joint ventures and OEM to partnerships with suppliers.

Company	Total	JV	Equity	Mktg	OEM	R&D	Int'l	Other
IBM	764	148	41	357	41	336	188	263
AT&T	386	85	16	186	17	147	151	156
Hewlett-Packard	337	40	12	197	33	162	96	125
General Motors	313	152	10	97	4	102	170	170
General Electric	305	167	10	93	7	76	186	159
Digital	291	25	7	180	22	107	74	82
Motorola	285	54	10	96	10	125	114	147
DuPont	231	106	6	91	2	65	120	142
Microsoft	212	16	6	85	15	123	48	95
Sun Microsystems	207	4	4	108	21	100	47	68

Source: The Alliance Analyst (July 24, 1995), p. 15.

THE AUTO COMPANIES: OPEN KIMONOS

The relationship between U.S. automakers and their suppliers provides a striking example of the new kind of collaboration. The old relationship might have been designed expressly to build bad cars expensively. The Big Three treated their suppliers remotely, gave them as little information as possible, chose them by competitive bidding based on price, signed contracts for just one year, and readily switched from one to another for pennies. As a consequence, suppliers didn't have the knowledge or motivation to improve their products, didn't want to make long-term investments, and had no sense of participating with the auto companies in making the customer happier. The brutal treatment of GM's suppliers in the early 1990s by José Ignacio López de Arriortua turned unhappy suppliers into enraged suppliers. He bullied price cuts out of them, summarily switched contractors, and committed the sin of showing one supplier's proposals to others.

While the Big Three inflated their costs by keeping their suppliers at a distance, the Japanese automakers profited from close relationships, based partly on the *keiretsu* system of families of companies. Toyota has managed its supplier relations particularly well. Toyota sends its people to work with the suppliers for days or even months, or transfers them permanently. In fact, 11% of the top executives at Toyota's affiliated suppliers are former Toyota employees. So the parent and its suppliers know each other and their needs intimately, and of course maintain long-term relationships. (It should be added that Toyota also owns a piece of equity in its *keiretsu* suppliers.) Moreover, Toyota sponsors a suppliers' association so that the suppliers can benefit from each other's knowledge. When Toyota started working in the United States it was disappointed to find the American suppliers wouldn't "open the kimono" and didn't even want Toyota people visiting their plants.[4] The Japanese system is far from perfect, of course. Suppliers outside the *keiretsu* enjoy the freedom to sell to anyone and have higher margins. Employees of the *keiretsu* supplier companies are second-class citizens beside the employees of the parent company.[5]

The U.S. automakers are working with considerable success to turn their suppliers from surly contractors into interested partners. Jeffrey Dyer, professor of management at Wharton, followed Chrysler's efforts from 1993 to 1996. In 1990, he says, Chrysler was the least trusted of the Big Three by suppliers. But the process and the attitudes have changed. Contracts have lengthened, from two years to five, and suppliers now sometimes work without a contract. Rather than being chosen from among at least three bidders after a part has been designed, suppliers are now "presourced" before the part is designed. Suppliers are chosen on the basis of performance and track record, rather than price. The "presourced" supplier then can participate in designing the part. Competitive bidding has disappeared almost completely at Chrysler, Dyer reports, and new cars are 97% presourced. The process helps speed the development of new models, because information flows more rapidly back and forth, parts are engineered concurrently with the rest of the car, and Chrysler doesn't lose time looking for contractors. Chrysler has reduced the development time for a new car from more than four years to three years and has cut the cost of development.

Although it is not written into the contract, Chrysler expects suppliers to help it cut costs by 5% a year. Chrysler encourages cost cutting by letting the supplier keep half the money saved. Under a program called SCORE (for supplier cost reduction effort) proposed in 1989 by the company's president, Robert Lutz, Chrysler does not audit suppliers' estimates of cost reduction. Instead, as a gesture of trust, Chrysler accepts their estimates. At first some suppliers took advantage of the trust, but Chrysler let them know it was aware that it was not getting the benefit of the reductions and the estimates improved. Chrysler also gives the supplier the choice of giving Chrysler more than half the benefit of the cost cuts and in return winning a higher rating as a supplier, which can mean more business from Chrysler. Magna International, a major Canadian supplier of many kinds of parts, chose to let Chrysler collect 100% of the $75.5 million savings resulting from its suggestions. As a result, Chrysler doubled its purchases from Magna in five years to $1 billion for the 1995 model year. Chrysler also rewards its suppliers with an extra $1 per car per pound of weight saved and with a prize of $20,000 for each part they can eliminate by simplifying design.

Dyer says that Chrysler's SCORE plan reduced costs by $269 million in 1993 and by more than $1 billion in 1996. These numbers went straight to Chrysler's bottom line. The new deal for suppliers also helped make Chrysler the lowest cost producer among the Big Three, raised the company's market share, and as mentioned, speeded the design process.[6]

The relationship between Ford and PPG Industries–Chemfil, described in *Business Horizons,* is another innovative kind of partnership. Chemfil cleans auto bodies at the Taurus-Sable assembly plant in Chicago before they are painted and afterward removes paints that have been oversprayed. In the bad old days Ford would simply negotiate the lowest price it could get for given quantities of cleaning fluids, Chemfil would deliver them (assuming it had won the contract for that year), and that would have been the sum of the relationship. Now Chemfil, which is designated a Tier I supplier by Ford, comes into the plant and assumes responsibility for cleaning the auto bodies for painting and then removing excess paint later. Chemfil runs the process and maintains the equipment. Just how much fluid Chemfil uses and how it does the job is Chemfil's responsibility. Ford doesn't pay by the quantity of chemicals Chemfil uses, but for the number of cars cleaned.

A proprietary booklet outlines the responsibilities of the two parties. Ford, for example, must train the Chemfil representative in the plant in statistical process controls so that he can keep improving the process. Ford also keeps Chemfil informed about changes in the paint process so it can adjust and improve. Money saved by improvements are shared by Ford and Chemfil. As a Tier I supplier, Chemfil takes on the responsibility for managing contracts with the Tier II suppliers who actually furnish the liquids. Like Chrysler, Ford accepts on trust the costs estimated by Chemfil. The agreement assumes Chemfil will improve productivity and therefore Ford is guaranteed lower costs. However, should external factors push Chemfil costs up, then the agreement can be renegotiated upwards.[7]

CORNING: PIECES OF THE EQUATION

The history of joint ventures is littered with famous disasters. The marriage between Renault and Volvo lasted just four months. Chrysler's partnerships with Renault and Fiat never led anywhere. Corning's joint venture with Dow Chemical ended with the Dow Corning Corporation seeking protection under Chapter 11 of the bankruptcy laws because of suits arising from silicone breast implants. Sill, the joint venture is a popular if formal way for a corporation to extend its strengths or acquire new ones. Unlike other types of alliances or partnerships, it involves the establishment of a new enterprise.

In spite of the Dow Corning experience, Jamie Houghton, Corning's CEO until 1996, says:

> We've been very successful with alliances and we've been at it a very long time. People are beginning to understand that alliances are going to be more prevalent in the future than they are now, or have been in the past. Things move too fast. You know, you can't do it by yourself anymore. Big Blue can't just do everything inside the walls of IBM. So I think alliances of one form or another are going to become more and more important and at Corning we happen to have a culture which says, "That's fine. If that's the best way to do business, let's go do it."

Corning, a veteran of 48 joint ventures since the 1920s, still had 16 active ones at the end of 1996. Three quarters of them have been a success, says CEO Roger Ackerman, and historically they have contributed 25% to 35% of Corning's income, although recently that was reduced to 20% as a result of the Dow Corning mess.

Corning has a joint venture with Samsung in Korea to make TV glass. Corning pioneered TV glass design and manufacturing, but without some form of local alliance, Korea remained a closed market to Corning. Now Samsung-Corning has sales of more than $900 million a year, Corning has access to the Korean market and to the rest of Asia, and Samsung has increased production and acquired know-how from Corning. In the 1970s, when Corning developed the first usable optical fiber, it realized also that phone companies would not buy optical fiber alone but would need cable fitted with optical fiber. Corning allied itself with a company that had first-class cable technology, Siemens, and formed 50-50 joint ventures with Siemens in Germany and the United States. To add to its capacity in North America, the joint venture, Siecor Corporation, acquired other cable manufacturing facilities in the United States. To give it access to other telephone markets, Corning created fiber joint ventures in the United Kingdom and Australia. "We had the optical fiber breakthrough," says Ackerman. "But that was one piece of the equation. We had the alternative of developing our own cable technology. That would have taken, who knows? Five years? But they [Siemens] were already in the business of cabling. With them we were instantly up to speed. Siecor is the largest supplier of optical cable in the world right now."

A more recent venture with the Vitro Group in Mexico started in 1992, seemed promising because of the free trade agreement with Mexico and because the two companies' lines of consumer glassware seemed

SEI Survey	
Skill in choosing and working with partners has become critical	75%
We have achieved that	25%

to complement each other. They set up joint ventures in both countries, with each partner owning 51% of the JV in its own country. But the double joint venture proved unwieldy, the collapse of the peso made it hard to export to Mexico, and "a much looser methodology for managing" at the Mexican company, as a Corning executive puts it delicately, proved uncomfortable, so the deal was killed quickly with a few phone calls.

Corning has developed a simple set of reasons for going into a joint venture. They include getting access to a geographic market that might otherwise be closed off, getting access to a new technology, getting help bringing new technology to market, finding an outlet for products that don't fit Corning's business, and sharing risks. To make a partnership work, Corning wants to know the partner well enough to learn whether both sides have the same values. Guy Di Cicco, Corning's director of globalization, says his company looks as a rule for a 50–50, win-win mindset that makes both sides feel comfortable and disarms tensions. (American companies that take comfort from insisting on majority control of an alliance, thinking that will give them the ability to step in and save the alliance if things go wrong, are still in the old control mode.) The owners of the joint venture should give its managers some autonomy and stay out of their battles. Corning avoids joining up with competing businesses, but the increasing global reach of many companies makes that harder because a partner in Europe may become a competitor in Asia. Therefore, says Di Cicco, Corning is now more cautious about the geographic implications of its joint ventures.[8]

SAP: PARTNERS BY THE HUNDREDS

While the traditional types of partnerships like Corning's joint ventures continue to grow, companies are finding new forms and new uses for alliances. SAP, the German software company, galloped around the world with literally hundreds of alliances, growing its business at a phenomenal rate. Rhône-Poulenc Rorer uses more than a dozen research alliances to get in a good position at the starting gate in the race for gene therapies.

Without its 500 alliances around the world, says SAP America's vice president for strategic partnerships, Alexander Ott, there is no way his company could have quintupled its worldwide business between 1991 and 1996. SAP is the world's leading supplier of "enterprise software," the big client-server systems that replace mainframes and tie a company together from shop floor to boardroom. By the end of 1996, SAP had installed 9,000 of its R/3 client-server systems around the world. "We have done this without mergers, acquisitions, royalties, joint ventures, or equity deals," says Ott. In fact, none of SAP's alliances are even exclusive.

SAP uses alliances in four ways:

1. To help consulting firms implement and install R/3 systems for their clients. Since the alliances are nonexclusive, the consultants are free to recommend to their clients SAP's competitors, mainly Oracle, PeopleSoft, and Baan, a Dutch firm. But in fact the consultants more often than not choose to push SAP.
2. To help hardware companies such as IBM and Hewlett-Packard develop platforms that work with R/3 systems.
3. To work with technology partners to develop software and applications. SAP has worked with Microsoft to make R/3 run on Microsoft's NT operating system, and with data base providers such as Informix and Oracle to make R/3 compatible with their data bases.
4. To encourage universities to use R/3 for research, and in their courses and workshops.

Among SAP's 500 partners, 13 are classified as global. They include the Big Six American accounting-consulting firms and Cap Gemini, a European consultancy, as well as Electronic Data Systems, IBM, and Hewlett-Packard. HP is a three-way partner, as a customer for R/3, as a hardware provider, and as a consulting company that helps others with R/3. Oracle is both a competitor and partner of SAP's. One of the things that makes SAP an attractive partner for these companies is that installing SAP, rewarding as it may be eventually, is extremely complex, expensive, and time-consuming. It takes years for a company like HP to get R/3 running properly. So when Arthur Andersen undertakes to help a global client install R/3, that can be a hugely profitable assignment. Andersen has 3,000 consultants trained and assigned to do nothing else— and SAP helps train those consultants. Ott claims that SAP's sales create an aftermarket for its partners worth $20 billion a year.[9]

RPR: A LOT OF BETS

Rhône-Poulenc Rorer, the American-based subsidiary that runs Rhône-Poulenc's worldwide pharmaceutical business, uses partnerships in an unusual way to have a shot at the gene therapy prize. RPR is strong in four fields (cancer, asthma, anti-infectives, and antibiotics), but as of 1994 had little capability in gene therapy. RPR's recently retired chairman, Robert Cawthorn, who had previously been president of Biogen, believes that gene therapy may become the therapy of the 21st century and wants RPR to be a major player. But how to play? Looking at gene therapy now is like looking at the pieces of a jigsaw puzzle without knowing what the whole picture looks like, says Cawthorn. RPR doesn't have the skills to undertake the research itself. It might have bought one or two genetic research companies, but then it might have spent a lot of money betting on the wrong technologies. Instead, RPR chose to make a small investment in many research partners and create an array of options in a flexible network of allies.

Thierry Soursac, a young French oncologist who also has a PhD in pharmacology and an MBA, runs RPR's alliances. He says the company has made limited up-front investments of $200,000 to $5 million in 19 research partners that were chosen to match a list of research capabilities RPR thought necessary. The partners are rewarded with further injections of equity when they reach certain milestones, but since the technology is changing so fast, RPR has defined these milestones carefully and Soursac says RPR pays only if the milestone is still meaningful when it is reached. The network is fluid. Partners come in and out every quarter. Should a partner's research prove successful, RPR would have first refusal rights to exclusive or nonexclusive worldwide licenses to the products.

The strengths that Soursac sees in this approach are that RPR got the first 13 partners for a bargain price of $12.5 million, that it has access to the work of more than 2,000 scientists around the world, and that the arrangement is a flexible one that can adapt to fast-advancing technologies. On the minus side, Soursac has many large egos to deal with, the network is widely dispersed geographically, and at the beginning lawyers created "nightmare" problems, mainly over confidentiality. And the future courses of gene therapy remain very hard to predict. "We are cutting our way through the jungle and we don't see more than ten feet ahead," says Soursac.[10]

"FARMING OUT THE FARM"

Outsourcing became the most common and most controversial way of extending the corporation in the 1990s. It is criticized as a new corporate villainy, a short-sighted way of cutting costs and a devious way of displacing union workers and other expensive in-house employees. Outsourcing was the hot button that set off a strike in 1996 at two General Motors brake parts plants in Ohio that lasted 17 days and closed 26 assembly plants for lack of parts. GM is determined to cut its costs by farming more work out to cheaper plants. The auto industry has traditionally bought parts for cars from outside manufacturers: Chrysler buys 70% of its parts, Ford 50%, and GM only 30%. GM's higher reliance on expensive inside suppliers put the company at a disadvantage when the automakers started cutting costs. GM wanted to move brake production from its own plants, where UAW labor costs $43 an hour, benefits included, to a nonunion Bosch plant in South Carolina, where labor costs from $16 to $23 an hour, including a fairly good benefits package.[11] The UAW, of course, wants to protect its members' jobs. The strike ended with both sides declaring victory and the issue unresolved.

Outsourcing is nothing new, but the outbreak of modern outsourcing—"farming out the farm," *The Economist* called it—began in 1989 when Eastman Kodak turned the bulk of its information services over to three other companies, IBM, Digital Equipment Corporation, and Businessland. The deal shocked corporate information officers, because it threatened their careers, and it flashed hope to CEOs, because many of them were fed up with information departments they didn't really understand but which consumed huge amounts of cash without producing any income. The Kodak deal showed outsourcing on its best behavior. IBM and the others wanted to demonstrate that outsourcing could work and they bent over backwards to please Kodak. Kodak described the deals as partnerships and said they were based on brief, simple contracts and gentlemen's agreements. The partners had to revise the agreements frequently as they learned how to work together and as their collaboration spread around the world, but they were reported to be satisfied.

After the Kodak deal, enthusiasm for outsourcing the work of those hard-to-control and often neglected information offices spread through big American companies. The companies that signed outsourcing agreements in the early 1990s announced expected savings of 20% to 50%.[12] But a study of the earlier partnerships by the Information Systems Research Center at the University of Houston found that some of them were having "severe problems" and were being unraveled at great expense.[13]

However, the hope of saving money lived on and companies saw other good reasons for turning their information systems over to others. If you were reengineering and cutting overhead, outsourcing gave you an opportunity to redesign your systems. If you wanted to focus on your "core competencies," turning the computers over to someone else relieved management of that responsibility. If you wanted to avoid the expense of replacing computers that became obsolete too fast, and the cost of retraining employees, it was nice to have someone else do it. So the outsourcing business grew.

CSC: CONSISTENCY WANTED

The worldwide market for outsourcing information systems has exploded by $10 billion a year each year since 1994, starting at $10 billion, and is expected to reach $40 billion in 1997.[14] Computer Sciences Corporation is winning a healthy share of that market. In 1996, J.P. Morgan and CNA Financial farmed out much of their data processing to CSC for $2 billion each over the life of the contracts and Du Pont signed a ten-year $4-billion deal, most of it going to CSC.

CSC agreed to take over all of Hughes Electronics' computer systems, including the hardware and the people, under a $1.5 billion, eight-year contract that went into effect at the beginning of 1995. Hughes badly needed to remodel and unify a motley collection of systems and equipment that had accumulated over the years—as happens at many companies—and get overhead costs under control. "Hughes wanted service levels to improve," says Heidi Trost, the CSC vice president who manages the contract. "Hughes' IT wasn't managed consistently and it desperately needed consistency." Hughes wanted to be able to transfer knowledge and information easily throughout the company, but couldn't do so while it had a hodgepodge of systems.

CSC took over the ownership, operation, and maintenance of everything connected with IT, from mainframes to desktops, from networks to data centers, even the telephone system. Hughes retained only the front end of the design of new systems, to keep connected to the information strategy. Under the terms of the agreement, all 2,000 IT people displaced at Hughes were offered jobs at CSC. The task was more difficult and complex than anyone at Hughes or CSC imagined, says Trost, and CSC did stub its toes. However, the pain was eased by a gradual transition, starting in the Southern California–Arizona area and spreading out to the rest of the country. The contract was flexible and did prove to need adjustments. Hughes engineers were accustomed to choosing whatever they thought they needed, and as a result CSC found no fewer than 2,000 different configurations among Hughes' 20,000 PCs. CSC distributed a catalog with just three configurations for Hughes engineers to choose from, but the engineers rebelled at that constraint. In the end CSC settled on 20 configurations. It will take some years for the transition to be completed, but so far it is meeting the goals set by the two parties.[15]

While outsourcing information technology has won the huge contracts in the 1990s, corporations have been farming out other more modest activities as well. Being dependent on others is not something brand new. In a sense, corporations, like everyone else, have never had any choice but to outsource utilities without which they couldn't work, such as water, electricity, and telephones. But today companies have the choice of sending out for many other needs. Clearly they don't want to outsource central competitive functions, such as customer relations, strategy, or leadership. But it is easy to see how many peripheral activities, like the mailroom, the cafeteria, and parts of the personnel department, are good candidates for outsourcing.

SEI Investments is ready to outsource as many activities as it can. When it broke up its human resources department some of its people were farmed out to the divisions to do the same work there, but others were encouraged to leave and set up a new company with an outsourcing contract with SEI. Two benefits administrators incorporated themselves to bid against others for the contract with SEI (they won). CEO Al West says outsourcing gives him a flexibility he didn't have and saves "a ton of management time."[16] Decisions to outsource become questionable when they relate to more critical activities such as manufacturing, distribution, and design, but these too are more likely to be farmed out today. Companies clearly are finding that many jobs can be done by others, better, more efficiently and even at a lower cost. Outsourcing has grown into a $100-billion-a-year business, and the proportion of major corporations using outsourcing increased from 58% in 1992 to 86% in 1996.[17]

Joe Neubauer, who built Aramark on the basis of doing things for other companies better than they could do it themselves, says "outsourcing is certainly not new, but the range of outsourcing possible is now immense and still growing." He sees outsourcing as a natural part of the shift from bureaucracy and central control to a better focus, flatter management, and more autonomy. Aramark itself has tightened its own focus on catering for others and got rid of businesses it had in trucking, school buses, construction, and retirement homes. Here are some of Neubauer's thoughts and cautions on outsourcing:

> Using a large company like General Motors as an example, at any of its facilities it would be easy to find the following employees: data processors, accountants, mail clerks, lawyers, janitors, cafeteria workers, artists, security guards, copywriters, nurses, painters. Their closest encounter with the car business is the drive home. How many actually make cars? Virtually none of them. Yet the company invests tremendous resources in those employees. . . . Outsourcing these kinds of functions would free up decision-makers. . . .
>
> Line functions are also becoming candidates for outsourcing. This presents a different kind of challenge for managers. The starting point is generally a discussion about something called the "value chain." . . . The question becomes, where is that core competency of the company, the genius around which the rest of the company must revolve? . . . Understanding that helps define which links in the chain are critical to retain and which are the ones to outsource.
>
> Make no mistake, outsourcing fundamentally challenges a central tenet of the old corporate culture: control. With outsourcing comes risks—from the loss of critical skills to loss of leverage over large suppliers. Morale may suffer as employees wonder if theirs will be the next function to be outsourced. Too narrow an outlook may leave a company too insulated—disengaged from

the reality of the marketplace. Finally, there is the concern that we will outsource our way to the hollow corporation. . . .

Companies that try to compete simply by cutting costs and overhead may be in for some surprises. Outsourcing is no panacea. It's often called the "make or buy" decision. Well, let me tell you, it can quickly become the make or break decision. It can make or break your human resource management, wreak havoc on your productivity, and ultimately hurt your profitability. There are plenty of examples of chopping overhead or "farming" out a function to save money only to find that expenses go up rather than down. . . . Outsourcing just to beat costs is a mistake. Outsourcing as a defensive strategy is a loser . . . it should be a positive strategic decision, measured by long-term strategic criteria. . . . And don't give away important learning opportunities that link you with customer preferences, supplier capabilities, or new technologies. . . .

There's an equally interesting human dimension to outsourcing as well. . . . Does a GM data processor have any chance of being the president of General Motors? Will the maintenance supervisor at IBM ever be tapped to head up IBM's R&D department? . . . No. They are effectively off the career track. . . . Outsourcing brings people into those enterprises that are geared to advance them. . . . Any employee . . . can advance to top management at Aramark.[18]

James Emshoff, whose medical transcription company, Medquist, exists by outsourcing, reinforces Neubauer's points. The interesting thing to ask when you consider the choice of doing something inside or outside the company, he says, "is can you hook into somebody as a partner who is going to take this thing to the next level of innovation? Too much weight is given to just a brutal cost reduction. Give it to someone who will squeeze 30% of the costs out! The more innovative approach is to give it to somebody who has that activity as their core and you will get three times the innovation could have done out of your own operation."[19]

What lies beyond outsourcing? Beyond joint ventures, partnerships, alliances, networks? Is the Japanese *keiretsu* a model for the rest of the world? Does the Chinese family-type concern have lessons for business in Europe and the Americas? The 55 million overseas Chinese are extraordinarily successful in business. *Fortune* describes them as "nothing less than the world's most vigorous capitalists."[20] Wong Yip Yan, chairman of WyWy House, a large, diversified company based in Singapore, sees the Southeast Asian economy overtaking that of the United States on the strength of those overseas Chinese who, he says, will produce the world's first trillionaires. Wong is one of the few overseas Chinese entrepreneurs who will not employ family members, and he would agree now it may have been a mistake not to hire other Wongs.[21] Good people are hard to get in Asia today, and you have to have people you can trust.

Much of the strength of the Chinese business derives from the intense cultivation of networks of family and friends: people you can trust; people you can deal with without bothering with lawyers and contracts. Overseas Chinese businesses tend to be family businesses (as are most of India's large companies) and the sons and occasionally the daughters work in the same room with the patriarch before they are sent off to run outposts of the empire. "Any Chinese organization is a learning organization because we all sit around the table and gossip about each other," says Wong. "That's a learning organization. No big office, no conference room. The chief sits at a table in the middle and everyone hears what he says."

At Kingston Technology Corporation in Fountain Valley, California, the two founders, David Sun and John Tu, sit in the middle of a bullpen in the company offices and while others don't sit at the same table, they can hear some of the conversation, especially when Sun, the boisterous partner, is talking. The immigrant founders have created what is probably the closest thing to a big Chinese family concern in the United States—and an extremely successful one. The employees are not relatives, but they are treated like family. Sun and Tu say that employees come first, before customers and suppliers. They believe employees should share in the profits. So when Kingston, a start-up in 1987, sold for $1.5 billion to Softbank Corporation in 1996, Sun and Tu shared a huge windfall. Kingston reinvested $500 million back into Softbank, leaving $1 billion clear. The partners didn't think the size of the profit was any reason to change their rule that employees should get 10% of the profits, so they set aside $100 million for bonuses to the 250 employees. The huge award nearly coincided and contrasted eloquently with the $90-million package awarded to Michael Ovitz upon his ignominious departure from Walt Disney.

The new owner, Softbank, described as the Japanese Microsoft, agreed not to change Kingston's philosophy. Like other overseas Chinese, Sun and Tu have no executive airs and trappings. They like to trust others. They have no lawyers on their staff and would like their relations with others to be based on trust and a handshake. In fact, they have no written contracts with the two manufacturers that assemble their products. But they have found it necessary to be a little more worldly in dealing with others. Big companies such as IBM, which is both a customer and a supplier, demand contracts. And Kingston has been let down by partners they trusted without a contract. So they have outside lawyers look at contracts today.[22]

Where Kingston departs from the overseas Chinese is in what Gary MacDonald, vice president of marketing, describes as "an almost frightening level of trust in the employees." The Chinese family firm trusts family and friends, but not the employees. In fact, Chinese firms may treat employees downright cruelly, as workers in sweatshops all over Asia (and in New York, for that matter) can testify. The Chinese firm is authoritarian and paternalistic. The boss fails in his responsibilities if he lets others make decisions. The idea of pushing responsibility down as low as possible, which is becoming the American way, does not fit the Chinese model.

Another obstacle to exchanging models across the Pacific is that most big American companies are public while the Chinese companies are mostly private. Kingston is private too, for that matter, and MacDonald agrees that Kingston could not be managed as it is if it had to answer to Wall Street every quarter. Wall Street would find the Chinese style too ad hoc and informal, too impenetrable.

The point is not whether Asia or the West can import models from the other side. They wouldn't work. But ideas can be adapted. Overseas Chinese companies are turning more to professional managers and the stock markets. And the *keiretsu* are loosening up. In the West, clearly, the idea has taken hold that partnerships, alliances, joint ventures, outsourcing—networks of companies—are becoming essential to business today. Western corporations have entered into alliances by the hundreds. They can serve to break into new markets, to spread risks, to acquire new technologies and products, to allow management to concentrate on the core of its business and let others do what they can do better. Partnerships need to be approached with some ambivalence. On the one hand, there must be a willingness to make a long-term commitment, which means getting to know your partners well enough to trust them. On the other hand, since many partnerships soon fail or lose their justification, you need the flexibility to withdraw quickly. You have to balance the need to know enough about what the partner or outsourcing company is doing to be satisfied it is working in your interest with the need to let the alliance work free of meddling. You need to let your partner know all he needs to know to work effectively, but not so much that he can turn around and become a rival. Partners can be allies in one market or in one part of the world and competitors in another. They can change from one to the other quickly. Managing a portfolio of partners is a subtle, demanding affair.

Pointers

- Before outsourcing or entering a partnership, have you figured out what you do best and what faculties you need to keep because they are the essence of your organization?
- Do you have important, sound reasons for going into a partnership, such as gaining entry into a new market, or bringing new products into your market, or gaining new technology?
- Is it a good deal for both sides?
- Is there trust and good chemistry on both sides?
- Will you learn from the partnership?
- Do you treat your suppliers as partners?
- Do you treat your customers as partners?
- If you are starting a joint venture, are you willing to let it operate autonomously?
- If you are outsourcing, have you tested the alternatives, including giving your own people a chance to bid on the work?

Links

- A partnership is an opportunity to learn about new markets, new ways of managing.
- Working for a catering company that runs corporate cafeterias, for example, gives people more opportunities than working in a company-

owned cafeteria, so outsourcing can create some better career prospects.

- Outsourcing saves management time.

Cautions

- Outsourcing should not be approached simply as a device to save money. It probably won't.
- Partnerships created imprudently may let critical knowledge escape and help set up a competitor.
- A company may let its critical skills drift away in a badly designed partnership.
- Although companies have always outsourced work, it has become a major and inflammatory issue between labor and management.

16

THE LEARNING LOOP

> I would argue that the rate at which individuals and organizations learn may become the only sustainable competitive advantage, especially in knowledge-intensive industries.
>
> —Ray Stata, CEO, Analog Devices Incorporated[1]

Jamie Houghton, who retired as CEO of Corning in 1996, makes a telling point about knowledge: if Corning takes one pound of glass and turns it into a Corelle dinner plate, the glass sells for 90 cents per pound. But if Corning turns the same amount of glass into optical fiber it sells for $550 per pound. The difference is knowledge. Applying a high level of skill to a simple product enhances its value, in this case, by more than 600 times. As we learn to add more value to products and processes by applying skills and knowledge, the more important it becomes to learn—and to learn how to learn. Houghton also relates that in 1972 one-third of Corning's work force was made up of people whose work was conceptual and two-thirds of people who worked with their hands. By 1994, the ratio had been reversed. Two-thirds of Corning's employees were conceptual workers.[2]

SEI Survey	
It is critical that an organization be flexible and dynamic, therefore continuously learning	83%
We are achieving that	15%

This is the age of the knowledge worker, as Peter Drucker named it. People with knowledge replace land, equipment, and capital as a company's chief asset. This means, of course, that today's employees have to be better educated and better trained than they were. As we said in Chapter 1, the work force of 1900, when only one American in ten graduated from high school, would have been useless in today's workplace. Today, 82% of the population has a high school diploma and 23% a bachelor's degree or higher. Even so, many employees need remedial education as well as job training to function in the new corporation. Managers foresee that finding and keeping qualified people will be crucial to competing in the 21st century.

The demand for knowledge is so intense today that it goes far beyond the education and training of individuals. If individuals learn but don't share that knowledge, it has only limited use for the organization. And if the organization does not record that knowledge, then it is not available for others in the organization. The whole concept of learning and knowledge is evolving, naturally enough, in much the same way as the concept of the corporation itself is evolving. We are moving from a functional to a systemic view of the corporation, and therefore our knowledge needs to be systemic too. We need to understand not just the parts of the organization, but also how they act on each other. As management's focus shifts from products to processes, we need to know more about processes. As organizations evolve from the command-and-control mode to the sense-and-respond mode, our attitude about information changes from seeing it as something to be controlled from the top to something that comes out of the market and pulls the company along.[3]

Traditionally, we have learned mostly by studying the past. But experience can be a bad teacher, and can become a hindrance to making the right decisions when the world is changing rapidly. If our experience fixes patterns in our minds that are no longer valid, then we are looking at the world through a distorted lens. Ford had ample evidence from its own research in the 1970s that a minivan would be a huge success, but the evidence didn't fit top management's view of the auto market. So it was left to Chrysler, pushed by defectors from Ford, to prove the appeal of the minivan. NASA satellites began picking up evidence of a hole in the ozone layer back in 1978 but the news of the hole was not published until 1985. The reason: scientists had programmed their computers to reject very low ozone readings on the assumption that these could only be the result of instrument errors. (Fortunately, NASA still had the original data and could go back and see that the ozone levels had been falling since 1978.)[4] The mind works the same way. When information doesn't fit a familiar pattern, it is likely to be rejected. We think we are seeing the facts, but we are actually seeing what the models in our head tell us to see. Therefore an important part of learning is to know what to discard.

Another problem with traditional learning is that it deadens the imagination and inclines us to distrust intuition. But intuition has always been important to leaders and remains so, in spite of all the information available today to decision makers. It's a matter of striking a balance between what you know instinctively is right and what you can prove with facts. Many important leaders have made fine decisions intuitively. Ray Kroc decided to spend $2.7 million he didn't have in 1960 to buy out the McDonald brothers in spite of the negative advice he was getting because "my funnybone instinct kept urging me on." Ronald Reagan didn't seem to care to know much about the details of government, or even the basic facts, but his political intuitions were superb. Bill Clinton revels in the details of policy and government, but he can't translate that knowledge into principled policy. Intuition is not uninformed guesswork. "It means knowing your business," says Ross Perot. "It means bringing to bear on a situation everything you've seen, felt, tasted, and experienced in an industry." So intuition is a different kind of learning that the executive needs.[5]

If business is in the van of education reform, the education establishment brings up the rearguard. Someone stepping out of 1900 into 1997 would probably find the workplace unrecognizable, but today's schoolroom would probably be comfortably familiar, give or take a few computers. Teaching is basically the same now as it was then. The teacher gets up and talks to the class. Bored students take some notes and forget most of what the teacher says. The education establishment is an enormous obstacle to change. Some educators, particularly those in private education, are beginning to believe a mass of research that shows there are better ways of teaching and learning. They talk of "student-centered learning," for example, which involves students in every aspect of their education, even the design of the curriculum. Students retain 15% of what they hear in a lecture, but they will remember 80% of what they experience.

BEYOND THE DISCIPLINES

In higher education, the business schools are changing, some of them radically. Perhaps they have more of a sense of the market and their customers' requirements than, for example, the liberal arts departments. The pressure to change business schools began in the mid-1980s, reflecting the competitive pressures that were changing business itself. If there was to be a new kind of management, there needed to be a new kind of business school. *Business Week* added to the pressure by starting a semiannual survey in 1988 to rank the top business schools. The schools compete keenly for a high ranking, which can translate into recruiting better students and making executive education programs more marketable.

It is hard to believe now, but four decades ago business schools had as little prestige as teachers' colleges and their professors had starting salaries below those of high school teachers. Two devastating reports issued separately in 1959 by the Ford Foundation and the Carnegie Foundation attacked the business schools for the low caliber of their teachers, research, and students, and for being out of touch with business. The resulting wave of reform raised standards and spending, and established some academic rigor. The schools fell into a pattern of teaching six basic disciplines: accounting, finance, human resources, marketing, operations, and strategy. In time the business schools' curricula acquired a monotonous sameness. The search for academic respectability led professors deeper into their specialties. Finance professors taught finance and did not concern themselves with marketing. The trouble with this approach, as the SEI Center studies pointed out, was that no business problem is solved inside a particular discipline. All business problems are cross-functional. Moreover, management is much more than the six disciplines. What about innovation, entrepreneurship, leadership, risk, information? And what about the rest of the world? The business school curriculum focused on the United States.

At Wharton, which ranked first in the *Business* Week surveys of 1994 and 1996, the SEI Center serves as a think tank to study the character of the 21st century corporation and hence its education needs. On the basis of the SEI Center's early work, Wharton began to move in 1989 under the then dean, Russell Palmer, to reflect the reality and the change in business. Under Palmer's successor, Tom Gerrity, Wharton added courses on quality, ethics, leadership, teamwork, information, and global business. Students are encouraged to take a one-month study excursion overseas. To break down the walls among the disciplines, the curriculum changed to include cross-functional courses taught by teams of professors from different departments. The traditional two-semester year was replaced by four six-week modules. Students work in teams of six, take on multidisciplinary case studies, and go out to the "field" on real consulting assignments. In the spirit of empowerment, students have more say in the affairs of the school. They sit on the committees that deal with the reforms and with administration. They also rate the professors in a formal "feedback" process that forces the faculty to be responsive. One professor has been removed from a course because of poor ratings by the students. Wharton recognizes it can't reform and then settle back into a static state if business continues to change, so the SEI Center continues to provide research for further reforms.

BREAKING ACADEMIC BARRIERS

It might be impossible to find a business school in the United States that didn't begin to make major changes in the last ten years or so. Under Joseph White, who came from Cummins Engine Company in 1990, the University of Michigan business school has experimented with a string of reforms, including a new requirement that teachers must get a "very good" rating from their students to win tenure.

William Glavin, former vice chairman of the Xerox Corporation, took some of the ideas developed at Wharton, where he had served as an adviser, and applied them vigorously as president of Babson College, an all-business school outside Boston. He was able to go further than Wharton has gone. Babson eliminated functional courses for first-year students. Instead they take modules of four, eight, and 13 weeks focusing on specific business problems. In the second module, for example, they go through the process of determining the potential for a new product. An accounting professor deals with the cost implications of the new product, and a law professor leads the discussion about the tax implications and what kind of organization could handle the new product. Many of the module classes have two or more professors in attendance. In their second year, the Babson students can concentrate on a functional discipline, but with the idea that when they graduate they will think of themselves not as finance or marketing specialists, but as entrepreneurial leaders. Glavin recalls that when he was still at Xerox at the end of the 1980s he told a Wharton board that the school was preparing people for jobs that no longer existed. Businesses were getting rid of their corporate staffs of specialized experts and looking instead for entrepreneurs and managers who could handle all the problems.

So much change is hard on the academic traditions of specialization, independence (not to say contrariness), and devotion to the principle of tenure through publication rather than teaching. How can you win tenure, much less the respect of your colleagues, by writing research reports on nonacademic subjects such as teamwork and the art of negotiating? Breaking through these academic barriers is hardest at the most prestigious schools, where the professors are armored with honors and tenure, and nowhere has it been harder than at the Harvard Business School. While other schools tried to make fundamental changes, Harvard steered the same course with mild corrections through the 15-year reign of Dean John McArthur.

However, Harvard-bred Kim Clark, who believes passionately that management really can make a difference, replaced McArthur in 1995 and started to apply vigorously to the school itself the new management ideas that some of the professors had been teaching. While McArthur had barely tolerated e-mail, Clark spent $11 million in six months to saturate the school with information technology. David Upton, a principal architect of the new system, explains that rather than make the reform with the typical large technology project that would deliver some monolithic system three years after it was needed, Harvard chose a dynamic approach that adds systems in small chunks. The chunks fit into a larger plan, which itself can evolve.

Harvard's new system is meant to be open, easy to use and pervasive. The school's intranet is the basic tool for running the school and for much of the learning. Professors can call up photos of their students in seating charts, and drill down to get a student's résumé and even hear the student's voice pronouncing his or her own name (important in a school with many foreign students). Each student has a home page which carries schedules, assignments, course outlines, much of the course material, and announcements and questions from professors. Although students still seem to prefer the famous Harvard case studies on paper, the cases are being digitized too, with video and audio components. In one case study students can see a Chinese factory in operation and listen to its American manager.[6]

Just as consultants talk of the virtual corporation, academics are talking about the virtual university. Information technology makes it possible to give an interactive, multimedia course to students far away. Dissatisfaction with the standard lecture-room delivery of knowledge and its cost is spurring professors to develop multimedia courses that can deliver to the Podunk student by CD-ROM or the Internet the same materials that the MIT, Stanford, or Wharton student gets. The material can be updated instantly, while it may take years to revise a textbook. It can be customized in the sense that the student can call up the material when and where he wants it. A combination of lectures, discussions, and interactive visual displays may get more into the mind of the student than a professor standing and lecturing for an hour. An interactive display can convey to an engineering student the hard-to-understand theory of how materials are distorted more clearly and rapidly than a lecturer can.[7]

One of the co-authors of this book, Jerry Wind, is co-founder of what could be described as a university halfway to being virtual, the new Interdisciplinary Center of Law, Business, and Technology in Herzliyya, near Tel Aviv. The school has a minimal staff (25 full-time teachers for 1,500 students) and a small library, but plenty of part-time teachers, many of them American professors, who can be called in to teach pieces of cross-functional courses. The center is developing the electronic delivery of instruction and material.

ADVENTURES IN TRAINING

"The irony of all this is that while universities become more like companies, companies are trying to become more like universities," as *The Economist* observed.[8] Indeed many businesses call their training centers universities. Corporate spending on training has grown hugely. The corporations in the United States with more than 100 employees spent $59.8 billion in 1996 to train a total of 58.6 million employees, according to a survey by *Training* magazine. Companies that employ more than 10,000 people spent on average $15 million on training in 1996.[9] Some companies involved in new technology and new management practices spent far more. For example, Andersen Consulting invested $290 million in training, Motorola $240 million.

The eagerness to find some magic formula for transforming and energizing their employees led some corporations to turn years ago to the "human potential movement," and take up "experiential adventures," New Age concepts, and even outright cults. In the 1980s, Werner Erhard, the founder of "est," and the "Church" of Scientology both established organizations focused on the business training market. Erhard replaced est with Transformation Technologies Inc., which licensed management consultants to use his materials. These materials, while purged of some of the more brutal aspects of the early est, exposed trainees to hours of unfathomable babble that was supposed to change their lives. Although Hollywood celebrities make the most enthusiastic converts to cults, business leaders proved gullible too. Transformation Technologies' clients in the late 1980s included Boeing, General Dynamics, IBM, and Lockheed. Happily, the corporate interest in cult training has subsided.[10] However, adventure experiences seem to have won a permanent place in the corporate training arsenal. Evidently an outdoor experience spiced with the thrill of a little danger (carefully limited with a short safety rope), turns office rivals into team buddies. If you fall backwards off a wall and your colleagues catch you safely in their arms, then you are going to trust them to protect you in the office too, aren't you? Motivational speakers also remain very popular. The enthusiasm they engender lasts for at least a week.

Putting aside the woo-woo stuff, the mainstream of corporate training is moving in directions that go to the heart of pedagogy. Business has reasons for changing and improving training that may be stronger and more urgent than the business schools' reasons for reform. While the most common means of delivering that training is still the classroom, businesses are trying many alternatives. There are several obvious reasons for doing so. One of them is simple and practical: in a downsized, speeded-up corporation there just isn't enough time for people to go off for a week or two or even a day, to take a course. If Hewlett-Packard's product cycle is as short as six months, one or two weeks' absence cuts into it too much. Microsoft, which, unlike many companies, has no formal management training and no "university" of its own, doesn't believe in heavy doses of training. "Going away for training goes against our culture," says Mike Murray, vice president for human relations at Microsoft. "Our work is so time sensitive that taking a day out of the office is impossible. Our people get antsy after half a day. So they stop listening even if the class lasts all day. Microsoft prefers to use job-specific training, rather than textbook or theoretical learning."[11]

The increasing demand for executive training at the business schools shows that formal courses lasting a week or more remain important for certain purposes. These courses work when they give the executive fundamental new skills or knowledge. The executive can go back to the office and use that platform of knowledge, augmenting and refreshing it with electronic, just-in-time training. The executive courses also fulfill a function which no amount of remote, just-in-time training could do: they connect the executive with a new network of colleagues. Like many aspects of the new corporation covered in this book, business training won't shift altogether from the old mode to the new, but will likely become a balance of the two, and each company will need to find the balance that fits its needs best.

XEROX: A SOCIAL EXPERIENCE

The reasons why formal corporate training often fails come vividly clear in an article in *Training* magazine about an attempt to cross-train people in a Xerox customer services center in Lewisville, near Dallas. The center had three departments and employees would often have to shunt customers from one department to another to solve a problem, an experience frustrating alike to customers and employees. Xerox decided to bring the three departments together and cross-train everybody so that each representative could deal with all of a customer's problems. There would be no more shunting. A consultant made the sensible suggestion that since the three departments already had all the necessary knowledge, the employees could train each other. The Xerox training headquarters in Leesburg, Virginia, was horrified and vetoed the idea. Its representatives made a quick visit to Lewisville to look at the training requirements, which they then passed on to curriculum designers in Leesburg. Months later the trainers brought detailed scripts to Lewisville and began an exhaustive series of courses. Trainees in billing and credit procedures had to sit through 11 weeks of lectures. The trainees complained they heard a lot about tasks they would never perform and little about critical parts of the job. They said the trainers had no real knowledge of what went on in the center, so when they returned to their desks their co-workers had to explain to them what they really needed to know. In any case, by then the trainees had forgotten what they had been told in class.

When the failure of the traditional approach became evident, the classes stopped. Xerox went back to the consultants, the Institute for Research and Learning, at Menlo Park, California, and followed their advice this time. The service reps were taken out of their solitary cubicles and put together in mixed groups of six or seven. They started teaching each other and handling customer calls from the first day. They learned socially, by talking, listening, and doing. They helped each other learn and they found the experience exhilarating. The training worked. (Unfortunately, they are all back in their departmental cubicles because after a two-year experiment Xerox decided in 1996 it couldn't afford the considerable cost of completing the merger of the three departments. So the operation was a success but the patient died.)[12]

MOTOROLA: DECAY IN 30 DAYS

Beginning with Robert Galvin in the early 1980s, Motorola's CEOs have made training one of the company's hallmarks. Motorolans are required to take five days of training a year and that may go up to 20 days by 2000, although there may be no formal mandate. Engineers already take that much training. The company spends 4% of its payroll on training (7% if you include the pay and expenses of trainees). Motorola University's budget of $120 million is about half the corporation's total training bill. Motorola University in Schaumburg, Illinois, has the staff and facilities of a sizable business school, as well as 11 branch offices around the world, and sales offices in Beijing, Tianjin, Tokyo, Yokohama, and Singapore (to sell course materials to its business units, suppliers, and customers).

Over the years, Motorola has learned a thing or two about corporate training. The first unpleasant surprise came when Motorola tried to train its work force in quality improvement methods and found that 40% of them were functionally illiterate and innumerate. So Motorola had to start again with some basic education. Then Motorola was surprised to find that training workers did no good if their supervisors hadn't also been trained. Middle managers just told the workers to go back to the old way of doing things. So Motorola started once again, from the top this time, with Bob Galvin taking the training himself. (At Xerox the "cascade" approach to training became a classic example of doing it right. The CEO in 1984, David Kearns, took the quality training himself, then trained his direct reports, who in turn trained theirs, and so on down to the bottom of the company. Thus everyone except people at the bottom rank of Xerox both received and gave training.)

Motorola's large, formal training structure conflicts somewhat with the new directions of corporate education, but has become more flexible. Motorola recognizes that there are many ways of delivering training, says Edward Bales, a consultant and former corporate director of education. Motorola University actually delivers only 50% of the company's training. Business units are free to pick their own training, which can be supplied by the corporation, by outside vendors, or by the units themselves. Training can be delivered on Netscape or the company's intranet. Motorola recently introduced the first interactive course on the intranet. Motorolans anywhere in the world can access it when they need it. Motorola U. sees its role as one of experimenting, leading, and helping as much as conducting training. The company has experimented successfully with virtual reality as a tool for training new assembly line workers. Normally, new hires would go straight to work on the line under supervision, but Bales says that after three days on a virtual line they have the proficiency of someone who has worked on a real line for five or six months. "There are huge, huge returns," says Bales. The idea is not as far-fetched as it may sound if you consider that much of the work in a plant today consists of operating computers.

Bales says training starts to decay immediately and usually disappears from the trainee's mind within 30 days unless used. The trainee also needs to go back to the right environment. If the manager does not understand what the trainee has learned, or the workplace hasn't been adapted to use the new training, then the training is lost. The complex coordination required by this just-in-time approach to training argues in favor of the electronic delivery of instruction at the trainee's workplace when he needs it.[13]

HEWLETT-PACKARD: TAKE WHAT YOU NEED

Hewlett-Packard puts almost as much effort into training as Motorola (and has devoted a steady 3.3% of its payroll to it for decades), but it uses a more informal process. HP has no university and has moved away from classroom training. Claudia Davis, director of training, questions the sense of taking a prescribed amount of training. "Why would you take 40 hours or 80 hours if you don't need it?" she asks. "Take whatever you personally need. People here are expected to learn but they are free to choose how to do it. It's not my job to make sure people do it. They are responsible for their own training. It's really as if you are your own employer. The company doesn't take care of you. We just make it easier for you." At the top level, HP puts its managers through what it calls "beachhead scanning," five-day sessions for different groups of executives to listen to people like C. K. Prahalad and think about strategy and future markets. But for others the training is more likely to be on the job, or through mentoring. "If a person takes a five-day course, 40% of his time is probably wasted," says Davis. "But if he takes it at his desk on a computer when he wants it after hours and can scan for key words to find out what he needs, then it becomes much more productive."[14]

HP follows up on the training not by asking the people who participated if they profited (they will usually say it was marvelous), but by asking the people they manage if they have seen any changes. Salespeople used to take time off for training on new products, but they found the training ineffective and now they are more likely to snatch bits and pieces of training at breakfast or lunch sessions. Now that they all have laptops they can also tie into training when it's most convenient, and search for the specific segment they may need.[15] Connecting the field representatives into a data base actually reduces the need for some training. HP now services all makes of equipment at its clients' offices, but the reps don't need to know all about all of them. From the site, they can call up the information they need to service a particular machine.

LEARNING TO LEARN

Training individuals is one thing. Teaching the whole organization to learn is another—it is more difficult, more complex, and subject lately to intense discussion from many angles, including New Age philosophizing that is hard to connect concretely with the business world. The hype and the ambiguousness shouldn't stop us from accepting the importance of creating a learning organization. This is not a vague concept. A learning organization opens itself to acquire, develop, and distribute knowledge rapidly so that everyone may have access to the newest and best ideas, practices, and products. It examines its own processes systematically and frequently to improve them. The case of how 3M expanded the use of microreplication to many uses unimaginable in the beginning, going from overhead projectors to abrasives to reflectors, is an example of a learning organization at its best (see Chapter 11).

Bureaucracies, among them classic Western corporations, are not learning organizations. They are resistant to learning. They close themselves off to the outside; they don't learn from their mistakes, and their people don't learn from each other. Instead of considering knowledge an asset whose value increases as it is shared, they consider it a weapon to be guarded in secrecy, as much from others inside as those outside.

When the enormity of the success of Japanese industry awoke the West two decades ago, it was evident that Japanese organizations had learned how to learn well and quickly. They had created learning organizations. Part of the reason was simply good organization. The Japanese assiduously attended and took notes and photographs at professional and technical meetings. Toyota employed hundreds of engineers to do nothing but visit its plants, picking up good ideas in one place and taking them to another. Since soon after World War II, the Japanese Union of Scientists and Engineers (JUSE) has served as a well-used forum for training and exchanging ideas about improving quality.

Beyond these obvious devices for promoting learning, Japanese culture seems more suited to spreading knowledge. In *The Knowledge-Creating Company,* Ikujiro Nonaka and Hirotaka Takeuchi, both American-trained professors at Hitotsubashi University, explain some of the differences between East and West. Westerners regard organizations as machines for processing information which is construed as hard data that is formal and systematic. The Japanese, they say, also recognize the importance of the kind of tacit knowledge that a master craftsman may have in his fingertips but which he cannot explain in words. The difference is the difference between viewing an organization as a machine and viewing it as a living organism. The tacit knowledge is subjective and intuitive, and hard to communicate, but the Japanese succeed in communicating it in subtle ways. They use metaphors and symbols which mean little to the Westerner but create insights for the Japanese. The tacit knowledge is also transmitted through the continuity of culture in Japanese corporations. In any case, the result is that the Japanese succeed in turning tacit knowledge into explicit knowledge, which helps explain how the best Japanese companies reached high levels of productivity and quality and turned out so many new products.[16]

Some of the management devices widely adopted now by Western organizations push them toward being learning organizations. Benchmarking, for example, has the bracing effect of showing corporate bureaucrats that someone else really has figured out a way of doing things better. As long as you don't look too closely at what others are doing, you can imagine that you know best. But a systematic study of other organizations can soon wipe the smug look off your face. What red-blooded American executive would have boasted 20 years ago that "we steal shamelessly" as Roger Milliken and others do now? Benchmarking also serves to rid you of knowledge that is no longer or never was true, an important part of learning. When teams bring together people from different parts of an organization, different disciplines, and different levels, they serve to spread knowledge and break down insular attitudes. The concept of the "boundaryless" organization promoted by GE has the same effect of breaking down barriers to spread knowledge. While the United States does not have its own JUSE, it does have the Baldrige quality award which since 1988 has established national criteria for good management practices. Many other organizations, such as the Center for Quality Management in Cambridge, the American Society for Quality Control in Milwaukee, and the American Productivity and Quality Center in Houston have also served to spread knowledge in industry.

THE LOGIC OF FEEDBACK

While some widespread new management techniques help a company to learn, they do not create a learning organization, that is, an organization that constantly improves itself by analyzing the results of its actions. Managers pride themselves on their logic and fact-based decision making, but in reality their thinking is no more logical than that of the rest of society. We live in a society that can't tell junk science from real science, in which people believe in astrology, effortless dieting, UFOs, the imminent threat of an airborne attack by United Nations troops, and the subversive threat from the Tripartite Commission. Why should business leaders be any different?

The simple idea of "feedback" is a powerful tool for bringing a measure of logic to an organization and, at the same time, turning it into a learning organization. We use feedback all our lives to learn. If a child touches a hot stove he learns never again to do it. It is a natural process for learning. When it comes to organizations, the feedback becomes more complex. John Dewey expressed the idea as a repetitious cycle of invention, observation, reflection, and action. The idea appears in management theory under many guises, the best known being W. Edwards Deming's "plan, do, check, act" (PDCA) cycle for achieving continuous improvement.

The "closed-loop feedback" doesn't work even when applied to a simple process if people don't know how to use it. When Deming first tried to help the Nashua Corporation in 1979 he found that the technicians producing coated copying paper made adjustments every time they saw any variation in the thickness of the coating because they didn't understand there was a natural variation. By misinterpreting the feedback, they actually made the variation worse. The machinery worked better without their meddling. Deming taught them how to take a series of measurements and use them in control charts so that they would know what adjustments, if any, were really necessary.

The messages delivered by feedback get derailed when the facts conflict with what we think we know. John Sterman, a professor at MIT's Sloan School, has done extensive work on learning in complex organizations, and points out that mental images can block out the knowledge that should come from "closed-loop learning." As an example, he points to NASA's failure to notice evidence of holes in the ozone layers picked up by its satellites, which we described earlier in this chapter. The mind works the same way. When information doesn't fit a pattern in our minds, it is likely to be rejected.

To remove the false models in our heads, Chris Argyris of the Har-

FIGURE 16.1

Learning Circles

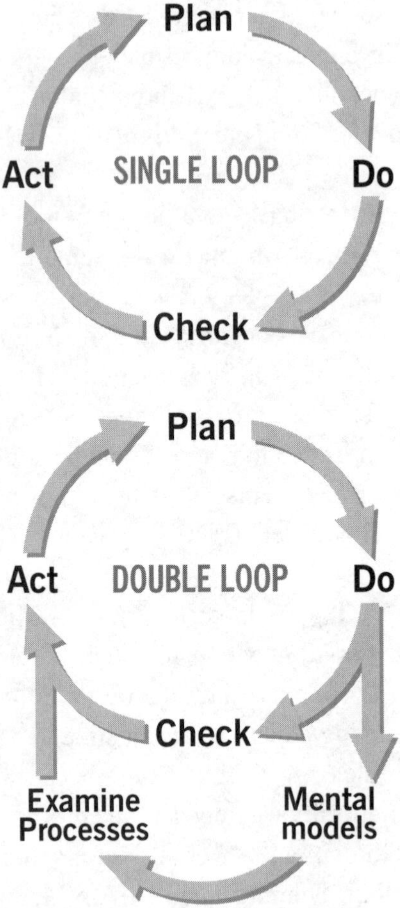

vard Business School proposed the idea of double-loop learning (see Figure 16.1.). Instead of having just one loop processed by our mental models, there should be a second part to the loop which would examine the models themselves. To put it very simply, we should look not only for what went wrong and make a correction, but we should examine why it went wrong and correct the system. Then the organization has acquired new knowledge and a new method for learning. In practice, of course, the use of feedback to help an organization is extremely complex, subject to many variables, distortions, and delays. Interactive models and virtual worlds can be very helpful. Flight simulators, used for many years, are an obvious example. They can throw more simulated emergencies at a trainee in a day than a pilot might encounter in a lifetime of flying.[17]

MICROSOFT: BRUTAL CRITIQUES

How Microsoft uses feedback to improve and learn is described in some detail by Michael Cusumano and Richard Selby in *Microsoft Secrets*. Beginning in the 1980s, Microsoft started to make it a regular practice to run a postmortem after each project had finished. The postmortems take about three months to complete and more than half of them result in detailed written reports which Bill Gates and other executives read closely. Microsoft people don't much appreciate instructions from above or advice from consultants, but they can be brutal when asked to critique their own work. Therefore the postmortems have teeth. The disastrous development of Word 3 for Windows, which was shipped four years behind schedule in 1989, produced some powerful postmortems that led to significant improvements in how Microsoft develops software. The earlier feedbacks looked only for the mistakes that had been made in the product, not the weaknesses in the process. In the 1990s Microsoft added the second loop to the postmortems by focusing on process. Attention shifted from what went wrong to why it went wrong.

In 1990 Microsoft also started to tap in to the vast number of contacts it has with customers—some 60,000 a day by computer or phone—to add to the feedback. That not only added market reality to what the postmortems produced, but also improved Microsoft's reputation for dealing unsympathetically with customers. To spread the benefits of what it was learning—so that the whole company, rather than individual teams, would learn and improve—Microsoft circulated reports and the postmortems themselves, used a videotape talk, arranged retreats, had lunches for the opposite numbers in different projects. In spite of these efforts to turn Microsoft into a learning organization—more than you would find in most companies—the development teams report the same kinds of problems show up in one project after another.[18] Becoming a learning organization is not simple or easy.

Pointers

- Do you have a culture that encourages learning?
- Are you creating a learning organization?

- Do you systematically monitor what you are doing so that you can do it better (single-loop learning)?
- Do you systematically examine your processes and your mental images of the business to see where they need to be revised and what needs to be unlearned (double-loop learning)?
- Do you have a structure and culture that encourages the transfer of knowledge from one part of the organization to others?
- Do you systematically look outside the organization for new ideas?
- Are you offering your employees the training they need to maintain the competitiveness of your organization?
- Are you using information technology to deliver just-in-time training to your people when and where they need it?
- Are you also offering the best mix of training methods, including classroom and university training, regional meetings, "virtual" instruction, refresher courses, and "social learning"?
- Are you testing the value of your training by examining changes in the behavior of the people who have been trained?
- Does the learning in your organization stretch all the way from the customer back through every process in the organization, so as to link the whole into a single system responding to the market?

Links

- Benchmarking, teams, information technology, and empowerment all have the effect of helping create learning systems.
- If people are trained but then go back to bosses and systems that are not prepared to use what they have learned, the training is wasted.

Cautions

- If training is not used within 30 days or so, it begins to evaporate.
- Managers in downsized, speeded-up companies don't have much time or patience for classroom training.
- Effective as many of the new training and teaching methods may be, multimedia training and virtual classes are unlikely to eliminate classic training. We can expect, rather, a balance of the two.

17

THE CIVIC ENTERPRISE

We simply want to do business in a responsible way and this,
we feel, will have a direct impact on the bottom line.
—Peter Jacobi, President, Levi Strauss

Y ou still hear the argument, from a few unreconstructed capitalist cowboys like Al Dunlap, that the corporation has no purpose other than to enrich its stockholders. The argument has lost most of its support, as outlined in Chapter 4. We expect more from business today. The corporation that forgets this is likely to find itself hard pressed by some combination of customers, lawyers, whistleblowers, unions, civil rights advocates, feminists, environmentalists, demonstrators, protesters, animal rights activists, tribal representatives, the media, local officials, and government agencies. The standards of the behavior expected of business are rising and the social and economic, not to mention legal, penalties of transgression are more severe.

Corporations are highly vulnerable to attack on the grounds of ethical failures, and they can most readily show their good faith by a demonstration of what Peter Drucker once dismissed as "ethical chic." In the last ten years American corporations have formally and rather seriously adopted ethics. General Dynamics reputedly created the first corporate ethics office in the United States in 1985.[1] Today more than half the *Fortune* 500 companies have them.[2] It would be hard to find a large corporation now that lacks a code of ethics, or a business school without a course in business ethics. KPMG Peat Marwick and other consulting firms have started giving their clients advice on ethics and performing "ethics audits" to head off potential trouble or to look at the effectiveness of existing ethics programs.

However, an aroma of humbuggery still surrounds the subject of corporate ethics, which is not surprising considering how many companies have been caught transgressing. A company may formulate a code of ethics, but if it lies tucked away in the general counsel's desk drawer it won't have much impact. When a company applies its code by firing an employee for a minor violation of a prohibition on using a company car for personal use while the chairman sends his wife to Paris on the company Gulfstream, ethics goes down the drain. That kind of behavior tends to get known around the company quickly. As the *Wall Street Journal* has revealed, one consulting firm, Towers Perrin, has handed out identical boilerplate ethics advice to many clients who thought they were paying for tailor-made services.[3] The subject of ethics does attract boilerplate prose and advice.

In spite of the aroma surrounding business ethics, companies have to take it seriously. As pointed out earlier in this book, the U.S. Sentencing Commission guidelines issued in 1991 specified lighter penalties for a company caught breaking the law if it had a working ethics code. That alert pushed many companies into adopting ethics codes, or revising existing codes, or pulling dormant codes out of the general counsel's files and trying to make them work. But apart from possible legal penalties, the furor that can be aroused today when a company is caught in a lapse can be devastating.

By contrast, corporations have learned that taking an ethical stance quickly, when a problem arises, is not only the right thing to do but may be best for business. Johnson & Johnson, which had always said that the welfare of customers and employees came before profits, set a famous example in the 1980s when without hesitating it spent $100 million to pull Tylenol off the shelves and warn the public after some bottles were found to have been laced with cyanide by a saboteur. The company earned enormous credit by this act. Contrast that behavior with the sullen stonewalling of many of the old command-and-control auto, oil, tobacco, and utility companies when confronted with an accusation of some environmental or safety transgression!

Texaco used to be one of those uptight companies. Like others in Big Oil, it was steeped in racism. Before Pearl Harbor, Texaco even tried for a while to help Francisco Franco and Adolf Hitler. But in 1996, when the *New York Times* revealed recordings of racist talk in Texaco, the reaction was that of a different company. Within weeks, Texaco's new CEO, Peter Bijur, had taken an extraordinary series of actions. The four executives involved in the meeting where racist talk had been recorded were punished. Texaco quickly settled a two-year-old discrimination suit which it had hoped earlier to win. Texaco agreed to pay $176 million to past and current employees and to fund various diversity programs. The company hired a black ad agency and set a goal for increasing purchases from minority-owned firms from $135 million annually to $1 billion by 2000. It set specific goals for hiring more blacks and women, said it would finance scholarships and internships for minority students, and would establish a mentoring program for employees. All employees would take diversity training. Managers' pay would be linked to achieving diversity goals. To supervise all these activities, Texaco added ombudsmen and set up an "equality and tolerance task force," and Bijur appointed a black personal assistant to monitor the company's progress. All this even though Bijur said an examination of the tape recordings of the meeting showed the racial epithets cited in the *New York Times* had not been uttered. Still, as Bijur said, the findings "do not change the unacceptable context and tone of those conversations." The extraordinary, probably unprecedented, reforms announced by Bijur moved the Reverend Jesse Jackson to call off a boycott of Texaco and the pressure groups eased off. Bijur might be faulted for going too far, but he stopped the damage and turned a disaster into an opportunity—at a cost that a $30-billion-a-year corporation can readily manage.[4]

LEVI STRAUSS: GLOBAL ACTIVIST

Texaco's actions seemed clear, decisive, and straightforward, at least in the immediate aftermath of the revelation. They were the right things to do. However, over the long run experience shows that being ethical is far from simple. The right thing is not always clear, nor is it always appreciated. Levi Strauss & Company probably has as long and good a record for ethical behavior as any company in the United States. With its rich history going back to mid-19th century San Francisco, when it made long-wearing pants for gold miners, and with its current prosperity based on the enduring worldwide popularity of its jeans, Levi Strauss is a highly visible company, vulnerable to public opinion. Levi Strauss began to set up college scholarships in the 19th century and when the 1906 earthquake destroyed its factory in San Francisco, it kept all its employees on the payroll for as long as six months until there was work for them to do. (However, in 1908 a company brochure advertised that "none but white women and girl operators are employed" in its factory. Diversity was not then an issue and anti-Chinese sentiment was strong in San Francisco.)

In the 1940s, long before it was required, Levi Strauss became what would later be called an "equal opportunity employer" and refused to locate plants in states such as Alabama and Mississippi, where they would have been segregated. Levi Strauss began helping the victims of AIDS in 1982, only a year after it was identified as a disease. When Robert Haas, the great-great-grand-nephew of the founder, became CEO in 1984 one of his first acts was to take the company private with a leveraged buyout. The company was floundering and Haas aimed to run it the way he wanted, without being badgered by Wall Street about short-term results. Among other things, he wanted to be free to insist on ethical behavior.

Haas made Levi Strauss's policy towards AIDS victims generous and sensitive. The company doesn't screen job applicants for AIDS, provides health coverage for them and their partners, provides counseling, keeps them working as long as possible, and holds managers accountable for how they deal with AIDS. Haas had thought the company was doing a good job of promoting women and minorities but when he had a lunch with several of them in management in 1986, he says, "my smug satisfaction with our progress was swiftly shattered." They told him they regularly encountered impediments to their progress because of their sex or race. Although LS reinforced its affirmative action efforts, it still hasn't reached where it would like to be.

LS made enemies outside by being helpful to AIDS victims, and made more enemies in the 1990s by cutting its contributions to the Boy Scouts after the organization banned homosexual troop leaders. The company has also had trouble coping with the ethical and public relations problems created when it has closed plants in the United States and picked up subcontractors overseas who can use cheap labor. LS makes no job guarantees in the United States, but it does have a more generous layoff policy than most companies.

While other companies have been attacked for using sweatshop labor overseas, LS has monitored its suppliers. In 1992 the company laid out a set of sourcing guidelines, applicable everywhere, that said it would not buy from contractors who used child or prison labor, who worked people more than 60 hours a week, and who did not give workers one day off a week. It would also not buy or sell in countries that abused human rights pervasively. Then, says President Peter Jacobi (who was then vice president for international affairs) LS spent 18 months on a massive audit of all its 600-odd suppliers. "Our mission is not to be the savior of human rights around the world," says Jacobi. "We simply want to do business in a responsible way and this, we feel, will have a direct impact on the bottom line."

On human rights grounds, Levi Strauss pulled out of Myanmar and began a withdrawal from China, closing Docker production there. It also stopped selling in China. LS plans to stay on in Hong Kong now that it has reverted to China, but will watch what happens there. In Costa Rica, Jacobi found a contractor who was automatically firing women when they got married and persuaded him to change the policy. In Bangladesh, Levi Strauss discovered a contractor who was employing some 40 children under 14. Simply firing them was not the answer because some were their families' sole support. LS persuaded the contractor to send the children to school and keep paying their wages, while LS picked up the costs of school—so long as the contractor did not replace the children with other children. Worldwide, LS dropped 5% of its contractors and told another 20% to improve.

Levi Strauss embeds what it calls its "aspirations" in the company with constant reminders, publications, and seminars, including a "leadership week" of training and three-and-a-half-day workshops on diversity. What really makes people take the aspirations seriously, however, is that managers are rated by their peers and the people who report to them. One-third of the evaluation relates to ethics and that figures in pay, promotion, and bonuses. If ethical behavior has hurt Levi Strauss, it doesn't show. Sales reached a record $7.1 billion in 1996, up 7% from the previous year and nearly three times the level in 1984, the year before the company went private. Haas agrees that public companies can have a conscience—he has named Cummins Engine and Herman Miller among them—but says it helps "not having Wall Street breathing down our neck." He avers, "In our company, ethical matters trump all other matters, including business."[5]

BEN & JERRY'S: CARING CAPITALISM

"Social cause marketing," as Wharton's Thomas Dunfee calls it, elevates ethical and socially conscious behavior to the point where it becomes the company's marketing strategy.[6] It can be extremely successful, as the righteous if quirky founders of The Body Shop and Ben & Jerry's Homemade, Incorporated, have discovered to their profit. Patagonia and Starbucks have also appealed strongly to that large part of the public that cares that the corporations which get their money should use all-natural ingredients, buy from worthy suppliers, help the downtrodden, and so forth. It is not an easy stance to maintain over the years and even a minor slip can open a company to charges of hypocrisy. The Body Shop took a beating on the stock market after several charges were aired or printed that questioned how genuine or valuable its policies were. (In one case, The Body Shop sued successfully for libel.)

Ben & Jerry's was established in Burlington, Vermont, in 1978 by Ben Cohen and Jerry Greenfield, friends since schooldays, determined to make great ice cream and, later, to fulfill a vision of what they called "caring capitalism." Of course, one might ask how socially useful it is to sell superpremium fatty ice cream that pads the flesh and clogs the arteries. But there's no question about Ben and Jerry's sincerity. Their annual reports, which at first glance could be mistaken for a child's play book, dissect with painful honesty and great detail the company's social performance for pages before making any mention of the business performance. The partners even use an outside auditor to write that part of the annual report. From these pages you learn that Ben & Jerry's contributes 7.5% of its pretax income to good causes (see Figure 17.1 on corporate giving), that it pays extra to get its milk from local dairymen in Vermont (provided that they don't use recombinant bovine growth hormone), that it buys chocolate fudge brownies from a bakery in Yonkers, New York, which employs the unemployed. The reports have also revealed that sulphur dioxide has been used to preserve the cherries in Cherry Garcia ice cream, and they have discussed at length whether their Rainforest Crunch flavor actually contains enough Brazil nuts from the rain forest to justify the label and whether buying those nuts really helped the indigenous people in the Amazon.

Ben & Jerry's grew but didn't grow up. In 1993, sales reached $140 million and profits $7 million. But the founders were out of their depth.

FIGURE **17.1**

Corporate Charity

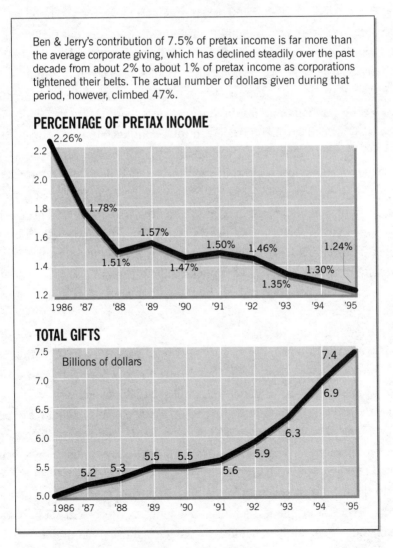

Ben & Jerry's contribution of 7.5% of pretax income is far more than the average corporate giving, which has declined steadily over the past decade from about 2% to about 1% of pretax income as corporations tightened their belts. The actual number of dollars given during that period, however, climbed 47%.

PERCENTAGE OF PRETAX INCOME

- 2.26%
- 1.78%
- 1.51%
- 1.57%
- 1.47%
- 1.50%
- 1.46%
- 1.35%
- 1.30%
- 1.24%

1986 '87 '88 '89 '90 '91 '92 '93 '94 '95

TOTAL GIFTS

Billions of dollars

- 5.2
- 5.3
- 5.5
- 5.5
- 5.6
- 5.9
- 6.3
- 6.9
- 7.4

1986 '87 '88 '89 '90 '91 '92 '93 '94 '95

Source: American Association of Fund-Raising Counsel.

As that year's annual report said, everyone in the company was talking of "lack of leadership, lack of direction, lack of clarity." The company told Milton Moskovitz, author of *100 Best Companies in America,* that it didn't deserve to be in his next edition. In 1994, with sales of super-premium ice cream stagnant, Ben & Jerry's lost money and the price of its shares tumbled.

The partners decided they needed a professional manager as CEO and in their whimsical way announced the applicant who could write the best 100-word essay on why he should be CEO would get the job. In reality, they used an executive search firm and picked a seasoned executive out of the ranks of consultants at McKinsey & Company. Here again they ran into trouble. Ben & Jerry's had a commendable rule that the highest-paid person in the company could not make more than seven times what the lowest-paid employee made (the ratio had been 5:1 until 1990). The cap had to go if Ben & Jerry's was to get a first-rate boss. The new CEO, Robert Holland, received total compensation worth $405,000 in 1995, about 18 times the pay of an ice-cream scooper. As Holland tried to expand the business, he ran into fundamental problems. Ben Cohen objected to an expansion into France because of the French government's policy on nuclear testing in the Pacific. Sorbets looked promising as a new market, but Ben & Jerry's venture in sorbets was held up because it threatened to reduce the company's purchases from the Vermont dairymen it wanted to support. Holland resigned towards the end of 1996 and was replaced in 1997 by Perry Odak, an executive at U.S. Repeating Arms Company (makers of Winchesters). Ben & Jerry's has supported gun control.[7]

The case of Ben & Jerry's is unusual because it's a company that was just too good for its own good. Ben & Jerry's now is working towards a new balance between business and ethics, which certainly doesn't mean it has to throw out the ethics. The case of Texaco is more what we expect of business—the company caught in serious misdeeds after successfully concealing them for years. But Texaco made the case unusual by getting all the bad news out quickly, apologizing fully, and cleaning up conspicuously. That kind of reaction is becoming more the norm. Levi Strauss might be considered a model for consistent, long-term ethical behavior, which almost certainly has done the business more good than harm, but which might be hard for a publicly owned company to copy.

TRAVELING ETHICS

Being ethical in business is neither simple nor easy. The chaotic and strident demands made by society don't show the way to clear, logical solutions. A global business has to work with another level of complication because ethics don't always travel well. When Michel Besson, as head of Saint-Gobain's businesses in North America, banned smoking on its premises the press in Paris denounced him as a tyrant and some senior executives in Paris vowed they would not come to America.[8] (While the rights of nonsmokers are now well established in the United States, smokers still seem to have the upper hand in France.)

Non-Americans are sometimes puzzled by American concern for corporate ethics. Why bother when this old world has always been so corrupt and always will be? That was the attitude in South Korea, for example. However, a new message came out of that country in 1996 when the heads of eight *chaebol,* the huge conglomerates that dominate South Korean business, were convicted of bribing government officials on a massive scale and sentenced to prison. They included the heads of Daewoo and Samsung. Four were given suspended sentences, but in fact, none of them are likely to serve any time. As business becomes more global, corporations can expect more pressure to conform to global ethical standards. There's a long way to go. In Japan, for example, the idea that sexual harassment, for which there is no expression in Japanese, might be wrong is just beginning to catch on.

So often is business cast in the role of villain—judging by TV fare, our criminal class consists mostly of businessmen—that we are creating a distorted image of business. As *The Economist* has said, "America is in danger of creating a society in which Big Business provides an excuse for every individual's mistake—where music companies bully troubled teenagers into suicide and hamburger joints force customers to spill hot coffee over themselves."[9] Even when a company is right, it may be tempted to plead guilty to avoid a costly fight or a publicity battle it may not win. Royal Dutch Shell couldn't take the heat from Greenpeace when it tried to dump the decommissioned Brent Spar oil rig at sea and towed it back to land, even though convinced that sinking it at sea would do the least environmental damage. That leaves 75 deep-water rigs in the North Sea that are coming to the end of their lives. What will be done with them?

As General Motors demonstrated when it took on NBC over a show about the danger of sidesaddle gas tanks on GM trucks and proved that NBC had helped the tanks blow up, business can win if it has a strong defense. Dow Corning and its two parents have written off hundreds of millions of dollars because of litigation over possible damage caused by breast implants. But Dow Corning, which at this writing continues to operate under the provisions of Chapter 11 of the bankruptcy law, decided at first to fight the suits in the belief that pending scientific studies would support its assertion that the implants were not harmful. In this case, in spite of the enormous pressure brought by lawsuits and by publicity about women who believe they were harmed, Dow Corning could reasonably claim its stance was right since it believes there's no scientific evidence that the implants caused the damage. But then, in 1997, Dow Corning decided the costs of fighting the suits was just too burdensome and it offered the claimants a $2.4 billion settlement.

The right road to diversity is also hard to follow. For Kingston Technologies in California diversity comes naturally. Its two Chinese-born founders have put together a work force consisting of 16 different ethnic groups. The company gives courses in English as a second language. But in Minnesota, 3M makes no special effort to recruit minorities, in the belief that recruiting the right people for careers at 3M takes precedence over choosing them for their race or sex. More than most companies, Corning has tried to bring in women and minorities. As mentioned in Chapter 4, Jamie Houghton made diversity one of his three chief goals (the others being better quality and performance). He did so, he said, if only because white men will constitute only 15% to 20% of the people entering the work force in the 21st century. Corning has no trouble hiring women or blacks, he says, but the trouble is that blacks "just leave faster than white males."[10]

Corning has two women among its corporate officers, others in senior corporate positions, and three who are plant managers. However, blacks have not done as well, partly because of the remote location of some Corning facilities. The small town of Corning, New York, is mostly white. Calvin Johnson, the team leader at the nearby SCC plant, a straight-backed West Pointer and a black, says that "attrition among blacks has been awful" maybe because of Corning's remoteness and maybe because of the fear of downsizing. He personally likes the area. It is a safe place for his family. But there are problems. It's hard to find a barber who can cut Afro-American hair. A friend of his drives the 40-odd miles to Ithaca just to get a haircut. Corning subsidizes a Society of Black Professionals, which does a nice job, he says, and tries hard to understand why blacks leave. Johnson thinks the attrition among blacks may have stopped.[11] Roger Ackerman, Houghton's successor, says diversity remains high on the agenda.

THE END OF GOOD OLD BOARDS

Just as companies have come under more scrutiny for their performance and behavior, so have their boards of directors. Boards had come to exemplify the old boys' network, the CEO's buddies who could be counted on to go along and not bother themselves too much about the performance of the company or the size of the CEO's pay. CEOs and ex-CEOs served on each other's boards and could be expected to reciprocate favors. In recent years, many boards added blacks and women. That is, they added one of each and expected them to represent their own constituencies but not to get too involved in the real business.

The whole fellowship of directors dissolved in the 1990s. The markets and society began to demand a higher level of performance and standards from boards of directors just as they had been demanding from corporations. The huge holdings of institutional investors, now amounting to about half the common stock of American companies, gave them a force and focus that puny individual investors never had. No corporation wanted to get on the annual list of ten companies targeted for special attention by the California Public Employees' Retirement System (Calpers) because of its poor performance.

The end of the era of good old boards arrived with four big bangs in a six-month period from late 1992 and to mid-1993 when the directors of four troubled giants, American Express, Eastman Kodak, General Motors, and IBM, finally got up the gumption to shuck their passive roles and throw out their CEOs. For more than a decade, business had been restructuring to meet the new demands of customers, employees, and technology, making the changes described in this book, and now, finally, it was the boards' turn to wake up and play their part in remaking business. With an aggressive push from stockholders and institutional investors, the boards began not only to be more independent and active, but also to look at their own conduct and makeup. No longer would boards be "parsley on the fish," or "ornaments on the Christmas tree," as they have been described.

No such uprising is remotely likely in Japan. "Directors in Japan are not directors in the American sense," says Masaru Yoshitomi, chairman of the U.S.–Japan Management Studies Center at Wharton. "Japanese directors are just high-ranking employees. There is at present no really effective mechanism for overseeing the CEO."[12] Japanese boards are enormous by Western standards, numbering 30 members or more. Toyota had 54 directors in 1995. Very few are outsiders, and even fewer are foreigners. Cutting the size of boards would be difficult because a directorship is considered the ultimate reward for good and faithful service (although Toyota has announced it will reduce the size of its board). The directors are usually old colleagues, if not classmates, of the president and they are not about to call him to account. Even the auditors are often insiders. The banks have lost much of the power they had over companies. However, Japanese CEOs are held in check by more of a sense of responsibility towards the workers than their American counterparts, and they don't expect to make the enormous fortunes that American CEOs take for granted.

John Smale, the former Procter & Gamble CEO who led the GM board rebellion that ousted Robert Stempel as CEO and who then served as GM's chairman, described what he had learned in a speech in 1993. After ticking off the basics of corporate leadership, he added, "there's one more element that did not get much attention until recently: namely, the role of the board of directors." He said the board must "act as an independent auditor of management's progress, asking the tough questions that management might not ask itself." The board must "recognize that beyond its responsibility to the stockholders, it also has a responsibility to the corporation's employees, customers, suppliers, and the communities where it operates." But the "paramount responsibility" remains the successful perpetuation of the business.[13]

New guidelines and recommendations for the board's behavior came from the National Association of Corporate Directors and other organizations, from the Cadbury report in Britain in 1992, and from the focus on the performance of the boards in the press and among academics.

Harvard, Stanford, and Wharton began giving seminars to help directors learn their jobs. *Business Week* began listing the best and the worst boards. Campbell Soup's ranked first in 1996—and was also selected "board of the year" at Wharton—and the Archer Daniels Midland board topped the list of the worst.[14] The ADM board, made up largely of friends and relatives of Dwayne Andreas, the CEO, took a public thrashing for its passivity as the scandal of ADM's price fixing played out, resulting in a $100-million fine.

THE NEW ROLE

Recommendations about how to improve the governance of corporations have been numerous and, on the whole, simple and clear, which is refreshing in the field of management theory. Boards should be fairly small (around a dozen seems right) and should include very few insiders. The independent board members should choose a lead director to give the group cohesion and they should meet regularly without the executive directors. Active executives should serve on no more than one or two outside boards and retired executives on no more than four or five. The compensation and terms of service of board members should be limited. The idea that the jobs of chairman and CEO should be separated does not get much support among reformers in the United States, although that arrangement is common in Europe and among nonprofit organizations in the United States. The Cadbury Report said British boards should add an audit committee (which American boards already have).

Are boards and companies responding to these recommendations? Not on one score. Directorship, a consulting firm, reports that the number of directors of *Fortune* 500 companies who sit on nine boards rose from 19 in 1991 to 35 in 1995, while the number sitting on ten or more boards went up from 17 to 33. The most charitable explanation of that trend is that the demand for first-rate directors has increased to the point where they need to serve on more boards. But in other respects, companies are responding to the calls for reform. The Korn/Ferry International annual survey of directors and chairmen reveals trends consistent with the recommendations about board reform (see Figure 17.2).

Commendable as they may be, these changes don't go much beyond

Figure 17.2

How Boards Are Changing

Korn/Ferry International's annual survey of 1,100 directors and chairmen of *Fortune* companies picked up these changes in the composition and procedures of boards that are mostly consistent with widely recommended reforms:

	1994	1995	1996
Average number of directors	12	11	11
Average number of insiders	3	2	2
Boards with women members	63%	69%	71%
Boards with minority members	44%	47%	51%
Boards with lead directors	22%	27%	24%
Outside directors hold executive meetings without the CEO	66%	73%	62%
Board formally evaluates CEO	67%	78%	69%
Board has a formal committee to evaluate itself and governance	41%	49%	51%

Source: Korn/Ferry International, *23rd and 24th Annual Board of Directors Study* (1996 and 1997).

attacking the structure of the board. They don't address more fundamental questions about the role and purpose of the board. As we argue in the next chapter, structural reform comes after, not before, more basic questions have been cleared up. The fact that more boards are formally evaluating the performance of the CEO should be good news, perhaps a portent of more reasonable compensation packages for CEOs. It's curious that one reform that doesn't figure on the lists of things that boards should do is to bring to heel the compensation of top executives. The inequity between the compensation at the top and compensation in the rest of the company continues to create outrage. However, in other respects and in spite of some enormous lapses, corporations are working their way towards better citizenship and better governance. Their new ethical standards, their growing acceptance of diversity, and their boardroom reforms all reflect the new demands of society and the recognition that the corporation doesn't exist solely to benefit the stockholder.

In fact, perhaps we can declare an end to the old argument about whether the corporation should serve all of society or only the stockholder. The two missions are coming together. It has become clearer that if a corporation is not a good citizen it probably won't serve its stockholders very well either. The penalties for unethical behavior, for creating risks to health or the environment, for abusing workers, are becoming so severe that they threaten not only the profits but sometimes the existence of the corporation. If anything could prove how risky it has become for a corporation to fail in citizenship it was the sudden collapse of the tobacco industry's intransigence in 1997. After decades of intensive lobbying, of denying that tobacco caused cancer or was addictive, of denying that its advertising was aimed especially at youngsters, the tobacco industry suddenly agreed to a settlement of the suit against it by 23 state attorneys general by putting enormous sums into a fund to help the victims of smoking. To be sure, the suits represented a big risk and certainly Big Tobacco had become increasingly unpopular, but what may have taken the fight out of the industry was the fact that tobacco shares went up every time there were rumors of a settlement. The interests of society and the stockholder had merged.

Pointers

- Are your corporate leaders, by speech and action, clearly committed to ethical behavior and good corporate citizenship?
- Do you have a clear set of ethical standards and do you visibly reinforce them with your actions?
- Does ethical behavior and good citizenship enter into the performance evaluations and compensation of your employees?
- Have you examined where your company might be vulnerable to charges of poor ethics, for instance, because of pollution or because a supplier is abusing child labor?
- Should the company or some of its employees be shown to have done something unacceptable, have you planned how you would react?
- Are you making a real effort to diversify the work force and keep the minority workers you do hire?
- Is your board of directors acting forcefully and independently to oversee the corporation?
- Has the board picked an independent lead director? Does it meet regularly in executive sessions without the inside directors? Does it evaluate the performance of the CEO regularly?

Links

• Ethical behavior and good corporate citizenship are becoming more closely tied to the long-term performance of the company's shares.

Cautions

• The intensified pressure to produce results, quickly and often with reduced staffs, may push managers to wink at ethical lapses.
• Keeping minority employees may prove harder than finding them and hiring them.
• Be careful not to make too much of your good deeds, because your halo may slip and choke you.

18

AN INTEGRATED
ARCHITECTURE

There is nothing easy, automatic, or formulaic about organizational architecture and design. Each situation is unique.
—David Nadler[1]

After all we have said about the characteristics of the 21st century corporation and the drivers of change, the new markets, the information technology, the stakeholders, and so forth, what can we say about what the new corporation looks like? What's its architecture? The conventional answer to that question would be to describe the structure of the corporation, to put everybody in boxes, and to define the chain of command. That would not work at all today. It would put the emphasis in the wrong place because today the formal structure becomes secondary. You don't report only to your boss in the new enterprise, you communicate with whoever you need to communicate with. The hierarchy is not primary. Therefore the nature of the next enterprise is more ambiguous, harder to pin down, harder to describe.

SEI Survey	
It is critical that a flatter, cross-functional organization replace the traditional hierarchy	77%
We are doing this	55%

To give the new corporation a face, to replace a rather abstract concept with a tangible identity, you might visit the new headquarters of SEI
Investments in the Pennsylvania countryside near Valley Forge. SEI
makes its living as an outsourcing company, handling the trust accounts
of banks and the investments of pension funds. Even before moving to its
new offices in 1996, SEI had acquired many of the characteristics of the
21st century corporation. The whole company was team based. The previous offices in Wayne were open, without partitions—even CEO Al
West sat exposed to whoever wanted to talk to him—and the jobs of secretaries had been abolished. The company had converted its information
system from a mainframe to an open client-server system which customers as well as employees can use.

The new offices in five factory-style buildings on a rural hillside stand
with all their innards of structural steel, pipes, and ducts exposed in vivid
colors, fuchsia and bright blue in one building, yellow, gold, and red in
another. What really catches the eye, however, are the thick coils of wire
dangling down from the overhead beams all over the buildings, like so
many snakes hanging from a jungle canopy. These "pythons," as SEI
calls them, contain phone, computer, and electrical wiring. West wants
people to move frequently and easily to form new teams and he was tired
of paying $2,000 per move to relocate desks and get the lines hooked up
under the flooring. Now when people need to move they simply unplug
their python, push their desk, chair, and filing cabinet to the new location
(everything is on wheels), reach up and grab the nearest python, plug in,
notify the computers where they are, and go to work. SEI people are expected to move themselves, even if it's from one building to another. The
paths and the rubberized flooring inside are easy to negotiate. In one
case, a new team was installed and ready to work two hours after starting the move. If a table of organization were drawn up for SEI, it wouldn't
be valid for long.

The team that redesigned Ford's worldwide auto operations in 1994
started by creating organization charts, but then realized this approach
was like trying to design a building before knowing what it was to be
used for (see Chapter 14). The team banned charts and began with principles and processes. Structure could come later. In a book titled *Organizational Architecture,* a group of consultants from the Delta Group
write that "in the network organization, patterns of interaction (flow of in-

formation, product, and people) are dynamic and established by need rather than by a rigid plan."[2] Some patterns last or are nearly permanent, others shift rapidly.

We don't cite the cases of SEI and Ford to establish a model for the 21st century corporation. There is not likely to be one model or even many models. They do however symbolize an approach to creating corporate architecture. We have already said (in Chapter 11) that corporations are becoming more complex and complexity requires a different way of organizing and managing. We quoted John Sculley as saying, "I don't think that it makes too much difference how you organize companies any more." Instead of being defined by a pyramid or a hierarchical table, the 21st century enterprise might better be defined as a series of related processes—all focused on creating value for the customer. Like other complex organisms—the human brain, or the environment, for that matter—this complex corporation cannot readily be commanded centrally. It derives its strength and unity from the interaction and cooperation among its parts.

Traditional companies did focus on structure, as did the management consultants who advised them. Executives are realizing now that if they don't break away from those tidy, reassuring tables of organization that put everyone in their place, they are going to fail. The whole quality improvement movement in the 1980s introduced business to the idea of focusing on process before structure, sometimes to excess. What we are saying today is that process, and structure, and other elements of an organization all have to be put in place and aligned with the vision, values, and objectives of the corporation.

FACING THE STAKEHOLDERS

We like to look at the 21st century enterprise as a circle of capabilities and assets which are connected to each other but which also all face the stakeholders, the focus of everybody's attention (see Figure 18.1). The stakeholders are principally the shareholders, customers, and employees—the order of importance varying with the company, its industry, and its nationality. Going around the circle in our illustration anticlockwise, the architecture of the new enterprise requires these capabilities and assets:

FIGURE 18.1

Changing the Organizational Architecture

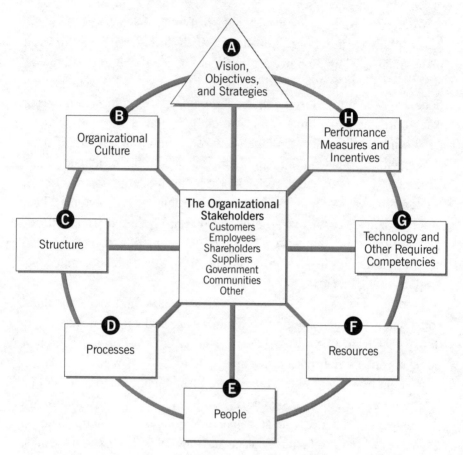

B. Organizational Culture. Several companies discussed in this book produced, by plan and example or by good fortune over the years, the kind of culture their businesses needed, and linked it to the values of the company. The 3M Company nurtures the innovative climate and the willingness to exchange information that has made it so successful at developing new products. From its beginning in 1912, L.L. Bean made a cult of going to extremes, if necessary, to serve the customer well. Hewlett-Packard's "HP Way" marked the company as a place where people are respected and trusted, but are expected to perform at a high level and as members of teams. Microsoft is working towards making itself a learning organization. In some companies we have looked at the old culture had to be scrapped and replaced before they could perform competitively today. That kind of switch certainly occurred at the Big Three automakers, and at IBM, Xerox, and Perot Systems.

C. Structure. Hierarchies and chains of command won't disappear altogether. Teams may make a lot more of the decisions, but somebody at the top has to be able to give orders at times, so old structures won't go away altogether. The more important role of structure today is to reinforce a company's strategies, changing with them as necessary. The strategy should be market-driven and so the structure should be built around market sectors. We have seen how KPMG Peat Marwick, Hewlett-Packard, and 3M reorganized to face their markets. VeriFone, much younger than the others, was organized—if that is the right word to use—from the beginning so that its executives faced their customers more than each other. As companies become global, they need a global structure. The matrix organization, which became popular in the 1970s and was soon discredited, even loathed, because it proved too bureaucratic and cumbersome as applied then, looks promising once again in the new context of business organization.

D. Processes. As mentioned earlier, the movement to improve quality in the 1980s focused management's attention on process, sometimes to the point of absurdity. Florida Power and Light became so wrapped up in following elaborate quality improvement processes, running meetings in exactly the prescribed way and reporting on them in excruciating detail, that FPL people got to hate the whole idea of quality improvement. But in many companies a commonsensical approach to looking at each process anew and eliminating its weaknesses yielded extraordinary results. By repeatedly setting new goals and improving its processes, Motorola reduced defects from 80,000 parts per million (ppm) in 1980 to 25 ppm in 1996 (although it did not reach its target of Six Sigma or 3.4 ppm). These and outstanding improvements at other companies were so convincing that it has become common for businesses to take a fresh look at all their processes, not just those for making products, and to do so frequently. The idea of setting objectives that would really stretch a company also started in the quality area and spread through the company and now is applied even to growth plans. Being competitive today means creating value from beginning to end, from raw materials to customers, with the best processes.

E. People. Some of the companies we have interviewed think that hiring and holding the best people will be the critical competitive advantage in the future. The information age raises the levels of skills and performance required of workers and managers. They need to be prepared to take on more work and responsibility as companies push authority downward, flatten out, and cut costs. Companies need to develop many leaders, not just a few for the top roles. At the same time, uncertainty, change, and job cuts have hurt morale and loyalty. As the baby boomers get closer to retirement age, labor scarcities are more likely. Finally, as technology and markets change, employers will need to review and update their people requirements. Staffing looks like one of management's more difficult problems in the 21st century enterprise. The key to customer loyalty, especially in the knowledge and service industries, will be to find ways to make employees satisfied and loyal.

F. Resources. The allocation of resources has always been one of management's critical responsibilities and that isn't likely to change, although the priorities assigned to different resources have changed. Capital allocation remains as important as ever, but becomes more complex as corporations spread around the globe. If an American company finds, as many have, that its overseas operations are its most profitable, then how does it divide its investments between foreign and domestic operations? Information has come to front and center as one of the most important resources of a corporation. The time of top executives and managers has become one of the scarce resources in the new enterprise. The people who run the lean and flattened corporations naturally have more to do, and they have added responsibilities—to provide and instill the vision, to lead the quality improvement efforts, to exemplify the team approach, to socialize with partners, to understand the customer, and to deal with the other stakeholders. Since there's still no substitute for face-to-face dealings, the time of the CEO has become more valuable than ever.

G. Technology. Executives who never had much need to understand technology stay awake at night worrying about the huge investments they have to make in technology. Ulrich Cartellieri, a managing director at Deutsche Bank, says he doesn't lose sleep over financial risks, which he understands, but he does over those $100s of millions that his bank spends now on information technology. Even if executives don't fully understand the risks of technology, they still have to make complex, fateful decisions. They need to study current technology, benchmark their own technology against what is available and what is possible on the frontiers of development. Then they need to look at their own needs and problems, and come up with solutions that serve their clients. They will face "make or buy" decisions to determine what can be developed internally and what should be done outside. They need to develop a vision, strategies, and objectives for their companies' technologies.

H. Measures and Incentives. Again and again in earlier chapters, we have said that measurement and incentives are what really bring about change. That applies to individuals and to organizations. What gets measured, gets attention. New measures can be used to improve quality and productivity, customer satisfaction, team performance, adherence to values. You set new objectives, stretch objectives if you really want to stimulate the organization, then you measure the performance against those objectives, and then you reward people and teams according to performance. Full 360-degree appraisal rather than the traditional appraisal from the top builds a more balanced picture of a manager's performance. Since they have so much influence in changing a company's behavior, new measurements need to be focused on what matters to customers (and other stakeholders) and since the measures may have unintended consequences they need to be monitored and adjusted.

A. Vision, Objectives, and Strategies. All of the elements of architecture described above should fall into line with the corporate vision, the objectives, and the strategies, which they support and execute. Although words like "vision" and "mission" have been abused and often amount to no more than corporate blather, we hope that in Chapter 7 on leadership we showed that these are genuinely important elements of the new enterprise. If properly defined, and if demonstrably supported by the leaders, they can help lift a corporation to a higher level of performance. If, as Bob Haas of Levi Strauss has said, ideas rather than orders control the new corporation, then a vision matters. The objectives, if they are challenging and doable, give the organization goals to work for and strategy provides the blueprint for getting there. As the circle of our diagram indicates, these three elements of vision, objectives, and strategies pull all the other parts of the architecture into an integrated effort to serve the customer, the employee, the shareholder and other stakeholders.

These stakeholders obviously do not hold equal rank, but the customer is the one who drives the company. All the elements in our diagram of organizational architecture connect and respond to the market. Strategy is driven by the answer to the question: Who are the customers and what do they need? The whole company, and not just the marketing department, needs a clear line of sight to the customer. The connection with the customer has become the universal concern of business.

As for the other stakeholders, we pointed out in Chapter 4 that their rank depends on which country you are talking about. In the United States and the United Kingdom, the majority of companies believe they exist primarily for the benefit of the shareholders, while in Japan, Germany, and France an even larger majority believe they exist to serve all stakeholders. You get the same results if you compare the importance of dividends to the importance of job security. But there is some movement towards a common view of the importance of the stakeholders. In Europe and Japan, the shareholder commands a little more respect than he did; in Japan, the interests of the employee and society are not quite as inviolable as they were, and in the United States and Britain the interests of society, the stockholder, and the employee are closer.

CREATING VALUE ALL AROUND

The perception of the shareholder's interest takes on a broader, more long-term aspect in the new enterprise. To get the best results, you look for ways of adding value throughout the enterprise, from the employee, to the customer, to the shareholder. Companies continue to use the usual bottom-line measures such as growth, profits, cash flow, market share, productivity, and the various "return" figures such as return on assets or sales, but they are also looking at new measures to see how the company is doing in a broader sense; not just at how the company is doing for itself, but how it's doing for the customers and for the employees (see Figure 18.2). Xerox looks at what it describes as a circle of value creation, passing from the employee to the customer to the shareholder and back to the employee (see Figure 18.3). By measuring economic value added (EVA), people value added (PVA), and customer value added (CVA)—three measures that some AT&T units have adopted—you can appraise the long-term performance of the whole company. Here's what the terms mean:

First, economic value added (EVA), the most widely used of these approaches, changes the way you look at a business. The cost of equity capital used not to figure in business results. But if the total return to the investor is below average, then the investor has suffered a real loss: the opportunity to earn more elsewhere. If you assign a cost of equity in the financial statements, based on the stock market performance of comparable companies, you get a different view of the company. If the company still shows a profit after subtracting the cost of equity, then it really is adding value for the investor. If your objective is long-term EVA, as it

FIGURE 18.2

Choosing Measures

The growing use of nontraditional, nonfinancial measures to judge corporate and individual performance helps to drive change and to put an emphasis on long-term rather than short-term indicators of success. Although the percentage of companies using nonfinancial measures in this survey did not increase, those that did substantially increased their use. Sibson & Company followed the trend for four years in the early 1990s (the company suspended the survey after 1994) and got these results:

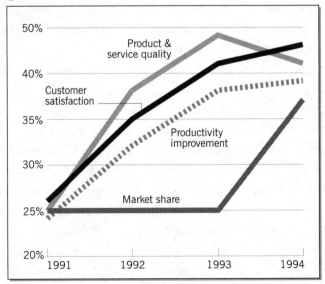

Source: Sibson & Company, Inc.

FIGURE 18.3

Circle of Values

Instead of measuring results just by the bottom line, some corporations are looking at broader measures which take into account not profits and losses, but how well the customer is doing and how well the employee is doing. The theory is that if all three parties are doing well, then the shareholder will benefit over the long haul. The diagram shows how Xerox looks at the circle of value.

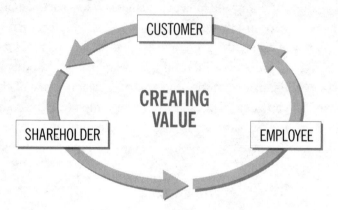

should be, then short-term tricks like shifting sales from one quarter to another make no sense.

Second, CVA, giving the customer more value, is, of course, central to a company's business. We have already explored, in Chapter 5, how the concept of satisfying the customer has evolved. It began simply with gauging customer satisfaction with the product or service and then evolved in sophistication to mean serving all the customers' needs, solving problems rather than moving products, trying to retain customers rather than just making a sale. That's why you see Merck and other pharmaceutical companies moving from peddling pills and discounting to focusing on wellness and offering business solutions to medical institutions (see Figure 18.4). Advertising agencies are looking beyond selling ads to providing an integrated public relations, advertising, communications, and marketing package, all over the world, and providing this package on the basis of sharing risks and rewards rather than collecting fees.

Third, people or employee value added (PVA), a less established concept, extends the idea of measuring employee satisfaction. Xerox now calls it employee satisfaction and motivation.[3] Do employees have the work environment, the training, the rewards, to produce the best results for the customer? The grouchy clerk drives customers away. Hiring and training

FIGURE 18.4

Changing the Model

The pharmaceutical industry example: From the old way of just pushing pills by discounting them, the drug companies are shifting to a new model that requires them to offer business solutions and medical solutions. If they hit the new shifting target they can charge premium prices and get on the hospitals' lists of preferred providers.

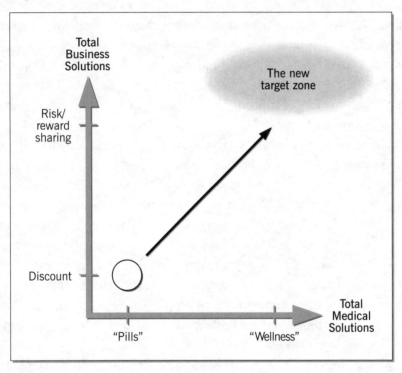

new employees is expensive, especially in knowledge businesses, so winning their loyalty is important. Are the employees adding to their own value, or future value, by their experience and learning? The measures of this kind of added value are not yet considered very reliable, but the idea that a well-treated, well-managed employee adds long-term value to a company is hardly a revelation. Even so, many executives ignore it.

LOOKING AT TOMORROW

Investment service companies have specialized in particular areas, such as financial consulting, trust administration, and specialized mutual funds and other investments. SEI started 25 years ago by offering computerized backroom services for banks and graduated to consulting for pension funds and trust administration. As the choice of investment ve-hicles multiplied, SEI saw that what these institutions needed was some-one to simplify the world for them by offering what it calls "integrated solutions." SEI offers a bundle of services to a client, including the de-sign of portfolios, selection of investment managers, and the administra-tion of accounts. SEI will pick money managers or mutual funds for a client, furnish the custodial and administrative services the accounts need, and actively supervise the performance of the funds and managers they select. SEI says that its institutional clients agreed that this was the kind of service they needed, but some hesitated to accept it because they fear a possible loss of control. Those doubters waited to see how the in-tegrated approach worked.

The integrated or bundled approach is one way of making the difficult transition into the future. People are most comfortable dealing with fa-miliar problems and applying familiar solutions, but when businesses don't focus on new problems that may require new solutions it is as if they were driving by looking through the rearview mirror—a dangerous way to travel. They need to look at tomorrow's opportunities and trends. Integrated solutions are a step into the future because growing numbers of customers are looking for partners who can provide solutions during an extended relationship rather than suppliers who just sell them a prod-uct, partners who help them find new ways to deal with new opportuni-ties (see Figure 18.5).

Wayne Huizenga, the entrepreneur who built up WMX Technologies and Blockbuster into billion-dollar businesses, does not get hemmed in by familiar solutions. He launched Republic Industries Incorporated in 1996 to create an integrated business in the fragmented auto retail in-dustry, pulling new and used car sales, rentals, leasing, servicing, recon-ditioning, and finance into one national network on a vast scale. Want a good used car? Go to one of his AutoNation USA superstores. They cover about 20 acres each and the showrooms alone measure three-quarters of an acre. They have toys and movies for children, snacks, and golf carts to take browsers around the lot. From a start with seven Auto-Nation locations in 1996, he planned to spread to more than 80 super-stores by 2000. Want a cheaper used car? Go to one of his ValuStop dealers. Want to buy or lease a new car? He began buying major dealer-

FIGURE 18.5

Strategic Scenarios

Like people, corporations seem most comfortable with things they know, so they like to apply familiar solutions not only to current problems but to new problems. This is a sure way to fail. Or they apply current solutions to new problems, which is highly risky. What the market demands today is new solutions to new problems.

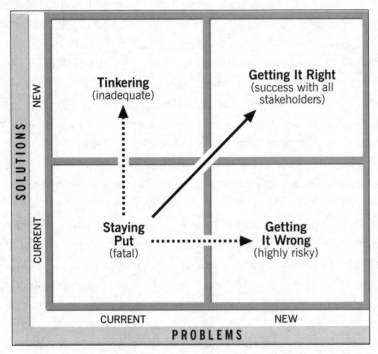

ships in late 1996 and within months was the biggest new car retailer in the country. Want to rent a car? Go to Alamo or National. Republic acquired them in 1996 and 1997, respectively. Need parts or financing? Republic has them too.

A big investment in information technology will allow Republic to track customers wherever they show up in the system and to try to keep them coming back. As the company grows, the pieces will become more integrated, although the exact form of the integration has yet to evolve. AutoNation and new car dealerships will often be close together, so customers can move from one to another. AutoNation customers will get "passports" entitling them to discounts which later may be available anywhere in the system. Alamo desks will appear at the AutoNation stores so that customers looking for a car or waiting for servicing can get a rental or even a loaner. Alamo and National will keep their brand names, but since Alamo caters more to weekend and leisure travelers and National to weekday business travelers, Republic may be able to reduce the total inventory of cars. The idea is to translate this kind of integration into lower costs and prices.

If Huizenga succeeds, he will build an integrated system that starts with buying new cars in great volume and then pulls together the other pieces of the auto retail business into a whole that fits both the car's life cycle and the needs of the owner and driver. The high risk of Huizenga's enterprise became apparent when Toyota and Honda sued to block him from acquiring their dealerships and Republic's shares fell sharply. However, whether or not he succeeds, the concept is one that is likely to be applied widely in many businesses in the 21st century.

The Wharton School is trying to anticipate future needs with new solutions not only by continuously updating its curriculum, but also with a new global strategy and the architecture to support it. Like many institutions that have taken a first step toward being global, Wharton is essentially centered on one campus and has a few exchanges with others. A program to help working executives and managers earn an MBA by coming to Wharton on weekends revealed a need and an opportunity because students travel so far to earn their MBAs. They come to Philadelphia for the two days not only from the mid-Atlantic region, as expected, but from the Midwest, the West Coast, even Mexico. Building on the popularity of that program, Wharton is planning to establish seven new affiliates for working MBA candidates in Asia, Latin America, Europe, and the Middle East. Companies will be able to send teams to each of the centers for four-day weekend sessions once a month for 18 months. The MBA students will also spend seven weeks in Philadelphia or on another campus. The centers will be linked electronically and students will be able to move from one to another.

XEROX: LOOKING INTO 2005

Xerox has reinvented itself repeatedly to meet the needs of the market; first in 1983 to focus on quality and then in 1992 to become a process-focused rather than function-based company. In 1995 Xerox regrouped to face the market, creating three divisions corresponding to its three major market segments (replacing divisions that corresponded to product lines). In 1997, Xerox regrouped again into five divisions corresponding to a newer view of the markets. The latest reorganization, in which the company replaced its Xerox 2000 plan with a Xerox 2005 plan, matched the kind of progression we have been describing in this chapter, beginning by peering into future markets and ending with a new architecture.

Xerox started the process early in 1996 by forming a worldwide team of 17 of its top leaders who met 11 times to listen to customers and experts talk about where they thought the markets were going. Although few of them could look as far ahead as 2005, they did convince the Xerox team that the needs of its customers are changing profoundly. Customers will want their documents managed across the enterprise. "We need to get coherence out of chaos," one customer said. Therefore Xerox should look for more opportunities like its $200-million deal with Owens-Corning to handle all its documents worldwide. Customers will want their documents managed digitally, but will want to view them in any format they prefer, whether it be on paper or on the screen. Customers are also getting more demanding and independent, more likely to tell Xerox what they want rather than listen to Xerox talk about its capabilities, and to acquire Xerox products through whatever channels they prefer. The planners also saw new opportunities to apply Xerox technology to commercial printing, to expand business in emerging markets, and to sell more of the supplies that copiers use.

Looking at these customer requirements as well as at changes in technology and the globalization of the markets, the Xerox team decided the company had to develop seven major new "strategic imperatives":

1. To provide enterprise-wide and complete document services and products. Xerox will now describe itself as a "document solutions" rather than a "document services" company.
2. To furnish customers with the three "Cs"—color, connectivity, and coherence.
3. To make all its offerings "citizens of the Internet" and the intranet.
4. To develop a full range of distribution channels beyond the direct sales force, from the Internet to telemarketing to superstores to mail order catalogs.
5. To move aggressively into emerging markets, especially China, Southeast Asia, Russia, and India.

6. To acquire the necessary new competencies, in marketing, in digital networks, and in managing indirect channels, for example.

7. To continue to change the way Xerox is managed, particularly "to be much faster in everything we do" and "to develop a stomach for risk taking."

Having decided where it was going and what it needed to get there, Xerox took the final step in pointing to 2005 by changing its structure. Xerox had divided its business into three groups in 1995—one to deal with the big, high-volume companies, another for regular businesses, and the third for stand-alone small business and home needs. From the new study five groups emerged:

1. "Production Systems" to provide high-volume digital production for the publishing and printing markets.

2. "Office Products" for stand-alone copiers and for office networks that can scan, print, fax, and copy documents.

3. "Document Services" for the large, integrated "document solutions."

4. "Channels" to complement the direct sales force by developing new channels through retailers, resellers, and distributors.

5. "Supplies" to give new attention to all the products that go with copying, such as paper, toner, inks, and cartridges.[4]

How well Xerox 2005 works remains to be seen, of course, and much of the outcome depends on extraneous elements such as luck, politics, and the economy. However, the Xerox initiative does illustrate what we think to be a sound approach to corporate architecture. Instead of starting by creating a structure, Xerox started by looking at how the world was changing and showing a willingness to change with it—again. Having examined the future—to the extent that it is possible—Xerox looked at what would be needed to deal with that future. Then Xerox determined what new competencies it would need. And only then, finally, did the company decide how to change its structure. Xerox did not try to fit its concept of the market to its structure or product line, or create what would be most convenient or easy to manage. In fact the new structure creates the potential for conflict among the five groups and among the channels. But the point is not to build a structure that suits management, but one that suits the customer, and the corporate vision, objectives, and strategy. It's a simple idea, but it's rare in business.

Pointers

- Do you still think of your company in terms of a table of organization, or pyramid or hierarchy?
- Do you have a clear vision of what your markets are going to be in the future?
- Have you analyzed the resources and capabilities you will need to compete in those markets?
- Have you planned how those resources and capabilities will all be linked and have a clear line of sight to the customer?
- Having made these determinations, have you created the right architecture to meet these needs and is it flexible?
- Do you use the right measures to know whether you are adding value for the customer and rewarding your people for doing so?
- Are you looking for new ways of meeting new customer needs?
- Are you changing the model of your business so that instead of simply making a sale you are solving the customer's problems?

Links

- The architecture has to support the vision, objectives, and strategy of the corporation.

Cautions

- You might as well accept that the new architecture is almost bound to be complex.
- Being complex, and subject to frequent change, the new corporation is going to be a stressful, difficult place to work.

CONCLUSION

The new enterprise we have tried to describe in this book does not exclude everything from the old corporation. Don't look for a clean break. There are no stark either/or choices; adopting new characteristics doesn't necessarily mean killing the old ones. Rather, as we said in the beginning, we see a shift in the balance. Hierarchies won't disappear. Teams won't become all-powerful. Executives won't defer to their employees for all decisions. We will have a mix of old and new, the balance varying from company to company depending on the leader, the industry, the market, and the country. Overseas Chinese and Indian family firms, Korean *chaebol,* Japanese *keiretsu,* entrepreneurial American corporations, and the constrained social model of business in Europe are going to react in different ways—though perhaps not so different as in the past. Organizations will be complex and diverse, flexible and restless. Each company will have its unique response.

Business is often accused, with reason, of faddism, but the management ideas stressed in this book, we believe, are not fads. They need to be used and tested for many years. They will evolve, but they need to be applied selectively. Change is all around us, but at times stability may be the right choice.

SEI Survey	
It is critical to create the unique balance of old and new characteristics that suits each business	68%
We are doing that	25%

The new enterprise will require you to be good at the old basics of running a business well: cash flow, finance, marketing, and timing. You will need to have the right instincts, and as ever count on good luck, too. No matter how well you have led a corporation through a transformation, it won't help if you are trying to sell an Edsel, or Corfam, or carbon paper, or the Susan B. Anthony dollar.

FOUR PRINCIPLES

In the introduction to this book, we contrasted 13 features of the old corporation with the new characteristics that we have seen emerging over the last decade and a half. The book has examined how companies went about adopting these new features and what lessons can be learned from their experience. And as we described the changes, we consistently saw four operating principles that we think need to govern the 21st century enterprise as it takes shape. The successful enterprise will be *dynamic, integrated, effective,* and *responsible.* To summarize points that have already been made repeatedly, here is why we think these principles are important:

Dynamic. Business faces so much change that old models made for a stable world probably won't work. The pace and scope of change have already reached levels where business executives who were comfortable until recently with five-year plans now are scared to predict what will happen next year. New technologies, especially information technology, new products, new competitors, new markets are all popping up so fast that the corporation must be ready to grasp the new before the old has even started to decline. The next enterprise must therefore be flexible and adaptable, ready to cope with radical or discontinuous change. It needs to try to invent its own future by going beyond adapting to new markets and by trying to create them. Business leaders, scholars, and consultants attending meetings at the Wharton School say they are especially preoccupied with the increasing difficulty of predicting the future and the need to deal with discontinuous change better. As we researched this book, we were struck—and somewhat handicapped—by the frequent reorganizations in the companies we were studying. Companies don't sit still long enough for you to take their portrait. What you say about a company may be valid only for that company and at that moment.

Integrated. James Emshoff, former chairman of MedQuist Incorporated, says, "there aren't enough leaders in corporate America who have the integrated vision that puts all the pieces of this 21st century corporation together in a balanced way to make the transition occur."[1] The leader must be capable of creating an integrated strategy, an integrated architecture, and be able to pursue cost reductions and efficiencies while also pursuing growth. The executive of the next enterprise needs a sense of relationships, a sense of how the new characteristics connect to each other. Vincent Barabba, head of General Motors' Strategic Decision Center, writes ". . . the activities performed by any company in a particular industry will be very similar. The unique differences between companies are in the execution of these activities—particularly managing the interactions. . . . Activities must be linked together as a total system."[2]

Effective. Today's executive might feel like the Iowa farmer who said, "Don't burden me with more ideas about how to farm better. I'm not farming as well as I know how now."[3] Our problems today do not come from a lack of ideas and theories. A number of them—total quality management, for instance, or even reengineering—provide a good perspective for creating a new kind of corporation, if properly applied. But they have failed to live up to expectations, mostly because of poor execution, as business leaders are well aware. A group of top Xerox executives were speculating recently about the relative importance of strategy and execution. They concluded that with good execution you could fix a poor strategy, but no amount of strategic thinking could overcome poor execution. This is a common opinion among executives. Of course, if the strategy calls for the production of something that people don't want, no

SEI Survey	
It is more critical to focus on good implementation than on creating new strategies	66%
We are doing that	26%

amount of great execution will save it. There probably are not more than a handful of top business leaders in the country who, like GE's Jack Welch, have the guts and consistency to hang in there long enough to make good ideas work.

Responsible. Business is forced by sheer self-interest if nothing else to treat its employees and the rest of society better than it has. American business has two personalities. The one usually on view is unfair, greedy, ruthless, dishonest. It is the business of mergers and layoffs, of shady deals, of stunned middle managers thrown out by callous CEOs whose pals on the board vote them obscene riches. The other personality is trying in an enlightened way to respond to a whole set of urgent pressures from customers, from competitors, from technology, and from society. At its best, this business is smart and innovative, supplies us with excellent products and services, responds intelligently to the customer, balances the needs of the other stakeholders, copes with globalization, has imaginative ways of getting the best out of its employees and making their work more satisfying, and contributes, sometimes generously, to charities and the community. Most companies are in fact a mixture of these two personalities, the good and the bad—if that is the right way to describe them. The new enterprise needs to be a good citizen.

ENGINES OF GROWTH

We should not expect that the new enterprise will carry us into a corporate utopia. Far from it. Business is going to be stressful, risky, and uncertain, possibly even more than it is today. The drive to innovate more and to do everything faster is bound to be stressful. Change is always stressful. The lack of job security and an assured future are stressful. Those looking for comfort in the new enterprise won't find it.

We may also find the new enterprise overburdens management. For example, the carrot-and-stick approach to changing corporate culture and behavior loads a lot of luggage on compensation plans. We want performance appraisals, promotions, salary, and bonuses to depend on managers' performance as team members *and* their contributions to improving quality *and* their focus on the customers *and* their willingness to learn *and* their contribution to diversity *and* whatever else their bosses may think is critical. That is a great deal to pack into a compensation plan.

The leader may be burdened similarly with an excess of new roles, all deemed essential. The leader must create the vision and work constantly to imbue the company with it. The leader must show by example that teams matter and spend time working with them. The leader must demonstrate a commitment to ethics, to quality, to alliances and partnerships. Without the leader's active intervention in all these and a few other areas the company won't change. That's a heavy load to carry.

Too many executives today have focused on immediate and selfish concerns, on deals and packages and payoffs, on cost cutting, and on quick fixes by fad. Leadership demands enduring qualities. It takes vision, courage, persistence, and a willingness to take risks to make the new management work.

It does work. American companies that were deemed dinosaurs a decade ago have returned to the world's markets in fighting trim because they have adopted some of the ideas described in this book. We can expect them and other companies, late starters, to become more competitive, more productive, more innovative, as they get better at the new management. The ideas of the new enterprise are applicable around the world, but the flexibility of American business has given it a huge advantage. Call it willingness to suffer pain now for gain later, or call it ruthlessness, but the American company has proven ready to do what it takes to change. Japanese companies remain so committed to lifetime employment, and European companies, with the exception of the British, so committed to their social contract that they haven't been able to extract any comparable advantage from the new management. We have seen some shifting toward a less rigid commitment. But Japanese business isn't creating new companies or new jobs at anything like the rate we see in the United States, while European companies are losing opportunities and contributing to a brutal level of unemployment. American companies may seem less human but they have created millions of new jobs.

After the years of downsizing and cost cutting, growth has become a key concern. Growth has always been an objective, of course, but for a while it took a backseat to increasing profits by cutting costs. Now business leaders have turned back to growth. The 21st century enterprise is particularly well placed to grow because its opens up new ways of doing business. Companies that innovate better can grow through new products and extensions of existing products. Companies that have speeded their processes can launch products and penetrate the markets faster. With well-developed alliances and partnerships they can enter new geographic markets or bring new products to old markets. With the right information technology and data about customers the new enterprise can grow through mass-customization, by segmenting the market more accurately, by selling on the Internet or through other new channels. The new enterprise focuses more clearly on the customer, does a better job of finding new customers, and builds the loyalty of customers who will make repeat purchases. The new enterprise knows how to look at itself and its markets, see where it is going, and build the kind of company that can find new solutions to new problems. The old corporation was the engine of prosperity. The new is even more promising.

The emergence of a vast middle class in China, India, and other countries of Asia and Latin America is creating huge new markets. Privatization and deregulation all around the world are opening up great segments of the world's economies to private enterprise. The loosening of tariffs and trade restrictions is making markets more global. Technology enables us to create a flood of new products, and information technology gives us more sophisticated ways of reaching the right customers with these products. New technologies and new approaches to management and training make people more productive. The new corporation, focused and designed to seize new opportunities, has an extraordinary future.

APPENDIX:
AN ACHIEVEMENT GAP

W hen you ask a group of senior executives what they need to do to prepare for the 21st century, there's little surprising in their goals. The aspirations are widely accepted and known. The surprise lies in how far they think they still have to go to achieve the transformation. To find out what senior executives consider will be the critical characteristics of a successful 21st century corporation and how well their companies were doing in adopting those characteristics, the SEI Center ran an informal survey in the fall of 1996.

The biggest gaps between aspirations and achievement surfaced when we asked executives about making their organizations flexible and innovative, and improving quality. Better quality, now defined not merely as making good products and services but creating a good all-around experience for the customer and providing solutions for the customer, rated the highest priority. The executives also gave a high priority to "reinventing" their companies and to making them flatter and more cross-functional, but thought performance was lagging there too. By contrast, they gave a relatively low priority to improving the ethics of business and heeding society's demands, and they congratulated themselves on coming very close to meeting their goals in these two areas.

We gave the survey to CEOs and other senior executives who attended Wharton's International Forum in the fall of 1996, and to a selection of *Fortune* 500 company executives. We received 53 answers to a set of 21 questions about the nature of the 21st century corporation. The respondents were almost equally divided among American, Japanese, and

European businessmen. They were asked to rate the characteristics on a scale of one to 10, first as to the priority they gave to the characteristic and second as to how close they had come to embracing it. Our idea was to compare priorities with achievements. Any answer of 8, 9, or 10 was counted as a critical priority or close to achievement. The accompanying chart shows the results.

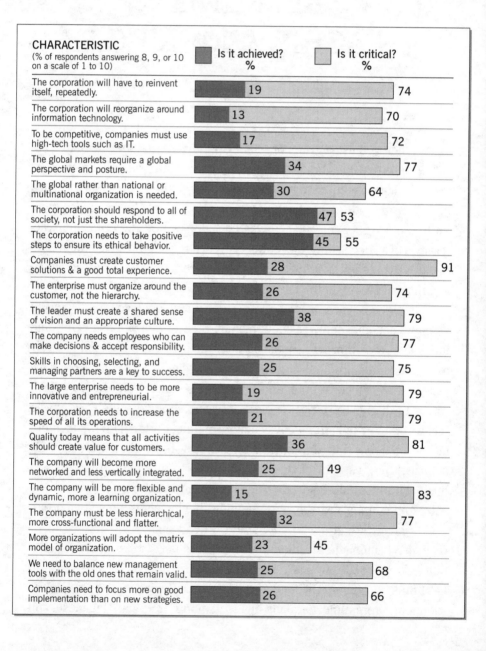

CHARACTERISTIC (% of respondents answering 8, 9, or 10 on a scale of 1 to 10)	Is it achieved? %	Is it critical? %
The corporation will have to reinvent itself, repeatedly.	19	74
The corporation will reorganize around information technology.	13	70
To be competitive, companies must use high-tech tools such as IT.	17	72
The global markets require a global perspective and posture.	34	77
The global rather than national or multinational organization is needed.	30	64
The corporation should respond to all of society, not just the shareholders.	47	53
The corporation needs to take positive steps to ensure its ethical behavior.	45	55
Companies must create customer solutions & a good total experience.	28	91
The enterprise must organize around the customer, not the hierarchy.	26	74
The leader must create a shared sense of vision and an appropriate culture.	38	79
The company needs employees who can make decisions & accept responsibility.	26	77
Skills in choosing, selecting, and managing partners are a key to success.	25	75
The large enterprise needs to be more innovative and entrepreneurial.	19	79
The corporation needs to increase the speed of all its operations.	21	79
Quality today means that all activities should create value for customers.	36	81
The company will become more networked and less vertically integrated.	25	49
The company will be more flexible and dynamic, more a learning organization.	15	83
The company must be less hierarchical, more cross-functional and flatter.	32	77
More organizations will adopt the matrix model of organization.	23	45
We need to balance new management tools with the old ones that remain valid.	25	68
Companies need to focus more on good implementation than on new strategies.	26	66

ACKNOWLEDGMENTS

I f any validation of the theme of change that runs through this book were needed it could be found in the corporate scene that kept shifting before our eyes as we worked on this book. So much changed during the two years we spent on the project that we had to go back to companies we had already interviewed to revise our findings. The companies kept trying to reinvent themselves, and as often as not the CEO we had first interviewed had moved on. We came to 3M just as it was starting a major change and we had to wait until the dust had settled a bit before conducting our interviews. Xerox, having reorganized in 1992 and 1995, did it again in 1997 (just in time for inclusion in this book). Frankly we lost count of the waves of change at AT&T. And so it went. To those we interviewed, and then reinterviewed, we are especially grateful.

The many people associated with the SEI Center for Advanced Studies in Management at Wharton as directors, senior fellows, faculty advisers, and as participants in seminars and workshops, helped create the background for this book and much of the specific research that went into it. The SEI Center directors who made important contributions include Alfred P. West, Jr., chairman of the SEI Center board and CEO of his own company, SEI Investments; Percy Barnevik, former CEO of ABB Asea Brown Boveri and now chairman of Investor AB; Michel L. Besson, executive vice president of Compagnie de Saint-Gobain; William F. Buehler, executive vice president of Xerox Corporation and his predecessor on the SEI Center board, Xerox CEO Paul Allaire; Ulrich Cartellieri, a managing director of Deutsche Bank; Pei-yuan Chia, former vice chairman of Citicorp; John Diebold, chairman of The JD Consulting Group Inc.; Gregory Farrington, dean of the School of Engineering and Applied Science at the University of Pennsylvania; Robert C. Holland, former president of the Committee for Economic Development; Reginald H. Jones, former CEO of the General Electric Company; Morton H. Meyerson, CEO of Perot Systems Corporation; Ronald A. Mitsch, vice chairman of 3M Company; Shaun O'Malley, former chairman of Price Waterhouse; John Sculley, co-founder of Sirius Thinking Entertainment and CEO of Live Picture Incorporated, and Wayne Yetter, former CEO of Astra Merck and now CEO of Novartis Pharmaceuticals Corporation.

Senior fellows at the SEI Center who were particularly helpful include Peter Brill, chairman of Compass Information Services, James R. Emshoff, CEO of IndeCap Industries and former CEO of MedQuist, Douglas A. Saarel, president of the Vantage Group, Paul J. H. Schoemaker, chairman of Decision Strategies International, and Michael von Brentano, chairman of Wickes PLC. Wharton faculty members who serve on the SEI Center faculty council and helped the authors include Professors Elizabeth Bailey, George Day, Paul R. Kleindorfer, Bruce Kogut, David Larcker, Marshall Meyer, and Jitendrah Singh. We also must acknowledge the contributions of professors Thomas Dunfee, Jeffrey Dyer, Robert House, Howard Perlmutter, and David Reibstein, as well as Masaru Yoshitomi, chairman of the U.S.–Japan Management Studies Center at Wharton, and Dean Thomas F. Gerrity of the Wharton School. Robert Gunther, who edited the SEI Center reports, provided much useful material. The members of the SEI Center staff, Pamela Byrnes, Lynn Galida, and Sandi Schultz, provided great support for the project. Edith Terry conducted our interviews in Japan with skill and understanding. Tina Teale of the International Forum processed our survey most efficiently.

Since this is a book more about execution than about theory, the heart of it came from the CEOs and other senior corporate officials we interviewed. In addition to those already mentioned, they were Gerald L. Good, executive vice president of the A&P, Ray Stata, CEO of Analog Devices, Joseph Neubauer, CEO of Aramark Corporation, Harold Burlingame, senior vice president of AT&T, former Vice Chairman Victor Pelson of AT&T, Alan Mulally, president of Boeing's Defense & Space Group, CEO Ryuzaburo Kaku of Canon, Roger G. Ackerman and

James R. Houghton, present and past CEOs of Corning, James Champy, former chairman of CSC Index, Robert B. Palmer, CEO of Digital Equipment Corporation, CEO Yotaro Kobayashi of Fuji-Xerox, CEO Nobuhiko Kawamoto of Honda, Bob Haidinger, president of the JJI Lighting Group, John Madonna, chairman of KPMG International, Chairman Kazuo Inamori of Kyocera, John McConnell, president of Labconco, Pete Jacobi, president of Levi Strauss & Company, Executive Vice President Hisao Tahara of Matsushita, Tom Urban, chairman of Pioneer Hi-Bred International, Peter Neff, former CEO of Rhône-Poulenc in the United States, Robert Cawthorn, former CEO of Rhône-Poulenc Rorer, Tokuichi Uranishi, General Manager of the corporate planning division at Toyota, and CEO Hatim Tyabji and senior vice president Will Pape at VeriFone.

We are also grateful to the many other corporate executives who shared their knowledge and time with us, including John Crewe, Alan Loren, Barry Murphy, and Susan Miller of American Express, Brian Gail and Brian Mulvaney of Aramark, Matt Emmens and many others at Astra Merck, Philip Scanlan at AT&T, Rob Michalak at Ben & Jerry's, Donna Mikov at Boeing, Heidi Trost at Computer Sciences, Norman Garrity and several others at Corning, Lucia Luce Quinn and others at DEC, Richard Parry-Jones, Charles Szuluk, and Robert Transou at Ford, Steve Kerr, Robert Muir, Jack Sprano, and Elizabeth Williams at GE, Vincent Barabba, Robert Hendry, and Arvin Mueller at GM, Claudia Davis, John Eaton, Dick Knudtsen, Richard LeVitt, and Kevin O'Connor at Hewlett-Packard, Takanori Sonoda at Honda, Steven Haeckel and Bob Talbot at IBM, Gary MacDonald at Kingston Technologies, Stephen Gound and others at Labconco, Richard Woo and Diana Woods at Levi Strauss, Mike Murray at Microsoft, Joseph Bailey, William Coyne, Drew Davis, Dick Lidstad, and Thomas Wollner at 3M, Rick Escherich at J.P. Morgan, Ed Bales, Chuck Blazevich, and Richard Buetow at Motorola, Jerry Armstrong and Tom Hanigan at Pioneer, John Abrams, Tom Kirk, and Robert Machin at Rhône-Poulenc, Alex Ott at SAP America, Scott Budge, Hank Greer, Karl Gurino, Rick Lieb, Murray Lewis, and Edward Loughlin at SEI Enterprises, T. R. Reid at Whirlpool, Judd Everhart, Hector Motroni, and Patricia Wallington at Xerox.

Among the academics, consultants, and others who were especially helpful were Jim Bamford of the Alliance Analyst, Ann Kaplan of the American Association of Fund-Raising Counsel, Charles Paulk, John

Rollins, and Tom Spahn at Andersen Consulting, William Glavin, president of Babson College, Vince Tobkin of Bain & Company, Bruce Pasternack and Al Viscio of Booz Allen & Hamilton, Tom Nardone of the Bureau of Labor Statistics, James Irvine of the Communications Workers of America, Ronald Berenbeim among others at the Conference Board, William Copeland of Copeland Associates, Richard Schroth of CSC Index, David Nadler, president of the Delta Consulting Group, Betty Jane Dunn at *Directorship,* Richard Hagberg of the Hagberg Consulting Group, James Harbour of Harbour & Associates, Jim Aisner, Christopher Bartlett, Joseph Bower, and David Quinn Mills at the Harvard Business School, Claudia Goldin at Harvard University, Russell Ackoff and Jamshid Garajedaghi at Interact, Dave Clay at the International Machinists, William Werhane at International Survey Research Corporation, Stephanie Rosenfelt at Korn/Ferry International, Harry Levinson of the Levinson Institute, Ann Gillespie and Stephen Rudolf of Arthur D. Little, Audrey Freedman of Manpower Plus, Bill Matassoni and Frank Ostroff of McKinsey & Co., David Gaylin, Dwight Gertz, and Pat Pollino of Mercer Management Consulting, David Cole, director of the Office for the Study of Automotive Transportation at the University of Michigan, John Sterman of the Sloan School at MIT, Donald Reinertsen, Chris Meyer of Strategic Alignment Group, Arthur Schneiderman, James A. Pierre, president of Seattle Professional Employees Association, and Mike Quinlan of Telular.

We owe special thanks to our editor at The Free Press, Robert Wallace, who used his expert knowledge of business books to encourage and support this project from the start, with much help from his assistant, Julie Black. We also thank the copy editors at The Free Press who helped this book through the delivery room, Celia Knight and Linnea Johnson. Samuel Velasco applied his fine talents to create the book's graphics, working with Iris Cohen, The Free Press's production director.

Our wives, Dina Wind and Patricia Main, gave us much useful advice and didn't complain about lost evenings and weekends. Their tolerance was admirable.

NOTES

Introduction

1. Astra Merck, *Capabilities + Solutions,* 1994. (Booklet reporting on a company meeting.)
2. Analogy suggested by Harry Levinson, retired chairman of the Levinson Institute, in an interview, April 26, 1995.

Chapter 1. Why Change?

1. Sumantra Ghoshal and Christopher Bartlett, "Changing the Role of Top Management: Beyond Structure to Process," *Harvard Business Review* (January–February, 1995), pp. 87–88.
2. Alfred D. Chandler Jr., *The Visible Hand: The Management Revolution in American Business* (Cambridge, Mass.: Harvard University Press paperback, 1977), pp. 79–203.
3. Frederick Winslow Taylor, *The Principles of Scientific Management* (New York: Harper & Brothers, 1911).
4. Chandler, *op. cit.,* p. 280.
5. Alfred P. Sloan Jr., *My Years With General Motors* (New York: McFadden Books paperback, 1965), pp. 139–140, 429–435.
6. Peter F. Drucker, *Concept of the Corporation* (New Brunswick, N.J.: Transaction Publishers, 1993 paperback edition).
7. William H. Whyte, *The Organization Man* (Garden City, N.Y.: Doubleday Anchor Books paperback, undated).
8. *Ibid.,* pp. 142–152.
9. A. Blanton Godfrey, Chairman, The Juran Institute Inc., speech at Impro94, November 17, 1994.
10. Claudia Goldin, "Egalitarianism and the Returns to Education during the Great Transformation of American Education," paper, November 15, 1996.
11. Ryuzaburo Kaku, chairman and CEO, Canon Inc., interview on December 7, 1995.

12. Nobuhiko Kawamoto, president and CEO, Honda Motor Co. Ltd., speech in Traverse City, Michigan, August 4, 1994.

13. Kawamoto, interview on December 15, 1995.

14. *Wall Street Journal,* "Elf Aquitaine's Chief Illustrates the Changes in Europe's Executives" (April 9, 1996), p. A1.

15. John Sculley, interview on July 22, 1995.

16. Margaret Wheatley, *Leadership and The New Science* (San Francisco: Berrett-Koehler Publishers paperback, 1994). The whole book is an interesting, intelligent "reach" for where the organization is going.

17. M. Mitchell Waldrop, *Complexity* (New York: Touchstone, 1992), p. 145.

18. Dee Hock, telephone interview on September 18, 1995.

19. Russell L. Ackoff, *The Democratic Corporation* (New York: Oxford University Press, 1994), pp. 117–118 *et al.*

Chapter 2. The Computer's Reign

1. Tom Urban, chairman of Pioneer Hi-Bred International Inc., speech March 7, 1994. Other material in this section was obtained in an interview with Mr. Urban on January 23, 1996, an interview with Tom Hanigan, vice president and director of information management, and Jerry R. Armstrong, director of sales operations, Pioneer, November 14, 1995, as well as Harvard Business School Case Study #9-193-010, *Pioneer Hi-Bred International Inc.: IT Support of Corn Research and Development* (revised June 11, 1993), and Harvard Business School Case Study #N9-596-029, *Pioneer Hi-Bred International, Inc.; Partnering in the '90s* (September 12, 1995).

2. Colin Crook, senior technology officer, Citibank, N.A., remarks at the Wharton conference on "The Impact of Computers and Information on Management: 1946–1996–2001," University of Pennsylvania, May 14, 1996.

3. Harvard Business School, Case Study #9-490-012, *People Express Airlines: Rise and Decline* (revised September 14, 1993).

4. Margaret Wheatley, *op. cit.,* pp. 101–110.

5. Peter F. Drucker, *Post-Capitalist Society* (New York: HarperBusiness paperback, 1994), pp. 1–8.

6. Paul Allaire, Chairman and CEO, Xerox Corporation, talk given at Wharton Conference, May 14, 1996.

Chapter 3. The Market's Impact

1. Robert Reich, *The Work of Nations* (New York: Alfred A. Knopf, 1992), p. 3.

2. United Nations Conference on Trade and Development, *World Investment Report 1996* (New York and Geneva: United Nations, 1996), p. 4.

3. Data taken from the International Monetary Fund's *World Economic Outlook,* May 1995, and the Bank of International Settlements' *Annual Report,* 1995–1996.

4. Howard Perlmutter, lecture to the International Management Association, December 9, 1994.

5. United Nations Conference on Trade and Development, *World Investment Report*

1993 (New York and Geneva, United Nations, 1993), p. 19, and *World Investment Report 1995* (New York and Geneva, United Nations, 1995), pp. XX and 8.

6. The Conference Board, *U.S. Manufacturers in the Global Marketplace* (New York: The Conference Board Inc., 1994).

7. *Ibid.*

8. *Inc.,* "The Inc. 500: Fastest-growing Private Companies," 1995, p. 31.

9. Hermann Simon, *Hidden Champions* (Boston: Harvard Business School Press, 1996), pp. 7–9, 67.

10. Council of Economic Advisers, *Economic Report of the President* (Washington, Government Printing Office, 1996), p. 402.

11. *The Economist,* "Economic Indicators" and "Emerging-Market Indicators" (April 26, 1997), pp. 108, 110.

12. Joseph T. Plummer, vice chairman, DMB&B, telephone interview on July 3, 1996.

13. Robert C. Holmes, executive director, strategic planning and management, Astra Merck, interview on June 16, 1995.

14. Walter P. Brooks, "Changing Uncertainties and Risks in Pharmaceutical R&D," *Spectrum,* November 16, 1994 (*Spectrum* is a private subscription publication of Decision Resources Inc.).

15. Tufts Center for the Study of Drug Development, Tufts University. Calculating the costs of drug developments is complex and controversial. However, various research documents prepared at the Tufts Center have substantiated these trends.

16. Robert E. Cawthorn, then chairman, Rhône-Poulenc Rorer, interview on December 18, 1995.

17. Tim Haigh, "U.S. Multinational Compensation Strategies for Local Nationals," *Compensation: Present Practices and Future Concerns* (New York: Conference Board, 1995), p. 15.

18. AT&T, *1995 Annual Report,* pp. 8 and 13.

19. Kenichi Ohmae, "Letter from Japan," *Harvard Business Review* (May–June, 1995), pp. 154–163.

20. David P. Hamilton and Norihiko Shirouzu, "Japan's Business Cartels Are Starting to Erode, But Change Is Slow," *Wall Street Journal* (December 4, 1995), p. A1.

21. Kenichi Ohmae, *Triad Power* (New York: Free Press, 1985), pp. 185–193.

22. Murray Weidenbaum, *Neoisolationism and Global Realities* (St. Louis: Washington University, 1996), p. 15.

Chapter 4. Society's Claims

1. A. J. Vogl, "Tough Guy," *Across the Board* (February, 1995), p. 16.

2. Kaku interview.

3. "Who's Next?" *The Economist* (July 13, 1996), p. 48.

4. "How High Can CEO Pay Go?" *Business Week* (April 22, 1996), pp. 100–101, and "Executive Pay," *Business Week* (April 21, 1997), pp. 58–59.

5. Vogl, *op. cit.*

6. Adolf A. Berle and Gardiner C. Means, *The Modern Corporation and Private*

Property (New Brunswick, N.J.: Transaction Publishers, 1991 paperback edition), pp. 113, 297–306.

7. Peter F. Drucker, *Concept of the Corporation,* p. 14, 20–21.

8. Donald S. MacNaughton, "A Responsible Business," speech on October 10, 1971.

9. Robert B. Reich, "How to Avoid These Layoffs?" *New York Times* (January 4, 1996), p. A21.

10. Bill Clinton, radio address, March 23, 1996.

11. Reich, *op. cit.*

12. Herbert Stein, "Corporate America, Mind Your Own Business," *Wall Street Journal* (July 15, 1996), p. A12.

13. William Safire, "The New Socialism," *New York Times* (February 26, 1996).

14. Jacob Wallenberg, presentation to the Wharton European Forum, London, March 29, 1996.

15. James R. Houghton, then CEO, Corning Inc., interview on October 26, 1995.

16. C. K. Prahalad, "Corporate Governance or Corporate Value Added? Rethinking the Primacy of Shareholder Value," *Journal of Applied Corporate Finance* (Winter 1994), p. 45. (The journal is a publication of Continental Bank.)

17. Andrew Stark, "What's the Matter with Business Ethics?" *Harvard Business Review* (May–June 1993), p. 38.

18. Joanne Ciulla, "Why Is Business Talking About Ethics," *California Management Review* (February 1991).

19. The Conference Board, *Corporate Ethics Practices* (New York: The Conference Board, 1992), pp. 11–13.

20. Ciulla, *op. cit.*

21. Robert C. Holland, senior fellow, SEI Center, "What Are the Prospects for a Global Code of Business Ethics?" Speech at the University of Colorado, December 8, 1994.

22. Robert C. Holland, "Integrative Social Contracts Theory," draft document, April 20, 1997.

23. John Rothchild, "Why I Invest with Sinners," *Fortune* (May 13, 1996), p. 197.

Chapter 5. The Customer's Demands

1. Peter Drucker, *Management: Tasks, Responsibilities, Practices* (New York: Harper & Row, 1973), p. 61.

2. National Quality Research Center (University of Michigan Business School), *American Customer Satisfaction Index.* The quarterly updates for November 1995 and February and May 1996 give low ratings to the airlines, newspapers, and network news, and much lower ratings to government services.

3. Richard J. Rosewicz, vice president of manufacturing, Labconco, interview on October 27, 1995.

4. A. Blanton Godfrey, CEO, Juran Institute Inc., interview on April 11, 1995.

5. Richard LeVitt, director, corporate quality, Hewlett-Packard, interview on October 11, 1995.

6. Ronald A. Mitsch, vice chairman, 3M, interview on January 15, 1996.

7. D. Drew Davis, staff vice president, corporate marketing and public affairs, 3M, interview on January 15, 1996.

8. Harvard Business School, *Apple Computer 1992,* Case Study #9-792-081 (Revised August 22, 1994).

9. Frederick F. Reichheld, *The Loyalty Effect* (Boston: Harvard Business School Press, 1996) and the *Harvard Business Review* (September–October 1990, March–April 1993, and March–April 1996).

10. Yoram (Jerry) Wind, "Market Segmentation," in *Companion Encyclopedia of Marketing* by Michael J. Baker, ed. (Andover, U.K.: Rutledge, 1995), p. 394.

11. Sculley interview.

12. Taiichi Ohno, *Toyota Production System* (Cambridge, Mass.: Productivity Press, 1988 edition).

Chapter 6. Absorbing the Customer

1. Quoted by G. Richard Wagoner Jr., president, GM North American Operations, in a speech at Traverse City, Michigan, August 9, 1995.

2. Hatim Tyabji, CEO, and William R. Pape, senior vice president and chief information officer, VeriFone, interviews on December 26, 1995, and September 12, 1995, respectively.

3. Alfred P. Sloan Jr., *op. cit.* pp. 282–283.

4. Mitsch and Davis, interviews.

5. Jon C. Madonna, chairman and CEO, KPMG Peat Marwick, interview on August 12, 1996.

6. Dick Knudtsen, sales force productivity & planning manager, computer sales operations for the Americas, Hewlett-Packard Company, interview on October 31, 1995. Also speech by Lew Platt, CEO of Hewlett-Packard, December 5, 1996, in San Francisco.

7. Dwight L. Gertz, vice president, Mercer Management Consulting, interview on March 1, 1995, and Dwight L. Gertz and João P. A. Baptista, *Grow to Be Great* (New York: Free Press, 1995), pp. 51–55.

8. John A. Crewe, president, international marketing and development, American Express, interview on October 10, 1995.

9. Sloan, *op cit.,* pp. 67–69.

10. Alex Taylor III, "GM's $11,000,000,000 Turnaround," *Fortune* (October 17, 1994), p. 70.

11. Arvin F. Mueller, group executive, Vehicle Development and Technical Operations Group, GM North American Operations, speech at Traverse City, Michigan, August 10, 1995.

12. David Cole, director of the Office for the Study of Automotive Transportation at the University of Michigan, interview on January 12, 1996.

13. Michael J. Rothman and Edgar L. Murphy, "Data Mining: A Practical Approach to Database Marketing," *IBM Consulting Group* (April 17, 1995).

14. Jeffrey F. Rayport and John J. Sviokla, "Managing in the Marketspace," *Harvard Business Review* (November–December, 1994), p. 41, and "Exploiting

the Virtual Value Chain," *Harvard Business Review* (November–December 1995) p. 75.

15. *The Economist,* "Home Shopping—Home Alone?" (October 12, 1996), p. 67.

Chapter 7. Reinventing the Leader

1. James O'Toole, *Leading Change* (New York: Ballantine Books, 1995 edition), p. 21.
2. Andrea Gabor, "Ross Perot: How He'll Make His Next Billion," *U.S. News & World Report* (June 20, 1988), p. 24.
3. The account of what happened at Perot Systems is based on Mort Meyerson, then chairman and CEO, Perot Systems, interview August 14, 1995, and Mort Meyerson, "Everything I Thought I Knew About Leadership Is Wrong," *Fast Company* (April–May, 1996), p. 71.
4. *Fortune,* "Rambos in Pinstripes: Why So Many CEOs Are Lousy Leaders" (June 24, 1996), p. 147.
5. Richard Hagberg, Hagberg Consulting Group, interview by telephone on September 26, 1996.
6. John Smale, speech to the Commercial Club of Cincinnati, October 21, 1993.
7. IBM, *Annual Report,* 1995.
8. Robert Howard, "Values Make the Company: An Interview with Robert Haas," *Harvard Business Review* (September–October, 1990), p. 134.
9. SEI Center for Advanced Studies in Management, *Visionary Leadership,* pamphlet published by the Wharton School in 1991.
10. Rick Escherich, managing director, J.P. Morgan, "Corporate Clarity Index," memo dated July 17, 1996.
11. Thomas A. Stewart, "Company Values That Add Value," *Fortune* (July 8, 1996), p. 147.
12. Harvard Business School, *People Express Airlines: Rise and Decline,* Case Study 9-490-012 (revised September 14, 1993), p. 3.
13. David H. Gaylin, vice president, Mercer Management Consulting Inc., interview on March 1, 1995.
14. *Measure,* "Framework for Our Objectives" (July, 1989), p. 22. (*Measure* is a Hewlett-Packard in-house publication.)
15. *Forbes,* "Boy Scouts on a Rampage" (January 1, 1996), p. 68.
16. Mike Murray, vice president, human resources & administration, Microsoft Corporation, interview on November 11, 1995.
17. James C. Collins and Jerry I. Porras, *Built to Last* (New York: HarperBusiness, 1994), p. 279.
18. Hermann Simon, *op. cit.,* p. 227.
19. General Electric Company, *1995 Annual Report.*
20. John F. Welch Jr., chairman, General Electric Company, speech to the annual meeting of stockholders, Charlottesville, Virginia, April 24, 1996.
21. Steven Kerr, vice president, corporate management development, General Electric, interview on May 30, 1995, and Robert E. Muir Jr., global human resources manager, General Electric Plastics, interview on February 15, 1996.

22. Kerr and Muir interviews.

23. Joseph Neubauer, CEO, Aramark Corporation, interview on October 10, 1995, and Brian Mulvaney, senior vice president, human relations, Aramark, interview on December 18, 1995.

24. Dee Hock, "Addendum to annual Bionomics Conference address," undated paper.

25. Robert N. Haidinger, CEO, JJI Lighting Group Incorporated, interview September 8, 1995.

26. Tyabji interview.

Chapter 8. The Dispensable Employee

1. *Newsweek*, February 26, 1996.

2. *New York Times*, "The Downsizing of America," March 3 through March 9, 1996.

3. Council of Economic Advisers, *Job Creation and Employment Opportunities: The United States Labor Market, 1993–1996*, April 23, 1996. This whole paragraph is based on the report.

4. *Ibid.*

5. Urban interview.

6. Michael Hammer and James Champy, *Reengineering the Corporation* (New York: HarperCollins, 1993), p. 200.

7. Dwight L. Gertz and João P. A. Baptista, *Grow to Be Great* (New York: Free Press, 1995), pp. 14–15.

8. Gene Hall, Jim Rosenthal, and Judy Wade, "How to Make Reengineering *Really* Work," *Harvard Business Review* (November–December, 1993), pp. 4–16.

9. International Survey Research Corporation, 1996 corporate survey.

10. James Champy, chairman, CSC Consulting Group, telephone interview, May 3, 1995.

11. Interviews conducted by Edith Terry in Japan in December, 1995.

12. Kenneth P. De Meuse, Paul A. Vanderheiden, and Thomas J. Bergmann, "Announced Layoffs: Their Effect on Corporate Financial Performance," *Human Resource Mangement* (Winter 1994), p. 522.

13. James Irvine, vice president, Communications Workers of America, interview on April 2, 1996.

14. Murray interview.

15. Alfred P. West Jr., CEO, SEI Investments, interview on December 5, 1995, and B. Scott Budge, senior vice president, interview on July 7, 1995.

16. Tyabji and Pape interviews.

17. Muir interview.

18. GE *Annual Report*, 1995.

19. Urban interview.

20. John McConnell, CEO, Labconco Corporation, and Michael Wyckoff, vice president for human relations and quality, interviews on October 27, 1995.

21. Houghton interview.

22. Roger G. Ackerman, president (now chairman), Corning Incorporated, interview on November 21, 1995.

23. Norman E. Garrity, executive vice president, Corning Incorporated (now president, Corning Technologies), interview on November 21, 1995.
24. These questions are suggested by Joel Brockner, "Managing the Efforts of Layoffs on Survivors," *California Management Review* (Winter, 1992), p. 9, and by Harry Levinson, *The Levinson Letter* (1993).

Chapter 9. The Indispensable Employee

1. Peter F. Drucker, *Concept of the Corporation,* pp. 298–301.
2. Irving Bluestone, interview on March 30, 1992.
3. Jeremy Main, *Quality Wars* (New York: Free Press, 1994), pp. 59–63.
4. Harvard Business School, Case Study #9-490-012, *op. cit.*
5. Sculley interview.
6. The Boeing paragraphs are based on interviews with Mullaly, McKinzie, James Pierre, president of the Seattle Professional Engineering Employees Association, November 3, 1995, and David Clay, shop steward, International Machinists Association, November 2, 1995.
7. Edward E. Lawler III, Susan Albers Morrison, and Gerald E. Ledford Jr., *Creating High Performance Organizations* (San Francisco: Jossey-Bass Publishers, 1995), pp. 9–29, 134–135.
8. *Training,* "Industry Report 1996" (October, 1996), pp. 37–69.
9. Chuck Blazevich, team director of corporate quality for business systems, Motorola Incorporated, interview on December 14, 1995.
10. Houghton interview.
11. Calvin V. Johnson, operations team leader, Specialty Cellular Ceramics plant, Erwin, New York, Corning Incorporated, interview on November 21, 1995.
12. Jack Welch, "To Our Share Owners," General Electric *1995 Annual Report,* p. 3.
13. Jack Welch, "To Our Share Owners," General Electric *1993 Annual Report,* p. 2.
14. Annette Ellison, Customer Center, GE Plastics Division, interview on February 6, 1996.
15. Jack Welch, *op. cit.,* p. 5.
16. Russell L. Ackoff, *op. cit.,* Chapter 4, "The Circular Organization."
17. Gerald L. Good, executive vice president, Great Atlantic & Pacific Tea Company, Incorporated, interview on March 19, 1996.
18. Tyabji and Pape interviews.
19. Lawler et al., *op. cit.,* pp. 18–26.
20. West interview.
21. Diane Woods, vice president, global strategy and organizational development, Levi Strauss, interview November 9, 1995.
22. Uranishi interview.
23. Kawamoto interview.
24. Budge interview.
25. Nadler interview.
26. Murray interview.
27. Tappas Sen, director of workplace of the future, AT&T, telephone interview on May 17, 1996.

Chapter 10. Mastering Information

1. Remarks at Wharton School conference on "The Impact of Computers on Information and Management, 1946–1996–2001," Philadelphia, May 13–14, 1996.
2. James Unruh, CEO, Unisys Corporation, remarks at the Wharton Conference, May 14, 1996.
3. Nikhil Deogun, "A Tough Bank Boss Takes on Computers, with Real Trepidation," *Wall Street Journal* (July 25, 1996), p. A1.
4. Material in this section was obtained in an interview with Thomas N. Urban, chairman of Pioneer Hi-Bred International Incorporated, on January 23, 1996, and an interview with Tom Hanigan, vice president and director of information management, and Jerry R. Armstrong, director of sales operations, Pioneer, November 14, 1995.
5. Charles Paulk, chief information officer, Andersen Consulting, interview on December 15, 1995.
6. John D. Rollins, Andersen Consulting, interview on June 12, 1995.
7. Wayne Yetter, then president & CEO, Astra Merck, interviews on January 25, 1995, and June 12, 1995. Other sources: Cathryn Gunther, manager of Astra Merck Metro New York Business Unit, interview on July 18, 1995; Harvard Business School Case Study #N9-594-045, *Astra/Merck Group* (March 23, 1994).
8. James R. Emshoff, then chairman, MedQuist Incorporated, interview on October 5, 1995, follow-up on May 22, 1997.
9. Jack A. Sprano, manager—information management operation, GE Plastics, interview on February 15, 1996.
10. Seth Lubove, "Cyberbanking," *Forbes* (October 21, 1996), p. 108.
11. Pape interview.
12. West interview and Mark Wilson, vice president, SEI, interview on July 7, 1995.
13. John Sculley, talk to a conference on "The Impact of Computers and Information on Management: 1946–1996–2001," University of Pennsylvania, May 14, 1996.
14. McConnell interview.
15. Michel Besson, president and CEO, Saint-Gobain Corporation (USA), interview on December 5, 1995.

Chapter 11. Spurring Innovation

1. Attributed to Hewlett by Lew Platt, CEO, Hewlett-Packard, in a speech at Yale University, February 28, 1997.
2. Harvey Golub, CEO, American Express Company, speech at World Financial Center, New York, February 7, 1996.
3. Lewis E. Platt, CEO, Hewlett-Packard, speech to Design SuperCon, March 1, 1995.
4. Gerald J. Fine, deputy general manager, Advanced Display Products, Corning Incorporated, interview on November 21, 1995.
5. Deborah Dougherty and Edward H. Bowman, "The Effects of Organizational Downsizing on Production Innovation," *California Management Review* (Summer, 1995), p. 31.

6. Ikujiro Nonaka and Hirotaka Takeuchi, *The Knowledge-Creating Company* (New York: Oxford University Press, 1995), p. 3.

7. James Brian Quinn, *Intelligent Enterprise* (New York: Free Press, 1992), p. 294.

8. Henry Mintzberg, *Mintzberg on Management* (New York: Free Press, 1989), p. 199.

9. Peter Drucker, *Post-Capitalist Society* (New York: HarperBusiness paperback, 1994), pp. 58–59.

10. The 3M material is based on interviews with Ronald A. Mitsch, vice chairman, William E. Coyne, senior vice president for research and development, Joseph T. Bailey, vice president for research and development in the industrial and consumer sector, and Thomas E. Wollner, vice president and head of the central research laboratories, all on January 15, 1996, plus additional telephone conversations and documents from 3M. Also Thomas A. Stewart, "3M Fights Back," *Fortune* (February 5, 1996), p. 94.

11. The Hewlett-Packard material is based on a speech by Lewis Platt, CEO, *op. cit.,* and on John H. Sheridan, "Lew Platt: Creating a Culture for Innovation," *Industry Week* (December 19, 1994), p. 26.

12. William F. Buehler, executive vice president and chief staff officer, Xerox Corporation, telephone interview on June 21, 1996. Also, "Nurturing an employee's brainchild," *Business Week* (Enterprise issue, 1993), p. 196.

13. American Express material based on speeches by Harvey Golub, CEO, on February 7, 1996, and June 11, 1996, Loren interview, and corporate documents.

14. Michael L. Tushman and Charles A. O'Reilly III, "Ambidextrous Organizations," *California Management Review* (Summer 1996), p. 9.

15. Stephen Rudolph, vice president for technology, Arthur D. Little Incorporated, interview on January 22, 1996.

Chapter 12. Stepping Up the Pace

1. The Andrew Grove quotation appeared in "Inside Intel," *Business Week* (June 1, 1992), p. 86, and the *Wall Street Journal* quotation appeared in "The Latest Thing in Many Companies Is Speed, Speed, Speed," (December 23, 1994), p. A1, and was attributed to Kim Sheridan, chairman of Avalon Software Incorporated.

2. Christopher Meyer, *Fast Cycle Time* (New York: Free Press, 1993), p. 7.

3. General Electric Company, *Annual Reports,* 1993 and 1994.

4. Gary MacDonald, vice president for marketing, Kingston Technology Corporation, interview November 7, 1995, and telephone interview, January 15, 1997.

5. Taiichi Ohno, *op. cit.,* pp. 26–42.

6. *Ibid.,* p. 42.

7. Jeremy Main, *op. cit.,* pp. 168–173.

8. *Daily News Record,* "Levi's Ups Ante on Reengineering Its QR Program to $850 Million" (March 9, 1995), p. 2.

9. *Women's Wear Daily,* "Seminar Takes Stock of QR Distribution" (April 23, 1996), p. 12.

10. *Industry Week,* "Lessons from Levis: Quick Response too Slow for the 90s" (May 2, 1994), p. A16.

11. *Business Horizons,* "The Implications of Time-based Competition on International Logistics Strategies" (September–October, 1995), p. 39.
12. Charles W. Szuluk, vice president for process leadership, Ford Automotive Operations, interview on November 20, 1995.
13. Kawamoto interview.
14. James P. Womack, Daniel T. Jones, and Daniel Roos, *The Machine That Changed the World* (New York: HarperPerennial paperback edition, 1991), p. 118.
15. Szuluk interview; Arvin F. Mueller, vice president and group executive of the Vehicle Development & Technical Operations Group, General Motors, interview on November 11, 1996, and *Wall Street Journal,* "Japanese Car Makers Speed Up Car Making" (December 29, 1995), p. B1.
16. Roy A. Bauer, Emilio Collar, Victor Tang, with Jerry Wind and Patrick R. Houston, *The Silverlake Project* (New York: Oxford University Press, 1992), pp. 115–128.
17. Donald G. Reinertsen, "Speed and Product Costs," *Electronic Business* (July, 1983).
18. Donald G. Reinertsen, Reinertsen & Associates, telephone interview on January 2, 1997.
19. Christoph-Friedrich von Braun, "The Acceleration Trap," *Sloan Management Review* (Fall 1990), reprint.
20. Main, *op. cit.,* pp. 129–130.

Chapter 13. Redefining Quality

1. Lew Platt, chairman and CEO, Hewlett-Packard Company, speech, Quality Forum XII San Francisco, October 3, 1996.
2. Kawamoto interview.
3. Yotaro Kobayashi, chairman, Fuji-Xerox Company, Ltd., interview on October 27, 1995.
4. Main, *op. cit.,* pp. 127–128.
5. Richard Buetow, senior vice president, Motorola Incorporated, interview on December 14, 1995, and telephone interview on January 23, 1997.
6. *Consumer Reports* issues of February, 1996 (top-freezer and side-by-side refrigerators, p. 40), May, 1996 (top-freezer refrigerators, p. 34), July, 1996 (washers, p. 38), August, 1996 (microwave ovens, p. 43), October, 1996 (ranges, p. 36), and January, 1997 (dishwashers, p. 43).
7. *Wall Street Journal,* "To Keep GE's Profits Rising, Welch Pushes Quality-Control Plan" (January 13, 1997), p. A1.
8. Welch speech, *op. cit.*
9. Xerox material based on Buehler interview, Hector J. Motroni, vice president for human resources and quality, interview on May 10, 1995, and on Richard J. Leo, "Xerox 2000: From Survival to Opportunity," *Quality Progress* (March, 1996), p. 65.
10. Hewlett-Packard material based on Lew Platt speech, *op. cit.,* and on LeVitt interview.
11. Martin R. Mariner, director of quality, Corning Incorporated, interview on November 21, 1995.

Chapter 14. The Global Reach

1. Hermann Simon, *op. cit.,* p. 74.
2. Besson interview.
3. Conference Board, *op. cit.*
4. Chandler, *op. cit.,* p. 368.
5. Kaku interview.
6. ABB material based on Percy Barnevik lecture at the SEI Center, November 26, 1991; an interview with Barnevik in *Across the Board* ("Making a Giant Dance," October, 1994, p. 27); Christopher A. Bartlett and Sumantra Ghoshal, "Beyond the M-Form: Toward a Managerial Theory of the Firm," *Strategic Management Journal* (Volume 14, Winter 1993), pp. 23–46; Sumantra Ghoshal and Christopher A. Bartlett, "Changing the Role of Top Management: Beyond Structure to Process," *Harvard Business Review* (January–February, 1995), pp. 86–96, and material supplied by Barnevik and ABB on March 5, 1997. Barnevik has since become chairman of Investor AB, the centerpiece of the Wallenberg family enterprises, which own a major share of ABB.
7. Whirlpool material based on "The Right Way to Go Global: An Interview with Whirlpool CEO David Whitwam," *Harvard Business Review* (March–April, 1994), pp. 135–145; *Business Week,* "Call It Worldpool" (November 28, 1994); and company reports and sources.
8. Uranishi interview and Toyota Motor Corporation, *Annual Report,* 1995.
9. Kawamoto interview and Kawamoto speech, *op. cit.*
10. *Automotive News,* "Trotman Passes the Word: Becoming No. 1 is Job 1," (November 11, 1994).
11. *Business Week,* "Red Alert at Ford" (December 2, 1996), p. 38.
12. Ford materials based mostly on interviews with Robert H. Transou, group vice president for manufacturing, Richard Parry-Jones, vice president, Small/Medium Vehicle Center, and Charles W. Szuluk, vice president, process leadership, all of Ford Automotive Operations, on November 30 and December 1, 1995.
13. GM material based on interviews with Vincent P. Barabba, general manager, Strategic Decisions Center, Robert W. Hendry, vice president and group executive, Business Support Group, and Arvin F. Mueller, vice president and group executive, Vehicle Development and Technical Operations Group, all at North American Operations, on January 11, 1996, and Wagoner speech, *op. cit.*
14. Conference Board, *op. cit.,* p. 21.
15. McConnell and Rosewicz interviews; Stephen Gound, executive vice president for finance, Labconco Corporation, and others interviewed at Labconco on October 27, 1995.
16. Simon, *op. cit.,* pp. 2, 78, 271–279.
17. Conference Board, *op. cit.*
18. *The Economist,* "Management Brief: Furnishing the world" (November 19, 1994), p. 79.
19. Neff interview.
20. Peter J. Neff, "Rhône-Poulenc's Global Odyssey," speech to a Conference Board seminar, March 30, 1994.

Chapter 15. The Extended Corporation

1. Joseph Neubauer, CEO, Aramark Corporation, speech to the Los Angeles Rotary, June 4, 1993.
2. Jordan D. Lewis, *The Connected Corporation* (New York: Free Press, 1995), p. xiii.
3. Jeremy Main, "Making Global Alliances Work," *Fortune* (December 17, 1990), p. 121.
4. Jeffrey H. Dyer and Harbir Singh, "The Relational View: Relational Rents and Sources of Interorganizational Competitive Advantage," draft paper at the Wharton School, October 13, 1996.
5. Lewis, *op. cit.,* p. xxi.
6. Jeffrey H. Dyer, talk to Wharton seminar, November 11, 1996. Dyer also wrote "How Chrysler Created an American Keiretsu," *Harvard Business Review* (July–August 1996), p. 42.
7. Thomas L. Zeller and Darin M. Gillis, "Achieving Market Excellence Through Quality: The Case of the Ford Motor Company," *Business Horizons* (May–June 1995), p. 23.
8. Corning material based on Houghton and Ackerman interviews, an article by Houghton, "Corning: Trust is the Key," *Across the Board* (November–December 1994), p. 42, and Guy Di Cicco, director of globalization, Corning Incorporated, talk to Wharton seminar, November 22, 1996.
9. Alexander R. Ott, vice president, global partnerships, SAP America, Inc., talk to Wharton seminar November 22, 1996, and interview on February 6, 1997. Also other published and company material.
10. Thierry Soursac, senior vice president, RPR, talk to a Wharton seminar, November 22, 1996, and Cawthorn interview.
11. *Wall Street Journal,* "A Rich Benefits Plan Gives GM Competitors Cost Edge" (March 21, 1996), p. B1.
12. Mary C. Lacity and Rudy Hirschheim, *Beyond the Information System Outsourcing Bandwagon* (Chichester: John Wiley & Sons, 1995), p. 20.
13. *Ibid.,* pp. 14–16.
14. Merrill Lynch research report on Computer Sciences, December, 1996.
15. Heidi M. Trost, vice president, Hughes Support Center, Computer Sciences Corporation, interview on November 7, 1995, and phone conversation on February 5, 1997.
16. West interview.
17. *Business Week,* "Has Outsourcing Gone Too Far" (April 1, 1996), p. 26.
18. Neubauer speech.
19. Emshoff interview.
20. Louis Kraar, "The Overseas Chinese," *Fortune* (October 31, 1994), p. 91.
21. Wong Yip Yan, chairman, WyWy House, remarks to SEI Center seminar, May 23, 1995.
22. Kingston material based on MacDonald interviews and company material.

Chapter 16. The Learning Loop

1. Ray Stata, "Organizational Learning—The Key to Management Innovation," *Sloan Management Review* (Spring, 1989).
2. James R. Houghton, CEO, Corning Incorporated, speech at Cornell University, November 3, 1994.
3. This paragraph is drawn largely from Vincent P. Barabba, *Meeting of the Minds* (Boston: Harvard Business School Press, 1995).
4. John D. Sterman, "Learning In and About Complex Systems," *System Dynamics Review* (Summer–Fall, 1994), pp. 291–329.
5. This paragraph is drawn principally from Roy Rowan, *The Intuitive Manager* (Boston: Little, Brown, 1986).
6. David Upton, "The Impact of Information Technology in Business Education," notes on a talk at the SEI Center on February 22, 1997.
7. Material on future learning came out of an SEI Center conference, "The Virtual University," January 11–12, 1995.
8. *The Economist,* "Re-engineering the MBA" (April 13, 1996), p. 65.
9. *Training,* "Industry Report 1996" (October, 1996), pp. 38, 45.
10. Jeremy Main, "Trying to Bend Managers' Minds," *Fortune* (November 23, 1987), p. 95.
11. Murray interview.
12. David Stamps, "Communities of Practice," *Training* (February, 1997), pp. 35–37.
13. Edward F. Bales, director of education—external systems, Motorola Incorporated. Interview on December 14, 1995 and by telephone on February 24, 1997. (Mr. Bales is now a consultant to Motorola.)
14. Claudia Davis, director of training, Hewlett-Packard Company, interview on October 31, 1995.
15. Knudtsen interview.
16. Nonaka and Takeuchi, *op. cit.,* Chapter 1.
17. This section is taken basically from Sterman, *op. cit.,* plus other material of his and an interview.
18. Michael A. Cusamano and Richard W. Selby, *Microsoft Secrets* (New York: Free Press, 1995), pp. 327–397.

Chapter 17. The Civic Enterprise

1. Gary Edwards, president, Ethics Resource Center, interview in *Prevention of Corporate Liability* (April 19, 1993).
2. Tim Bell, director for business ethics services, KPMG Peat Marwick, telephone interview on August 14, 1996.
3. *Wall Street Journal,* "Consultant's Advice on Diversity Was Anything But Diverse" (March 11, 1997), p. A1.
4. Peter I. Bijur, CEO, Texaco Inc., letter to shareholders, November 26, 1996, plus various published reports.
5. Levi Strauss material based on Peter Jacobi, president of Levi Strauss, interviews on November 1, 1995, and March 6, 1997; Harvard Business School, *Levi Strauss & Co. and the AIDS Crisis,* Case Study #9-391-198 (revised March 1, 1995);

Robert D. Haas, CEO, Levi Strauss, speech on diversity, July 1991; *San Francisco Focus,* "Mr. Blue Jeans" (October 1993), p. 65; and company documents.

6. Thomas W. Dunfee, "Marketing an Ethical Stance," *Financial Times,* November 17, 1995.

7. Ben & Jerry's Homemade, Incorporated, *Annual Reports, 1993, 1994,* and *1995;* other company documents; *Business Week* (July 15, 1996), *Wall Street Journal* (January 3, 1997).

8. Besson interview.

9. *The Economist,* "White Smoke, and Black": (June 28, 1997), p. 16.

10. Houghton interview.

11. Johnson interview

12. Masaru Yoshitomi, chairman of the U.S.-Japan Management Studies Center, Wharton; remarks at a Wharton seminar, March 27, 1997.

13. Smale speech, *op. cit.*

14. *Business Week* (November 25, 1996), p. 82.

15. *The New York Times,* "Ties That Bind: His Directors, Her Charity" (March 21, 1995), p. D1.

Chapter 18. An Integrated Architecture

1. David A. Nadler and Michael L. Tushman, *Competing by Design* (New York: Oxford University Press, 1997), p. 223.

2. David A. Nadler, Marc S. Gerstein, Robert B. Shaw and Associates, *Organizational Architecture* (San Francisco: Jossey-Bass Inc., 1992), p. 32.

3. Xerox Corporation, *How We Run Xerox (Employee Handbook)* (1996), pp 33–34.

4. This section is based on various Xerox Corporation documents, particularly *Xerox 2005,* issued March 18, 1997.

Conclusion

1. Emshoff interview.

2. Vincent P. Barabba, *op. cit.* p. 82.

3. The authors thank Arthur Schneiderman for bringing this piece of wisdom to their attention.

INDEX

ABOUT THE AUTHORS

JERRY YORAM WIND is the Lauder Professor and Professor of Marketing at the Wharton School of the University of Pennsylvania. He is the founding director of Wharton's think tank, the SEI Center for Advanced Studies in Management. He is also currently leading Wharton's efforts to become global, and he led the development of the new Wharton MBA curriculum. Previously, he headed the development of Wharton's executive MBA program and the Wharton International Forum. In 1983, he founded the Joseph H. Lauder Institute of Management and International Studies, which he directed until the establishment of the SEI Center in 1989.

Dr. Wind is one of the most cited authorities on marketing, having written or coauthored fourteen books and more than two hundred papers and articles in the field. He was editor-in-chief of *The Journal of Marketing*. He has served as a consultant to many of the *Fortune* 500 companies and currently lists AT&T, Bristol-Myers Squibb, Edward Jones, Price Waterhouse, and SEI Investments among his clients.

He joined the Wharton faculty on receiving his PhD from Stanford University in 1967. At present, he is a trustee of the Philadelphia Museum of Art, a director of Enhance Financial Services Group, chairman of the international advisory board of the new Interdisciplinary Center for Business, Law, and Technology in Herzliyya, Israel, and vice chairman of the International Academy of Management.

Dr. Wind is the recipient of various awards, including the prestigious Charles Coolidge Parlin Award (1985), the first Faculty Impact Award by

Wharton Alumni, the 1993 AMA/Irwin Distinguished Educator Award, and the 1996 Paul D. Converse Award.

JEREMY MAIN, a member of *Fortune's* Board of Editors from 1981 to 1992, specializes in the related fields of management, productivity, and quality. *Quality Wars,* his account of the difficult but essential experience of American companies in attempting to improve quality, was published by The Free Press in 1994.

Mr. Main was born in Buenos Aires, educated at schools in Argentina and Canada, and received an A.B. degree from Princeton University. He served as a Washington and foreign correspondent for International News Service and as an editor and correspondent for *Pacific Stars & Stripes* during the Korean War. After joining *Time's* Washington bureau in 1958 to report on space and defense news, he subsequently moved to the Paris bureau, where he specialized in diplomatic news. He joined *Fortune* in 1966 in New York and worked there, as well as at *Money* magazine, as a writer and editor until 1992. His many articles called attention to the new management.

He won a University of Missouri Business Journalism Award in 1982 for articles on quality and productivity. In 1988, he taught at Yale University as a visiting lecturer. He is a Senior Fellow at the SEI Center at the Wharton School.